Wirtschaft + Gesellschaft

Wirtschaft und Gesellschaft ist ein wichtiges Themenfeld der Sozialwissenschaften. Daher diese Buchreihe: Sie will zentrale Institutionen des Wirtschaftslebens wie Märkte, Geld und Unternehmen sowie deren Entwicklungsdynamiken sozial- und gesellschaftstheoretisch in den Blick nehmen. Damit soll ein sichtbarer Raum für Arbeiten geschaffen werden, die die Wirtschaft in ihrer gesellschaftlichen Einbettung betrachten oder aber soziale Effekte des Wirtschaftsgeschehens und wirtschaftlichen Denkens analysieren. Die Reihe steht für einen disziplinären wie theoretischen Pluralismus und pflegt ein offenes Themenspektrum.

More information about this series at http://www.springer.com/series/12587

Giacomo Bazzani

When Money Changes Society

The case of Sardex money as community

Springer VS

Giacomo Bazzani
Department of Statistics, Computer Science,
Applications "G. Parenti"
University of Florence
Firenze, Italy

ISSN 2626-6156 ISSN 2626-6164 (electronic)
Wirtschaft + Gesellschaft
ISBN 978-3-658-28532-6 ISBN 978-3-658-28533-3 (eBook)
https://doi.org/10.1007/978-3-658-28533-3

Planung/Lektorat: Cori Antonia Mackrodt
This Springer VS imprint is published by the registered company Springer Fachmedien Wiesbaden GmbH part of Springer Nature.
The registered company address is: Abraham-Lincoln-Str. 46, 65189 Wiesbaden, Germany

Acknowledgements

This book is the result of research undertaken in the PhD programme in Social and Political Change at the Universities of Turin and Florence. My supervisor was Prof. Carlo Trigilia who accompanied the research in all its parts with passion, availability and professionalism. The entire PhD programme board has always encouraged and followed all the research with useful tips. In particular, I must thank Prof. Marco Bontempi who provided constant help, support and encouragement at every stage of the research.

Thanks are due to Sardex Ltd, its founders and all the staff whose willingness and availability made this research easier.

The research benefited from a One Year Research Grant (91660080) obtained from the DAAD (German Academic Exchange Service) which made it possible to refine the interpretation of the results during the 2017/2018 academic year while visiting the Max Planck Institute for the Study of Societies in Cologne and the University of Trier. An earlier version of the thesis was discussed at the Max Planck Institute for the Study of Societies in Cologne and benefited from the helpful advice of the Director, Prof. Jens Beckert, Wolfgang Streek, Fritz Scharpf, John Wilkinson, Benjamin Braun, Gregory Ferguson as well as numerous researchers at the institute. An earlier version of the research was also presented at Trier University and it benefited from the useful suggestions of Prof. Andrea Maurer's research group, especially Michael Anger and Clemens Schmidt. Special thanks go to Prof. Andrea Maurer for her constant feedback which helped identify the social mechanisms and for her enthusiasm throughout the research.

Parts of the research were also discussed at conferences and seminars at the Panteion University of Social and Political Sciences in Athens, The New School in New York, the University of Constance, the University of Florence, the University of Lyon 1, Universitat Oberta de Catalunya of Barcelona, the University of Helsinki, the University of Oslo, the University of Rome "La Sapienza" the many comments received were beneficial. I had the opportunity to discuss the research and receive very useful advice from Patrick Aspers, Delia Baldassarri, Filippo Barbera, Jérôme Blanc, Maurizio Catino, Dimitri D'Andrea, Nigel Dodd, Alberto Gherardini, Giorgio Grossi, Peter Hedström, Lars Mjøset, Paolo Perulli, Aaron Pitluck, Francesco Ramella, Roberta Ricucci and Akos

Rona-Tas. Useful advice also came from the two reviewers who contributed to the final version of the text through two review rounds.

The English language manuscript editing was funded by the Inter-University Centre for Political Sociology of the Universities of Florence, Perugia and Genoa. Jane Ferguson Simpson has done an excellent and accurate job of translating and proof-reading which led to the current version of the text.

This project has taken five years and I would never have been able to carry it out on my own: I wish to thank all my family who accompanied me with trust and generosity during this extraordinary experience.

Contents

Abbreviations

F.	Founder interview n°
E.	Entrepreneur interview n°
CC	Complementary currency
Sardex currency	The circulating money expressed in Sardex
Sardex Ltd	The company which founded, promotes and manages the circulation of Sardex currency
Sardex network or network	The network of companies using the Sardex currency
Sardex device	All the technological and social elements involved in the functioning of the Sardex currency
Sardex project	The functioning of the Sardex currency and the economic and political form of regulation of the economy embodied

List of Figures

List of Tables

1 Introduction

Gold is a treasure, and he who possesses it does all he wishes to in this world, and succeeds in helping souls to paradise.
(Christopher Columbus)

It is well enough that the people of the nation do not understand our banking and monetary system for, if they did, I believe that there would be a revolution before tomorrow morning.
(Henry Ford)

Many countries have struggled to recover from the economic crisis in 2008, which began in the United States and then spread to Europe. To deal with this economic crisis and its social effects, central regulatory institutions implemented two main types of public policies: (i) central banks introduced quantitative easing programmes, and (ii) central governments introduced austerity policies to reduce public spending and make markets more dynamic. The Federal Reserve in the United States invested 29 trillion dollars in monetary policies, the Bank of England 325 billion pounds; while the British government spent more than a thousand trillion pounds on bank bailouts, the European Central Bank spent more than a trillion euros providing banks with low-interest loans (Dodd 2014, p. 2). Despite the creation of such enormous quantities of new money to deal with the economic crisis, the social consequences have been harsh, partly because of the effects of the crisis itself and partly because of the policies adopted to deal with it.

Southern European countries, in particular, have not recovered from the economic crisis and the gap between rich and poor regions, that already existed in these countries, has been exacerbated by the effects of the crisis. In Italy for example, the southern regions have felt the effects of this crisis more keenly than their northern counterparts, and they are finding it harder to recover. One of the many social consequences of this

G. Bazzani, *When Money Changes Society*, Wirtschaft + Gesellschaft,
https://doi.org/10.1007/978-3-658-28533-3_1

phenomenon is that emigration of young well-qualified people from Southern Italy to Northern Italy and Northern Europe has increased in these years of crisis (Piras and Lobina 2018).

Sardinia, for example, is one of the least economically developed Italian and European regions and between 2007 and 2016 its GDP decreased by 9.1% (Banca d'Italia 2018, p. 13) and there was a steady increase in youth emigration. In this context of insufficient economic development and growing social distress, due in part to the economic crisis, the Sardex complementary currency (CC) was created in 2009. The currency was founded by five young Sardinians, four of whom had emigrated to various Northern European countries for study or work. The founders were interested in returning to their region of origin to try and "do something useful" for their land, and to "build" a job with which to earn their living. Although none of them had any formal economic education, they were passionately interested in studying how money functions: this lead them to learn more about the experience of the Wir, a CC created in Switzerland in 1934 and still operating as a bank. This research, combined with a considerable dose of entrepreneurial courage, led to the creation of the Sardex CC which, over the next few years evolved into a complex, well-organised monetary system that registered a significant increase in member numbers and monetary transactions every year.

Sardex, like Wir, is a CC created to facilitate exchanges between companies (b2b). It takes the form of a mutual credit system which means there is no need to use ordinary currency (in this case the euro). Mutual credit between companies is a very specific form of CC which differs from ordinary money and also from most CCs (e.g., crypto-currencies). Companies use Sardex to buy goods and services; this exchange in Sardex is not "issued" by a central authority but is in fact a form of credit that entrepreneurs belonging to the Sardex network make to each other. This type of exchange is similar to bartering, but the presence of a central authority (Sardex Ltd) which tracks all transactions, enables multilateral "bartering" between companies. This multilateral "bartering" enables the mutual credit between these companies to function as a means of payment and exchange in the same way as the ordinary currency does (see Sect. 3.4). Sardex Ltd therefore, acts as a clearing house in a similar way to the clearing houses for international transactions between different currencies. Sardex Ltd records the purchases and sales of products and services among member companies and ensures that each company has its own Sardex account. This account functions in a similar way to a bank account, and can have either a positive or negative balance, depending on the balance of purchases and sales in Sardex.

After a difficult start-up phase, when only a few companies signed up, the Sardex project gathered momentum and in 2017 the value of transactions in Sardex reached the equivalent of eighty million euros and there were 4000 member companies, covering practically all sectors of the Sardinian economy. In 2013 Sardex began to expand into other Italian regions, creating similar regional CCs (e.g., Venetex in Veneto, Marchex in Marche, Piemex in Piemonte, etc.). By 2018 twelve new regional currencies had been launched with the aim of creating a CC similar to Sardex in every Italian region. Similar CCs have also been set up in other EU countries: the ones operating in Nantes (France), Barcelona (Spain), Bristol and Brixton (Great Britain) are well known.

However, Sardex remains a CC that cannot, and does not, aspire to be an alternative currency to the euro. In order to avoid imbalances in their company's balance sheet, entrepreneurs are aware they cannot increase their business in Sardex beyond a certain limit (around 20% of the total). Beyond this limit, they would run the risk of insufficient euro liquidity for the purchase of raw materials not produced in Sardinia, or for the payment of taxes and utilities that cannot be paid in Sardex. The limitations to using Sardex, on the one hand, make it dependent on the euro, but, on the other, they enable Sardex to fulfil functions that the ordinary currency cannot achieve. Sardex facilitates access to credit and promotes exchanges between local companies through an economic system that entrepreneurs consider virtuous for their own company and for the socio-economic development of their region (see Chap. 4.).

The coexistence and circulation of different currencies was normal in pre-modern times. Then, with the coming of nation states, coinage became an exclusive feature of the modern state and the circulation of other currencies was prohibited. For the modern state, having the exclusive right to issue money was a way to strengthen its authority over the territory, and to better control tax collection and economic exchanges with other countries. Although the literature currently documents the presence of more than 4500 CCs (Place and Bindewald 2015), these continue to be viewed with a certain distrust by the central authorities, especially by the central banks. The traditional approach of economic science towards CCs certainly plays a role in perpetuating this diffidence: from the point of view of general equilibrium theory, in fact, the presence of a CC can appear to be dysfunctional to the economic system. The traditional approach of economic science tends to consider money as a "neutral veil" between individuals' desires and the goods to be purchased. A consequence of this approach is that the coexistence on the market of more than one currency can easily be considered a further transaction cost: in fact, exchanges between the currencies may be necessary and this would make the exchangeability between goods and money less immediate.

In order to challenge this traditional view of CCs, empirical research was undertaken to assess the economic and social effects of Sardex. The author carried out the fieldwork in 2017, visiting and interviewing the Sardex founders and Sardex employees from every sector of Sardex activity as well as entrepreneurs who were members of the Sardex network (see Appendix A for sample selection and interview analysis details). Interviews were designed to investigate how Sardex functioned (technical and relational), to ascertain the mechanisms that determined the expansion of the Sardex entrepreneurial network and to assess the economic and social effects of using Sardex from the entrepreneurs' perspective.

Research results show that companies that use the Sardex CC increased their customers by an average of 23% and their revenues by 26%, net of the estimated substitution effect between the euro and the Sardex (see Sect. 5.1). These economic results are very encouraging for member companies: in fact, despite the rapid membership increase, the drop-out rate is very low, between 3 and 4% per *annum* of the total number of members. In a period of severe recession, in an economically weak region such as Sardinia, the excellent economic results generated by using Sardex make this CC a worthwhile policy tool for local development.

The economic growth of firms that use Sardex cannot be explained within the traditional interpretation of money as a "neutral veil". The classical economic interpretation of how money functions, still present in the monetarist approach, interprets money as a neutral veil over the real economic values expressed by price trends, labour costs and economic transactions motivated by exogenous desires formed outside the economic sphere (Patinkin 1987).[1] On the contrary, research shows that the Sardex *modus operandi* and its provision of low-cost credit have a real effect on the economy, and the CC is not simply being used for business that would have been conducted, in any case, in euros. The way the CC functions increases the number of new economic transactions and also contributes to the orientation of entrepreneurs' preferences (see Sub-sects. 4.3.1 and 4.3.2).

The research findings allow the author to advance the following propositions: (i) the effects produced by Sardex in increasing exchanges between economic actors can be explained by social mechanisms that cannot be attributed solely to traditional utilitarianism; (ii) the social mechanisms promoted by Sardex encourage economic development by fostering cooperation between economic actors, whereas current economic policies advocate increasing competition (see Sect. 4.2); (iii) the way in which a currency functions determines a wide range of economic and social effects which are not normally attributed to money (e.g., reciprocity, solidarity, etc.).

Classical sociology considered money as central to the functioning of modern society, relating it to a progressive expansion of instrumental rationality and the emergence of weaker social ties. Modern money, the universal equivalent described by Simmel (1990), facilitates the exchange of goods and values by providing a single unit of account. This "frees" people and things from traditional social ties and makes them free to "sell" their work and trade goods on markets that increasingly erode national borders. Modern money thus frees the individual from traditional social ties and facilitates the creation of ever larger and more inter-connected markets. Sardex money, on the other hand, seems to work in the opposite direction: the weak social ties of ordinary economic transactions are replaced by strong ones, characterised by a high level of reciprocity (see Sub-sect. 4.1.3)

[1]Keynesian interpretations of how money functions, though, do accept that the manipulation of the cost of money by the central banks can have effects on the economy, at least in the short term.

and by an ethical code (see Sub-sect. 4.1.4). Furthermore the movement of goods is restricted to the regional level and much is done to promote economic exchanges between member companies.

In order to explain how Sardex functions the different elements that constitute the Sardex device as a whole need to be disentangled: (i) the specific characteristics of the Sardex currency; (ii) the manner in which Sardex Ltd regulates the circulation of this currency and (iii) the social effects that these elements produce. The different social mechanisms triggered by Sardex are used to analytically identify the single steps in the action chain that produces the social effects. This use of social mechanisms refers to a form of sociological explanation that seeks to ascertain which are the key elements, and how they interact with each other to bring about individual and collective action within specific social contexts. In particular, social mechanisms try to explain how specific forms of individual action interact with contextual elements, producing social effects that are not directly related to the intentionality of the individual actor. The social effects of the Sardex currency generated by specific mechanisms, can be divided into (i) effects on trust, generated by selection, signalling, reciprocity, monitoring and sanctioning mechanisms; (ii) effects on cooperation; (iii) effects on solidarity, generated by opportunity, desire, belief and collective action mechanisms.

In short, the main argument of this book is that the characteristics of Sardex, and the way in which its circulation is regulated by Sardex Ltd, trigger numerous social mechanisms, and sustain a high level of interpersonal trust among entrepreneurs, as well as trust in the Sardex Ltd management (See Chap. 4.). This high level of trust - based on an ethical code of conduct as well as horizontal and hierarchical monitoring and sanctioning systems - together with the low cost of transactions, facilitates a high level of cooperation between entrepreneurs which can explain the large number of transactions. Horizontal and hierarchical selection, together with monitoring and sanctioning mechanisms, facilitate exchanges, limit opportunistic behaviours and allow entrepreneurs to place a high level of trust in other entrepreneurs in the network. This high level of trust and cooperation, together with the limited circulation and use of the currency, encourage solidarity among entrepreneurs and between entrepreneurs and their region of origin (for an introduction to the generative mechanisms of Sardex see Sect. 4.4). Entrepreneurs thus begin to associate the use of Sardex with "local development" because they believe that Sardex operations have positive effects on the socio-economic development of the region. This attitude also creates specific forms of promotion of the Sardex project by entrepreneurs which are not undertaken for their direct economic interests. In this sense, Sardex is able to combine the individual interest of the entrepreneur with a collective interest defined by the regional boundaries of currency circulation. Although the economic benefits for member companies remain the principle motivation for using the Sardex currency, member entrepreneurs believe their transactions in Sardex will also benefit the socio-economic development of their region. This does not happen when transactions are conducted in the euro.

Such evidence hints at the power money has to change society. Moving beyond the idea of money enhancing impersonal, market relationships, the Sardex currency facilitates the creation of new social ties where individuals perceive themselves and their economic activity as deeply involved with a collectivity. Despite this power, our understanding of the capacity of money to change social ties is underdeveloped, and this is reflected in academic research, as well as in policy making. The study of how money functions, in fact, is mostly limited to macro-economics, and policy making is the exclusive domain of the central banks. The author hopes this book will stimulate further research to better understand money's potential for changing society and that it will also promote public debate on the issue of introducing some form of democratic control over money production and regulation.

The chapter dedicated to 'A mechanism approach for money', places the research in the context of the sociology of money and explains how social-action models can be used to describe the influence of money in society. The chapter 'The Sardex experience' briefly presents some Sardex precursors, and then relates the history of the Sardex CC, its technical operations and how it is regulated by Sardex Ltd. The chapter 'Social mechanisms influenced by Sardex' describes how the Sardex device generates social effects on trust, cooperation and solidarity. A brief introduction is provided for all the social mechanisms discussed, explaining how they operate within Sardex. The chapter ends with a brief overview of how the currency's characteristics, its regulation and the social mechanisms presented earlier in the chapter, link together to produce social effects.

The 'Conclusions' discuss some of the implications of this type of currency operations. Sardex can be considered as an unconventional development policy tool because of its economic effects, on both transaction costs and the demand-side. Positive and negative influences on the competitiveness and cooperative capacity of the economic system are also discussed with regard to the effects on economic innovation. If its economic and social effects are properly understood, Sardex can play a role as a tool for local development and as an economic stimulus during economic downturns. Finally, Sardex operations are discussed as an example from which to draw analytical categories for describing the social functioning of money. Starting from the social mechanisms examined in Sardex operations, it is possible to describe how, currencies with different characteristics support different social effects. A preliminary typology of the social functioning of money that compares the characteristics and social effects of a modern state currency with Sardex and with a crypto-currency is proposed. The Sardex currency seems to be an emblematic case that makes it possible to describe the performative role of money in generating specific forms of social ties that link individuals and society and that lead to general considerations about the functioning and the economic and social effects of contemporary monetary policies.

References

Banca d'Italia. (2018). *Economie regionali. L'economia delle regioni italiane nel 2017*. Roma: Banca D'Italia.

Dodd, N. (2014). *The social life of money*. Princeton NJ: Princeton University Press.

Patinkin, D. (1987). Neutrality of money. *The new palgrave dictionary of economics, 3,* 639–644.

Place, C., & Bindewald, L. (2015). Validating and improving the impact of complementary currency systems through impact assessment frameworks. *International Journal of Community Currency Research, 19*(D), 152–164.

Piras, M., & Lobina, E. (2018). *Emigrazione giovanile qualificata in Sardegna*. Cagliari: Fondazione Sardinia.

Simmel, G. (1990). *The philosophy of money*. London: Routledge. (First Publication 1907)

A Mechanism Approach for Money

2

This chapter briefly presents some sociological studies of particular value for the study of money. These studies will be used to identify theoretical and methodological elements useful for making hypotheses with which to analyse the Sardex case.

2.1 The Origins of the Sociology of Money

Geoffrey Ingham argues that the study of money in the social sciences was affected by the intellectual labour division that followed the Methodenstreit (2004, p. 59). The intellectual debate and controversy surrounding the validity of the methodology adopted in the social sciences led to the formation of the "Austrian" school of economists. It also meant that henceforth the study of money would be divided between Sociology and Economics, each with their own interests and their own methodologies. The economists abandoned all theoretical interest in the nature of money, while the sociologists turned their attention to the cultural and social conditions that allow money to circulate (ibid). The theoretical debate on money, though, already existed and had been well developed in classical sociology so it is still possible to ascertain the heuristic questions and the instruments required for a contemporary understanding and interpretation of money, its uses and effects.

In Parsons' (1950) idea of society, money is considered a generalised symbolic medium of communication and social interaction which contributes to the functional differentiation of various parts of the social system. As a symbol, money is considered a "neutral" veil over other elements and therefore has no tangible effects on either the economy or on society, which are both left in the background of money's field of action. Money, therefore, has no value in itself, but only embodies the values of the goods to which it refers. From this point of view, money recalls an idea of a transcendent society

G. Bazzani, *When Money Changes Society*, Wirtschaft + Gesellschaft,
https://doi.org/10.1007/978-3-658-28533-3_2

as opposed to the immanence of the social interaction in which money is involved. In the resulting intellectual labour division, sociologists have the role of addressing the integrative functions performed by money, leaving to economists the dynamics of money that affect the economy.

Parsons' approach to the study of money greatly influenced authors such as Habermas, Luhmann and Giddens (Dodd 1994; Ganssmann 1988) in the second half of the twentieth century. These authors consider money as a means for promoting social differentiation because of its role as mediator between goods and services, even over long distances in space and time. Money's existence, and the functions it performs in society, are seen as an outcome of historical and macro-social processes that overhang the immanence of the social interaction mediated by money. The explanatory model of functionalist money accepts a teleological view of money which is parallel to the economists' view that money is a mere tool for maximising individual utility. Ingham argues that modern sociology and economics have not grasped a key point of this approach: "*money is not merely a symbolic token that integrates 'disembedded social systems' (Giddens* 1990*); it is also* value *in itself. Control of money's production is a pivotal social institution*" (Ingham 2004, p. 61).

Marx also sees money as a neutral medium for goods within the more general framework of labour commodification (Marx 1904). The analysis of money belongs to the broader theory of the historical dynamics of capitalism. Marx, however, distanced himself from contemporary economists in explaining money, and did not consider that money was a mere symptom of the real economy, but rather that it was a symptom of the social structure behind the economic relations. Marx had grasped the capacity of credit to create money that went beyond economic productive activities in the strict sense. He believed that bank credit could expand beyond reasonable limits and become "*the most powerful means of driving capitalist production beyond its own limits, and this has become one of the most effective vehicles of crises and swindle*" (Marx 1981 [1894], p. 739). Despite the relevance of this prediction, Marx's analysis of the social and financial dimension of money does not include the self-generative capacity of money activated by the relationship between creditors and debtors, primarily between commercial banks and entrepreneurs. Money as a medium for exchanging goods does not capture the complex social relationships that underlie the ability of commercial banks to create money through the provision of loans. This capacity does not simply concern the gathering and transmission of pre-existing economic values, but refers to the creation of new values that did not previously exist (Schumpeter 1994 [1954], p. 113, quoted in Ingham 2004, p. 63). This point of view also makes it possible to describe the origin and economic and social effects of money by tracing the social mechanisms that money generates, not as a mere symptoms of pre-existing values, but as an institutional actor capable of producing their own effects.

Among the classical sociologists, it was Simmel who studied money most systematically. In his book, *The Philosophy of Money* (1990 [1907]), he describes how daily life in modern society is increasingly becoming fragmented and impersonal and how this quality finds a perfect expression in money: "*the more the life of society becomes dominated by monetary relationships, the more the relativistic character of existence finds its expression in conscious life*" (ibid, p. 518). This modern form of sociation is also constituted by the calculating character of money, which has introduced high precision and security in the convertibility and in the definition of equivalences and inequalities in social life. The privileged place for monetary exchange developments was in the late nineteenth-century metropoli, where everyone could perceive that everything was a potential object of purchase and exchange for a monetary value. Simmel rejects all the economic theories, including the Marxist one, which place the value of money in something substantive that refers to its material, to its production process, to the encounter between supply and demand or to the value of work. Money represents an abstract value (ibid, p. 126) that has an essentially relational nature: it represents an exchange based on an attribution of value that transcends the nature of the things exchanged and uses money as a mediator. Money creates a corresponding value between exchanged things, through its role as a mediator, without any real external referent to the attribution of value other than the social relationship itself. This analysis of money recalls both the immanence of the social interaction and the transcendence of the patterns of sociation (in Simmel's language) that shape society. Though this representation of money is successful in describing many of the characteristics of money and modern social relations, it does not explain how value is assigned, nor how it is linked to the forms and uses of money. In any case, Simmel's theoretical contribution to the sociological explanation of money is pivotal because money emerges from his analysis as a pattern of social as well as economic relations (Dodd 2014, p. 93). However, as in the marginalist economic approach, Simmel places the attribution of value beyond the interaction to which money gives form, placing it in an "elsewhere" that, although it is not only culturally formed as in the marginalist approach, is socially determined by the patterns of sociation through a process that is not sociologically described or explained.

In Weber's analysis, money expands the market and allows both indirect and long-distance spatial and temporal exchanges between supply and demand. For Weber, it is crucial that money creates a unit for the value attribution for all goods or services (Weber 1978 [1922], p. 81). This increases the possibilities of exchange, bypassing the problem of the need for spatial and temporal contiguity of the goods and subjects involved. In a new way for the time, Weber's economic reading holds together the economic view of the match between supply and demand and the socialist criticism of the power struggle. In Weber's analysis, prices are the effect of the encounter between supply and demand but they are also the "*product of conflicts of interest [that] result from power constellations in the struggle for economic existence. Money is primarily a weapon in this struggle, and prices are expressions of this struggle*" (ibid, p. 108 cited in Ingham 2004, p. 67). Money for Weber is not a mere spectator of competition in the market: it is "*a weapon*" that influences market dynamics. In this perspective, money plays an active part in determining prices. Far from being just a neutral veil covering economic or social dynamics, money contributes to shaping them. As a unit of account, money produces a rational computability of economic activity and establishes equivalences between goods and services that would otherwise be impossible. In addition, Weber recognises that the quantity of money circulating is not neutral but generates effects. In fact, if monetary policies are the legitimate expression of a ruling government, they necessarily respond to power and interest groups, which are unlikely to produce the "right" amount and the "right" type of circulating money (ibid, p. 183) for society as a whole. Monetary policies are always under the pressure of interest groups in the struggle for survival. Weber helps us recognise the essentially political nature of money creation and the social and political effects necessarily generated by the quantity and quality of money in circulation.

Classical sociology clearly identified the political, social, and economic nature of money production and use, although, with the exception of Simmel, little effort was made to trace the micro-level social mechanisms through which money operates in society. Instead, money was usually described at the macro-social level as a significant actor in the dynamics of social change in modernity, within the different theoretical perspectives of the authors mentioned above. Sociologists and economists tended to share the view of money as a neutral medium, convertible into almost all goods and services, indifferent to the attributions of value for which it could be used. The neoclassical economic approach went so far as to assume a full and constant convertibility between time, money and utility. In classical sociological analyses the social effects of the use of money tend to converge towards a flattening and impersonality of social relations mediated by the use of money. The convertibility of the value attributed to each good or service into units of money is seen as a progressive flattening of the variety of social relations that are always emotionally, affectively, intentionally and intellectually characterised. Such relationships seem to be progressively emptied of these qualities in order to converge towards forms of relationship mediated and characterised by their monetary value.

2.2 The Contemporary Sociology of Money

Viviana Zelizer, in her book, *The Social Meaning of Money* (1995), completely reverses the traditional interpretation of the social effects of money. For Zelizer, social life itself changes money. First of all, the author notes that money is essentially not a homogeneous entity. She includes in the money category "*all the objects that have recognised, regularised exchange value in one social setting or another*" (ibid., p. 21). Furthermore, people can use the currency in different ways, according to specific social customs and meanings. Gifts, wages, coupons and stamps are all examples of money substitutes, which can perform the function of exchange and of equivalence in a similar manner to money, but with very specific and different social uses and meanings. For example, a salary may have a value equivalent to that of a gift but its use and social meaning are very different. Zelizer focuses on three specific cases of differentiated money: domestic money, gift money and poor people's money. Her research focuses on the United States in the period between 1870 and 1930: her wide variety of sources includes songs, sermons, articles in women's magazines, newspaper ads, guides for charitable institutions and court rulings on disputes between husband and wife. In this wide-ranging research, Zelizer reconstructs how money became differentiated and specialised in specific social uses and meanings. The analysis of the changes that took place over several decades in the quantity, quality, use, meanings and family relationships that had brought "pin money" into being, is very relevant for a sociological understanding of money. Pin money is the currency that husbands used to give their wives money. At the beginning of the period of Zelizer's study, the husband's work was pratically the only source of money for the family. How this money was spent, by whom and for what purposes, was sometimes subject to family disputes and changes over time. By combining the recommendations for the good housewife in women's magazines, with the court records of cases that involved disputes between spouses over pin money, Zelizer reconstructs the socially shared horizon within which money performed specific functions, one of which was regulating authority and power within the family. Pin money has been used over time and among different social groups in different ways for the purchase of family essentials, for the purchase of the wife's own personal goods or for children's or for everyone's needs without distinction. The use, from time to time, depending on the situation and the historical period, was imposed by the husband, chosen by the wife, decided by negotiation or dispute, capable of fracturing the family and of consolidating it. Money as described by Zelizer is both an effect of cultural values and a producer of specific forms of social relations. Money is not always the same in different contexts: a sum of money given as compensation for damage is not the same as money given for the support of children, or the same sum given in memory of a dead person. Zelizer's money is far from being a mere vehicle for uniforming and levelling social relationships: it is immersed in and gives shape to specific forms of social relationships. Considering it as a single neutral equivalent of exchange would be a reductionist operation that hides its true social nature.

Geoffrey Ingham conducted extensive research on the origin of money in his famous book *The Nature of Money* (2004). His research seeks answers some general questions regarding the nature of money, its essence, its genesis and its ability to be worthy of its value. Like Zelizer, Ingham rejects the vision of money as a mere facilitator of monetary transactions without any real influence in the economy. In the traditional interpretation of economics, money spontaneously emerged from the market to facilitate transactions, replacing bartering because of its efficiency and flexibility. For Ingham, this interpretation fails for two reasons: firstly, it does not recognise the influence that money can have on the economy and, secondly, it ignores the fact that money came into being as the result of political and social struggles. Ingham follows Weber's suggestion regarding the political nature of money and the economy and Knapp's interpretation of the genesis of money through the state (1973 [1924]). In this perspective, Ingham identifies two fundamental characteristics of money. The first sees money not only as a means of exchange, but also as a unit of account with capacity for accumulation and transfer (Ingham 2004, p. 69). The second fundamental feature of money is its capacity to trigger a relationship between debtor and creditor. The potential of money to transform itself into credit, and the different ways it can be produced, highlight its nature as a social relationship: "*Different modes of production of money may be identified. These consist in social relations between issuers, between issuer and users, between users and in the technological means available for the storage and transportation of abstract value —from clay tablets to coins, pen and paper, magnetic traces and so on*" (ibid., p. 77–78). Ingham stresses that a currency can only emerge in the presence of an authority which guarantees the stability of the value of the currency itself, because interpersonal trust is insufficient to ensure the value of the currency over time and space. The value of a currency is ultimately given by the confidence placed in the state, especially in its ability to repay its debts by taxing its citizens. In this sense, the value of money is "*the enacted outcome of social and political conflicts between the main interests in the economy*" (ibid., p. 81). Ingham identifies four historical ideal-types for creating the value of money: "*different modes for the production of money entail … typical struggles which are also involved in establishing the value of money. For example, in capitalism, a central conflict is between the debtor classes, who demand 'soft credit', and the creditors, who want safe 'hard money'*" (ibid., p. 78). Ingham describes how different forms of money, linked to major social changes, have emerged throughout history with the creation in recent times of nation states with centralised currency emission. This concentration and depersonalisation of credit paves the way for the emergence of financial markets and the expansion of credit leverage or, in the case of economic downturn, a general reduction of credit leverage. Ingham takes up the analysis of substantialist Weberian money, examining the historical, social and political conditions which led to the emergence of specific forms of money. From this point of view, money is not a neutral vehicle of modern rationalisation or a mere facilitator of exchanges, but instead it is the effect of political and social struggles and a mediator of specific forms of social relations in the provision of credit.

Nigel Dodd expands the analysis of the possible social effects of money by examining the utopian dimension in which money is created and develops (Dodd 1994, 2005, 2014, 2015). Referring to Simmel's concept of perfect money (1990), Dodd describes how essentially all currencies were designed and implemented for the purpose of shaping a utopian society. In the literal sense of the term, a utopian society is a society which does not exist and money, with its design, at the same time foreshadows and favours its creation (Dodd 2015, p. 79). Dodd discusses the many social dimensions embodied in currencies immersed in the past, emphasising their utopian tension through the classification of five main parameters (ibid., p. 81). The first parameter concerns the type of criticism that recently reformed currencies level at existing ones. This ranges from the belief that the currency in use is producing injustices, excessive or reduced wages in the criticism made by Ruskin—which led to the formulation of "Labour money" (Ruskin 1928)—to Fisher's criticism that it created financial instability—the Chicago Plan proposed a 100 % Reserve Plan as an answer to the great depression (Fisher 1935). The second classifying parameter is the definition of money which underpins the purposes of the reformers. This ranges from being just a medium of exchange in Gesell's Rotting money (1958 [1916]), to being considered as a debt in the Social credit money projects of Douglas (1979) or Riegel's Private enterprise money (1944). The third parameter, the level of implementation and governance of the new money, ranges from the local level in Ruskin's Labour money to the state level in Douglas' Social Credit to the global level in Bitcoin (Nakamoto 2008). The fourth parameter, the type of money created, ranges from endogenous credit, in Proudhon's People's Bank project (1927), to being exogenously created through a peer-to-peer payment system, as in Bitcoin. The final parameter, perhaps the most important one, concerns the goals that underlie the creation and design of the money. These goals reveal underlying social projects, but are also a form of response to pressing social problems that existed at the time a particular currency was designed. The utopian goals include: attaining real liberal equality (Gesell's Rotting money project), promoting social justice with anti-capitalist under-tones (Proudhon's People's bank project), attempting sustainability and monetary equilibrium (Douthwaite's 2006 Ecological money).

Perhaps the best developed project of utopian money is the Euro which is currently in a re-evaluation phase. The Euro was introduced in 1999 and it represents the most ambitious attempt at monetary unity among developed countries. It can be seen as the last step in the process of European integration that commenced after the Second World War, in accordance with the integration model proposed by Monnet. The advancement of European economic, social and political integration had been achieved until then primarily through a *de facto* integration of economic and governance structures, and it was assumed that this progressive integration would lead to the establishment of a common political and constitutional ethos of the European peoples (Habermas 2012). Thus, the ambitious Euro project was organised around the idea that "*you can create a European society through economic means*" (Swedberg 2013, p. 2). The supranational integration and economic prosperity produced by the new currency is seen as a means of fostering social and political integration between citizens of different nation states. Krugman clarified the terms of the utopian Euro project: "*The point is to deliver a series of economic integration plans that do double duty: they're economically productive, but they also create* de facto *solidarity*" ("The Euro and the European Project" cit. in Swedberg 2013, p. 13, cit. Dodd 2015, p. 97).

The utopian dimension contained in specific forms of money leads us to consider the central role that expectations play within the capitalist dynamic. Jens Beckert (2015) has described how a theory of capitalist dynamics cannot only be based on the analysis of macro-phenomena such as technological progress, the division of labour, institutional change or the growth of production factors: "*What we need to be explained is how these aspects are related to social action. Ultimately, it is what actors do that gives a social system its dynamism. A theory of capitalist dynamics therefore requires a micro basis*" ibid., p. 75). Beckert identifies four fundamental elements to explain capitalist dynamics: money and credit, investments, innovation and consumption. These elements contribute to the capitalist dynamic thanks to the fundamental role that expectations play among entrepreneurs and consumers in each of the four key factors. Expectations are socially and institutionally supported and they play a central role in market coordination. In order for markets to function, they must resolve three fundamental problems of coordination: value attribution, competition and cooperation (Beckert 2009). From this point of view, money plays a role in the attribution of value with the function of unit of account, together with exogenous factors, and in promoting interpersonal and institutional trust and stabilising cooperation. The social role played by money in stabilising cooperation is evident in the national state unification projects and the centralisation of money described by Ingham (2004), as well as in the socio-political unification project of the European Union mediated by the Euro, described by Dodd (2015) and Swedberg (2013).

Classical and contemporary sociologists have developed valuable research bases that make it possible to affirm that money is an effect of specific socio-historical conditions but is also capable of producing relevant economic and social effects. Evans synthesises this double movement in the metaphor of money-change-value and value-change-money (Evans 2009 cit. Sartori 2016, p. 285). This metaphor represents the two-way dimension of the interaction between money and society well. Looking at the analysis of money made by the above mentioned classical and contemporary sociologists, it seems reasonable to extend the metaphor of the double movement of money to wider social forces beyond the mere analysis of values. Following the analysis of the classics, it is possible to affirm, in general, that *society-changes-money* (Parsons, Weber, Marx and also Ingham and Zelizer) and also that *money-changes-society* (Simmel, Weber and also Dodd and Beckert). Both directions of movement are significant for understanding how money is—and can be—created and used.

An analysis of the classic texts that discuss the evolution of the relationship between money and society shows they usually have the origin of modern society as their historical reference, except for Simmel who primarily focuses on the late nineteenth century metropolis. This type of analysis, also accepted by Ingham, make it possible to elaborate macro-theories of modern social change and its relationship with money. Even Zelizer, though her work is recent, analyses United States society in the late nineteenth and early twentieth centuries. Her analysis is much more detailed when she describes the social mechanisms linked to the double social movement of money at the level of family interaction. Within this theoretical framework of the double movement between society and money, there are only a few examples of analysis of how this double movement functions in contemporary society. Among the authors mentioned, only Dodd goes so far as to search for the utopian dimension of money in contemporary currencies (i.e. euro and bitcoin) while Beckert describes the influence of money on the capitalist dynamic: both authors follow the money-change-society direction.

The study of contemporary money is therefore useful for testing the validity of social macro-change theories described by classical sociologists in relation to money, but also for developing fine-grained explanations of the social mechanisms that explain the reciprocal influences between money and society.

2.3 An Analytical Approach to the Study of Money

Simmel was the first to undertake sociological analysis of the functioning of money at the micro level (1990 [1907]). Money is considered a pattern of sociation which determines the form of social interaction and which has the well-known effects of depersonalising and freeing the subjects involved (ibid., p. 298 ff.). A contemporary approach to the sociological study of money should attempt to identify the mechanisms which link money to contemporary social phenomena. The authors cited provide suggestions on the reciprocal influence between money and society but, given the contextual nature of social phenomena, specific forms of money and different historical and geographical contexts may reveal different mechanisms for the functioning of money.

> Different modes of production of money may be identified. These consist in social relations between issuers, between issuer and users and between users and in the technological means available for the storage and transportation of abstract value — from clay tablets to coins, pen and paper, magnetic traces and so on (Ingham 2004, pp. 77–78).

The mutual influences between money and society need to be investigated using a fine-grained approach that is able to identify which elements affect the social interaction and in what direction. To this end, the methodological debate recently developed around social mechanism and analytical sociology can provide useful insights for the study of money.[1]

The explanatory aim of analytical sociology is based on the idea of social mechanism. The concept of mechanism requires that, by observing a specific social dynamic, the explanation is able to identify the elements generating the phenomenon described. For example, by observing that, as wealth changes, consumption habits change, researchers should be able to describe which elements, after varying the amount of money available, lead to a change in consumption habits. From this point of view, money would no longer be the cause of the observed social phenomenon, but only one of the elements at stake that can be used to explain *how* the action is brought about. The generative mechanism can therefore be a set of elements that need to be understood in order to explain how the action is brought about. The statistical correlation between the amount of money and new consumption styles is not a sufficient sociological explanation of the phenomenon in itself, but the statistical correlation itself is treated as a black box whose functioning

---

[1]Although the term and the use of social mechanisms have been debated for some time, the research program became clearer and more coherent in the mid-1990s. The book *Social Mechanisms: An Analytical Approach to Social Theory* (Hedström and Swedberg 1998) quickly become a point of reference for the debate on social mechanisms and the most cited text in the field. The next most relevant contribution is *Dissecting the Social: On the Principles of Analytical Sociology* in which Hedström (2005) proposes a coherent and organic research program for an analytical sociological approach. For recent developments see Maurer (2016), Demeulenaere (2011), Hedström and Berman (2009).

needs to be described. The concept of mechanism is however an empty concept in itself, which needs to be associated with specific elements that vary in each situation: "*social mechanism, as here defined, describes a constellation of entities and activities that are organised such that they regularly bring about a particular type of outcome*" (Hedström 2005, p. 25).[2]

Despite the intense debate about the conditions of validity of this approach and its correct interpretation, some principles appear clear enough to be used for the study of the social mechanisms of money. First of all, the concepts used should be as clear and precise as possible in describing the phenomena observed.[3] Although clarity and precision in the use of concepts may lead to the loss of part of their semantic richness, this precision of the concepts, used in relation to the external referents they wish to describe, is an essential feature. Otherwise, the evidence provided would not be able to clearly interpret the interactions between different elements involved in the observed social processes. The conceptual clarity of the *explanandum* should lead to a clear identification of the indicators to be used, both qualitative and quantitative (Hedström and Swedberg 1998, p. 136–137). The social mechanisms approach does not deny the validity of statistical analysis, but warns against an overly relaxed use of multivariate analysis in order to elaborate sociological explanations:

> The crucial point here is that no matter how carefully the variables entering a statistical model are chosen; no matter how resistant the structure of the model's estimates is to different model specifications; no matter how large the amount of outcome variability accounted for by the predictors' variability—the model's coefficients cannot provide a detailed representation of the entities, the activities, and the relations among those entities and activities that are likely to be responsible for the observed outcome(s) … No matter how carefully specified and sophisticated a statistical model may be, it can only provide a parsimonious description of a set of relations that represents the individual or social-level signature of a (set of) social mechanism(s). But it cannot provide an explicit, detailed, and dynamic representation of that mechanism and of its high-level consequences (Manzo 2014, p. 13).

Different social phenomena require the analysis of the role of different elements, their characteristics and how they connect with each other. The same social phenomenon could be the subject of different levels of analysis. The case of the diffusion of wealth can be described in generative mechanisms, for example, both in the functioning of regulatory institutions and at the level of social interaction or at the level of psychological dynamics. Different elements and mechanisms carry out the action simultaneously at

[2]"*Explaining the behaviour of a social system by means of three components: the effects of properties of the system on the constraints or orientations of actors; the action of actors who are within the system; and the combination or interaction of those actions, bringing about the systemic behaviour*" (Coleman 1990, p. 27).

[3]"*Precise, action-based, abstract, and fine-grained explanations*" (Hedström and Swedberg 1998, p. 25).

different levels of analysis (Goldthorpe 2001; Hedström 2005, p. 62–63). It is also reasonable to assume that within complex social phenomena, such as the functioning of money, articulated sets of different social mechanisms are simultaneously involved in bringing about the action. The aim of this research is to describe the sets of social mechanisms that explain the observed economic effects of using Sardex money.

For these reasons, the explanatory program of analytical sociology concerns the basic elements that bring about the action. These basic elements must be described in terms of their characteristics, functioning and interaction with other elements. The basic element of social functioning that is usually considered in analytical sociology is the individual (Hedström 2005; Hedström and Bearman 2009), in the wake of the methodological individualism of Boudon (1986). Although the observation of individual behaviour and the use of the individual as a unit of analysis can be a valid starting point for the explanation of many social dynamics, this theoretical approach has often been criticised for the risk of reductionism in the explanation of social phenomena (Abbott 2007; Sampson 2011; Sawyer 2011).[4]

The sociological explanation of how money functions is a situation in which the explanation cannot consider only the characteristics of the individuals involved, but must also consider the characteristics of money. In fact, as the central banks that regulate the money supply well know, even the variation of a few tenths of a point in the cost of money can generate relevant changes in individual behaviour regarding savings or investments. The social mechanisms that bring about these phenomena cannot be adequately understood without considering the characteristics of money (in this case the discount rate), its mode of operation (the lending of bank credit) and the motivations and constraints of the individuals who use money. So it can be argued that, for the analysis of the social mechanisms regarding how money functions, the analysis of the characteristics of money and its rules of functioning are as important as the action model that explains the economic actions of entrepreneurs.

2.4 Socio-Material Mechanisms

When Jens Beckert (2015), analysed the role of expectations in determining capitalist dynamics, he explained how a theory of this dynamic cannot only be based on an analysis of macro-phenomena such as technological progress, the division of labour,

[4] "*Hedström has made important clarifications and, in effect, relaxed the requirements for the kinds of mechanisms that can be used in solid social mechanisms-based explanations. For example, in stressing that the idea of social mechanisms, "does not tell us how to conceptualise human action" (Hedström and Ylikoski* 2010, *p. 60), he emphasised that intentional action manifested in desires, beliefs, and opportunities (DBO) are not the only things that qualify as micro foundations. Habits, routines, scheme-following, and other more or less unconscious behaviours may also be evoked as micro-level mechanisms. Moreover, the level of complexity, or inversely, the extent to which social-mechanism-based explanations should build on abstractions and simplifications, is now seen as a choice of the analyst*" (Edling and Rydgren 2016, p. 1138).

institutional change or the growth of the factors of production, but: "*what we need to be explained is how these aspects are related to social action. Ultimately, it is what actors do that gives a social system its dynamism. A theory of capitalist dynamics therefore requires a micro basis*" (ibid., p. 75). Likewise, for the sociological analysis of the functioning of money, an understanding of how the different characteristics of the elements involved interact with each other is essential in order to understand the social mechanisms that bring about the action, in the terms described in the previous section. Individuals who interact with money find themselves involved in a socio-technical network for which interactions among individuals—ascribable to values, norms, beliefs and preferences—are, by themselves, insufficient to explain the role that the characteristics of money have.

Analysis of the distribution of roles among the different elements that contribute to the functioning of the markets is a well-established area of sociological research (Callon 1990; Cetina and Preda 2006; Muniesa et al. 2007; Cochoy et al. 2016; Brewer 2017; Hopkinson 2017; Stigzelius et al. 2018), which has been extensively developed in the research field using the theoretical approach of *performativity* (Aspers 2007; Hawkins 2012; MacKenzie and Millo 2003; MacKenzie 2004). Michel Callon suggests, for example, using the carbon trading market as a specific case of a device capable of distributing roles (2009). Using the idea of performativity of economic theories,[5] the author shows how the implementation of the carbon trading market is a clear case of transition from an *in vitro* experiment to an *in vivo* one.[6]

Carbon trading can be considered as a very specific form of money (Bazzani 2019). In fact, carbon trading certificates are a form of money that performs the function of a unit of account and this functioning cannot be traced back to any hypothetical exchange system that arose "naturally" among the economic actors as the result of preferences generated independently of how the regulatory bodies had designed these exchanges. The carbon trading market exists only because it was intentionally designed by the policy maker in the wake of precise economic theories and the exchange object itself—the issuance certificate—exists only as a means of exchange designed to be traded in the carbon trading market.[7]

---

[5]For an introduction, see Mitchell (2005), Callon et al. (2007), Çalışkan and Callon (2009) and Muniesa (2014).

[6]*In vitro* experiments are those realised by economists when they mathematically model the functioning of a market and try to hypothesise how it would function best. *In vivo* experiments are when from theory the next step is a regulatory government body designing the functioning of the market (Callon 2009, p. 357; Callon et al. 2002).

[7]Although in many cases the hypothesis of economic theories having performative effects on market functioning may be the subject of debate, in the case of carbon trading their effects appear evident. This does not detract from legitimacy, nor does it exclude the possible relevance and complementarity of other explanatory models of the phenomenon (e.g., neo-institutionalism, rational choice, social networks, etc.) but it focuses attention on aspects and explanatory links that are often

This process of designing the functioning of the currency to be exchanged and the functioning of its market is obviously not neutral with respect to the results and effects that carbon trading will produce. The regulatory body defines the internalities and externalities of the system as well as the operating rules: these can activate, or not activate, specific chains of action and social mechanisms among actors in the field which can produce results that may, or may not, be in line with expectations and can also throw up unexpected effects (see Pettenger 2016; Kuch 2015).

The socio-technical device category (socio-technical *agencements*), is the one that most effectively lends itself to describing the complexity of the network of elements involved in the implementation of a specific form of money and the effects it can produce.[8] The carbon trading market, as a specific form of money, can be considered a socio-technical device: a complex social and technical network made up of actors (politicians, economists, jurists, entrepreneurs, workers, citizens, etc.) and objects (molecules, certificates, measuring instruments, regulations, software, etc.) that interact with each other in a way that is not completely predictable compared to what might be expected from a stabilised theory of social action.

To understand how a socio-technical device functions, the network of interactions that it creates needs to be observed and described.[9] In the case of currency design, the distinction between internality and externality is a decisive element for its functioning, especially in relation to the possible difference between the lines of demarcation set by the designers and the lines of demarcation between internality and externalities observable when the currency is used. The way money operates as a socio-technical device is designed so as to prescribe roles for the actors involved, including some actors in the device and in the frame of the action envisaged (e.g., investors) while, at the same time, excluding others (e.g., entrepreneurs without collateral as a guarantee or without consolidated financial statements). The design can also include or exclude specific interaction frames (e.g., usury or gift exchanges between banks and customers). In this perspective, money as a socio-technical device contributes to distributing roles among the actors involved, defining the boundaries of the network of actors involved and stabilising the forms of social action (Bontempi 2018). The description of the roles assumed by the different social and technical elements involved in the functioning of the device is fundamentally important for an effective understanding of how the currency functions which then allows hypotheses to be elaborated to verify the social mechanisms present.

---

little considered. In fact, in the case of carbon trading, scientists—despite disagreeing with one another on various aspects of this subject—provide the definition and quantification of the good that has to be exchanged in the market (the emissions), while the policy maker, with the advice of economists and jurists, designs and implements the functioning of the market, identifying the internality and the externality of the system.

[8]For an introduction to this concept see Muniesa et al. (2007) and Callon (2007).

[9]For an introduction to this argument see Akrich and Latour (1992). For conceptualising the forms of agency within the socio-technical network see Bontempi (2017).

The way in which money is designed to function describes an audience of actors who could potentially become involved, outlines the characteristics of the actors who have access to money, establishes a horizon of legitimacy of access to the commodity and, in sociological terms, a specific frame of social interaction (Goffman 1974; Cetina and Preda 2001). Setting aside a deductive approach to the explanation of social action—which uses particular innate or intrinsic human qualities (e.g., *Homo oeconomicus* or social Darwinism)—and adopting a neutral gaze towards observable models of action, it is possible to describe how money as a socio-technical device can favour specific models of social action linked to the way in which the roles are distributed and to the lines of demarcation between internalities and externalities linked to its mode of functioning.

It is necessary to have a neutral point of observation for identifying the elements, which from time to time are significant for explaining the social mechanisms of money, in order to understand their real influence and their characteristics. Chap. 4, *Social mechanisms* influenced by Sardex, shows how it is necessary to consider specific, sometimes different, characteristics of the elements involved so as to explain each single social mechanism. Using the utilitarian action model as only one of the possible models of social action, not as the only model in the economic sphere, it is possible to describe which elements among those identified—individual (e.g., preferences and beliefs), institutional and regulatory (e.g., Sardex Ltd and broker team) and technical (e.g., interest rate and mode of money circulation)—contribute, and to what extent they each carry out the observed social effects. In this way, a neutral starting position is used with respect to the elements to be considered in the analysis and in relation to the mechanisms that explain the use of money and the way in which this can change society.

References

Abbott, A. (2007). Mechanisms and relations. *Sociologica, 1*(2), 1–22.

Akrich, M., & Latour, B. (1992). A summary of a convenient vocabulary for the semiotics of humans and non-human assemblies. In W. Bijker & J. Law (Eds.), *Shaping technology, building society: Studies in sociotechnical change*. Cambridge, MA: MIT Press.

Aspers, P. (2007). Theory, reality, and performativity in markets. *American Journal of Economics and Sociology, 66*(2), 379–398.

Bazzani, G. (2019). Teorie del denaro e carbon trading: Il frame dell'azione sociale per fronteggiare il riscaldamento globale. *Jura Gentium, 16*(1), 74–96.

Beckert, J. (2009). The social order of markets. *Theory and society, 38*(3), 245–269.

Beckert, J. (2015). Re-imagining capitalist dynamics. Fictional expectations and the openness of economic futures. In P. Aspers & N. Dodd (Eds.), *Re-imagining economic sociology*. Oxford: Oxford University Press.

Bontempi, M. (2017). Networks of actants. Conceptualizing agency and actor as networks' effects in actor-network theory. *Politica & Società, 6*(1), 7–30.

Bontempi, M. (2018). Concetti socio-materiali e critica sociale. Alcune implicazioni per la teoria sociologica a partire da un contributo di L. Gallino. *Quaderni di sociologia, 3*(18), 81–100.

Boudon, R. (1986). *Theories of social change: A critical appraisal*, Berkeley, CA: University of California Press.

Brewer, B. D. (2017). Making the 'handmade' bike and trying to make a living: Market objects, field-configuring events and some limits to market making. *Consumption Markets & Culture, 20*(6), 523–538.

Callon, M. (1990). Techno-economic networks and irreversibility. *The Sociological Review, 38*(1_suppl), 132–161.

Callon, M. (2007). An essay on the growing contribution of economic markets to the proliferation of the social. *Theory, Culture & Society, 24*(7–8), 139–163.

Callon, M. (2009). Civilizing markets carbon trading between in vitro and in vivo experiments. *Accounting, Organizations and Society, 34*(3–4), 535–548.

Callon, M., Méadel, C., & Rabeharisoa, V. (2002). The economy of qualities. *Economy and Society, 31*(2), 194–217.

Callon, M., Millo, Y., & Muniesa, F. (Eds.). (2007). *Market devices*. Oxford: Blackwell.

Çalışkan, K., & Callon, M. (2009). Economization, part 1: shifting attention from the economy towards processes of economization. *Economy and Society, 38*(3), 369–398.

Cetina, K. K., & Preda, A. (2001). The epistemization of economic transactions. *Current Sociology, 49*(4), 27–44.

Cetina, K. K., & Preda, A. (2006). *The sociology of financial markets*. Oxford: Oxford University Press.

Cochoy, F., Trompette, P., & Araujo, L. (2016). From market agencements to market agencing: An introduction. *Consumption Markets & Culture, 19*(1), 3–16.

Coleman, J. S. (1990). *Foundations of social theory*. Cambridge: Belknap Press.

Demeulenaere, P. (Ed.). (2011). *Analytical sociology and social mechanisms*. New York, NY: Cambridge University Press.

Dodd, N. (1994). *The sociology of money*. Cambridge: Polity.

Dodd, N. (2005). Reinventing monies in Europe. *Economy and Society, 34*(4), 558–583.

Dodd, N. (2014). *The social life of money*. Princeton, NJ: Princeton University Press.

Dodd, N. (2015). Utopianism and the future of money. In P. Aspers & N. Dodd (Eds.), *Re-imagining economic sociology*. Oxford: Oxford University Press.

Douglas, C. H. (1979). *Social credit*. Pamplin, VA: Institute of Economic Democracy.

Douthwaite, R. (2006). *The ecology of money*. Cloughjordan: Feasta.

Edling, C., & Rydgren, J. (2016). Social mechanisms in empirical sociology: Introduction to special issue. *American Behavioral Scientist, 60*(10), 1135–1145.

Evans, M. S. (2009). Zelizer's Theory of Money & the Case of Local Currencies. *Environment and Planning, 41*, 1026–1041.

Fisher, I. (1935). *100% Money: Designed to keep checking banks 100% liquid; to prevent inflation and deflation; largely to cure or prevent depressions; and to wipe out much of the National Debt*. New York, NY: Harper and Row.

Ganssmann, H. (1988). Money – A symbolically generalized medium of communication? On the concept of money in recent sociology. *Economy and Society, 17*, 285–315.

Gesell, S. (1958). *The Natural Economic Order*, London: Peter Owen Ltd (First Publication 1916).

Giddens, A. (1990). *The consequences of modernity*. Cambridge: Polity.

Goffman, E. (1974). *Frame analysis: An essay on the organization of experience*. Cambridge, MA: Harvard University Press.

Goldthorpe, J. H. (2001). Causation, statistics, and sociology. *European Sociological Review, 17*(1), 1–20.

Habermas, J. (2012). *The crisis of the European Union*. Cambridge: Polity.

Hawkins, G. (2012). The performativity of food packaging: Market devices, waste crisis and recycling. *The Sociological Review, 60*(2), 66–83.
Hedström, P. (2005). *Dissecting the social: On the principles of analytical sociology*. Cambridge: Cambridge University Press.
Hedström, P., & Bearman, P. S. (Eds.). (2009). *The Oxford handbook of analytical sociology*. Oxford: Oxford University Press.
Hedström, P., & Swedberg, R. (Eds.). (1998). *Social mechanisms: An analytical approach to social theory*. Cambridge: Cambridge University Press.
Hedström, P., & Ylikoski, P. (2010). Causal mechanisms in the social sciences. *Annual Review of Sociology, 36*, 49–67.
Hopkinson, G. C. (2017). Making a market for male dairy calves: Alternative and mainstream relationality. *Journal of Marketing Management, 33*(7–8), 556–579.
Ingham, G. (2004). *The nature of money*. Cambridge: Polity.
Knapp, G. F. (1973). *The state theory of money*. New York, NY: Augustus M. Kelley. (First Publication 1924).
Kuch, D. (2015). *The rise and fall of carbon emissions trading*. London: Palgrave Macmillan.
MacKenzie, D. (2004). The big, bad wolf and the rational market: Portfolio insurance, the 1987 crash and the performativity of economics. *Economy and Society, 33*(3), 303–334.
MacKenzie, D., & Millo, Y. (2003). Constructing a market, performing theory: The historical sociology of a financial derivatives exchange. *American Journal of Sociology, 109*(1), 107–145.
Manzo, G. (Ed.). (2014). *Analytical sociology: Actions and networks*. Chichester: Wiley.
Marx, K. (1981). *Capital* (Vol. 3). Harmondsworth: Penguin.
Marx, K. (1904). *A contribution to the critique of political economy*. Chicago, IL: Charles H. Kerr.
Maurer, A. (2016). Social mechanisms as special cases of explanatory sociology: Notes toward systemizing and expanding mechanism-based explanation within sociology. *Analyse & Kritik, 38*(1), 31–52.
Mitchell, T. (2005). The work of economics: How a discipline makes its world. *European Journal of Sociology/ Archives Européennes De Sociologie/ Europäisches Archiv Für Soziologie, 46*(2), 297–320.
Muniesa, F. (2014). *The provoked economy: Economic reality and the performative turn*. London: Routledge.
Muniesa, F., Millo, Y., & Callon, M. (2007). An introduction to market devices. *The Sociological Review, 55*(s2), 1–12.
Nakamoto, S. (2008). *Bitocin: A Peer-to-Peer Electronic Cash System*. https://bitcoin.org/bitcoin.pdf. Accessed 1 March 2020.
Parsons, T. (1950). *Social system*. New York, NY: Free Press.
Pettenger, M. E. (Ed.). (2016). *The social construction of climate change: Power, knowledge, norms, discourses*. New York, NY: Routledge.
Proudhon, J. F. (1927). *Proudhon's solution of the social problem*. New York, NY: Vanguard Press.
Riegel, E. C. (1944). *Private enterprise money: A non-political money system*. New York, NY: Harbinger House.
Ruskin, J. (1928). *Time and tide and Munera Pulveris*. London: Macmillan.
Sampson, R. J. (2011). Neighborhood effects, causal mechanisms and the social structure of the city. In P. Demeulenaere (Ed.), *Analytical sociology and social mechanisms*. New York, NY: Cambridge University Press.
Sartori, L., & Dini, P. (2016). From complementary currency to institution: A micro-macro study of the Sardex mutual credit system. *Stato e Mercato, 36*(2), 273–304.
Sawyer, K. (2011). Conversation as mechanism: Emergence in creative groups. In P. Demeulenaere (Ed.), *Analytical sociology and social mechanisms*. New York, NY: Cambridge University Press.

Schumpeter, J. A. (1994). *History of economic analysis*. London: Routledge. (First Publication 1954).

Simmel, G. (1990). *The Philosophy of money*. London: Routledge.

Stigzelius, I., Araujo, L., Mason, K., Murto, R. Palo, & Palo, T. (2018). Kitchen concerns at the boundary between markets and consumption: Agencing practice change in times of scarcity (Husmodern, Sweden 1938–1958). *Consumption Markets & Culture, 21*(4), 347–372.

Swedberg, R. (2013). *An elephant in the room or can you create a European Community through economic means?* Ithaca, NY: Cornell University, Dept. of Sociology.

Weber, M. (1978). *Economy and society*. Berkeley, CA: University of California Press. (First Publication 1922).

Zelizer, V. (1995). *The social meaning of money: Pin money, paychecks, poor relief and other currencies*. New York, NY: Basic Books.

3 The Sardex Experience

This chapter provides a brief introduction to complementary currencies, focussing in particular on the forerunners of the Sardex currency. Subsequently it describes the background to setting up the Sardex complementary currency and explains how this currency functions.

3.1 Money and Complementary Currencies

The use of just one currency within a vast geographical area is a relatively recent historical development. As nation states formed in Europe their new sovereign authorities attempted to centralise power and affirmed their exclusive right to issue money. Prior to this it was common for different currencies and circulating exchange units to co-exist, often in competition with one another. The rise of nation states seemed to have definitively brought to an end the simultaneous presence of different circulating currencies. Research reveals, however, that thousands of complementary currencies have come into being, some of them in recent years. Their creation is often in response to economic, political, social and, more recently, environmental crises and their objective is to prefigure new models of social regulation that respond to emerging needs (Amato and Fantacci 2013, 2015).

Over the last thirty years 4500 complementary currency systems, community credit and alternative financial systems have been documented in the literature (Blanc 2013; Servet 2013). These systems have brought into being a large variety of currencies which have sought to address a wide range of aims and objectives, in the following areas: cultural, governmental, economic, social and environmental. Place and Bindewald (2015) summarise the principal categories of aims and objectives that emerge from these currencies by analytically distinguishing meta, macro, meso and micro levels within each of

G. Bazzani, *When Money Changes Society*, Wirtschaft + Gesellschaft,
https://doi.org/10.1007/978-3-658-28533-3_3

the five areas. In this way they define 37 wide-ranging objectives of a cultural, economic, environmental and social nature (ibid., pp. 158–159).[1]

The common denominators of such different experiences are the geographical restrictions placed on currency circulation and the attempt to respond to economic or social needs which, in the eyes of the actors involved, are not being met by the current ordinary currency. Complementary currencies usually arise in response to specific economic, social or environmental needs and carry with them expectations of results in line with these needs. Unlike the many recent virtual currencies (e.g., Bitcoin), complementary currencies do not aspire to replace the current currency but "only" to fill gaps in the functioning of the current currency, so some monetary functions continue to be carried out by the ordinary currency.[2] Indeed some complementary currencies have ceased to exist when the functions they performed were reabsorbed by other regulatory systems. Some historical examples of currencies will help to clarify the complementary role that can exist between different types of money.

3.2 The Currency Forerunners to Sardex

The Sardex belongs to a restricted typology that excludes most of the known complementary currencies. Like most complementary currencies, though, the Sardex only circulates at a local level, although it potentially extends to the entire region of Sardinia. Unlike the more common complementary currencies, the Sardex currency has no store-of-value function. The idea of using money as a means of payment and a means of exchange but not as a store of value is not new in economic history: examples can be found prior to the advent of modern state currencies and the gold standard, as well as subsequently, in more recent years, especially during periods of economic crisis. Some of these examples will be presented in the following sub-sections.

3.2.1 Medieval Currencies

The Roman empire managed to impose the same unit of account and the use of the same currency throughout its territory. Rome minted coins that were acquired by the regions of the empire when they sold their products in order to pay taxes to Rome. This enabled the

[1]Over the years specific studies have evaluated the effects of these complementary currencies. The bibliography on complementary currencies prepared by Schroeder et al. (2011) includes 76 publications dedicated to "impact assessment": these represent 18.7% of all the titles published in English (Place and Bindewald 2015).

[2]For the different functions of money, including a comparison of Bitcoin and Sardex, see Sect. 5.2 The Social Functioning of Money.

empire to finance its development and sustain its military expenses (Goldsmith 1987). In the middle of the fourth century AD, after the fall of the Roman empire, money almost disappeared (Ingham 2004, p. 109): the empire had guaranteed the value and exchangeability of money and, without it, money gradually became redundant to trade and was avoided. It was the medieval kings, dukes and feudal lords who began to mint money again and circulate it, primarily within their own territories (Bloch 1962). Although these new currencies were based on the Roman Denarius, the weight of the coins and the quality of the silver deployed by the various local authorities in power varied.

During his reign Charlemagne established a common unit of account for the currencies of all his territories with the purpose of creating a uniform tax regime for all the territories of the Holy Roman Empire. However, this unit of account was only an abstract value which ascribed the same value to currencies whose weight and value varied. The value of the currencies in circulation, although the quality and quantity of the silver they contained varied, was standardised by the unit of account imposed by the emperor. The functions of currency—a unit of account, a means of exchange and a store of value—that had been unified in the Roman currency were now separated, making the unit of account value independent of the currency's material characteristics. The abstract value of money was defined in such a way that each silver pound corresponded to 20 shillings and each shilling was divided into 12 pence (Einaudi 1953 [1936], p. 230). Despite the fact that in the following centuries the effective weight of the silver in each pound was reduced to just 3% of its nominal value, the exchange rate with other currencies remained unchanged, based on the rate established by Charlemagne's decree.

Einaudi described the decoupling of the value of the medium of exchange from that of the unit of account as the constitution of an "imaginary currency" (ibid.).[3] The myriads of different currencies, minted with different weights and values, circulating in the provinces of Europe of the period found a mutual convertibility in the value established by the imaginary currency which was able to establish equivalences of value. Only in the thirteenth century the nascent French state imposed its own new unit of account for the different currencies circulating within its territory, making the convertibility between the various currencies circulating in the territories of Europe more complex (Bloch 1954 [1936]).

Monetary policies had two courses of action available when the unit of account was uncoupled from the medium of exchange. They could reduce the quantity of precious metals used for minting coins so as to preserve precious-metal ingots as a store of value, or they could modify the unit of account value in order to devalue or revalue the value of the coins in circulation (Day 1999) thereby facilitating or dampening inflationary or deflationary tendencies. The possibility of revaluing or devaluating nominal currency values could have a limited impact on purchasing power due to the prices of

[3] Such use of an abstract unit of account as an exchange medium dates back to Babilonian times (Ingham 2004, p. 110).

goods realigning with currency values, but it had a substantial impact on the value of debts contracted, immediately devaluing or revaluing them (Einaudi 1937, p. 264). From a redistributive point of view, the devaluation of debts would certainly impact the distribution of wealth between landowners and weaker social groups (Fantacci 2013, p. 131).

These operations on the unit of account also made it possible to facilitate or hinder the circulation of currencies and the functioning of the economy: currencies that were depreciated or at risk of depreciation might appear to be fragile store-of-value instruments thereby facilitating their exchange for goods considered to be more durable or more attractive. As the more recent Wörgl case demonstrates, faster monetary circulation at the macro level results in increased economic development.

3.2.2 Wörgl: "Relieve Need, Provide Work and Bread"

Stamp scripts, a form of local currency issued by municipalities, were widespread during the Great Depression in Europe and the United States. Local administrations used them to hire unemployed workers to work in their city, for example in the construction of roads, bridges or aqueducts (Fisher 1933). Through agreements with local merchants, the money workers received could be spent on buying goods and services; this money would then circulate among the city's businesses. Faced with the difficulties of matching supply and demand for goods and labour during the economic recession, the use of stamp scripts helped create employment and made the economic system work better.

The city of Wörgl in Austria is one of the best known examples of the effectiveness that stamp scripts had at that time. Between 1932 and 1933 Wörgl experienced a severe economic crisis with high unemployment levels and poverty among families. The mayor of the city followed the economic and monetary theories of Silvio Gesell (1958 [1916]): he deposited 40,000 shillings at a local bank and printed an equivalent value of local currency which he used to hire the unemployed and pay them a wage to carry out public works that the city needed.

The purpose of this complementary currency was clearly indicated on the banknotes: "Lindert die Not, Gibt Arbeit und Brot" (Relieves need, provides work and bread). The Wörgl stamp scripts had the peculiarity that to maintain their current validity—and therefore their value—it was necessary to put a stamp on them every month which confirmed their current validity but depreciated their value by 1%. The depreciation *(demurrage)* of the banknotes resulted in them circulating more rapidly[4]: those who received these notes as payment tried to spend them as soon as possible so as not to see their value reduced over time. The positive economic effects did not depend only on the expenses directly paid by the municipality or on the payment of the relative salaries but, above all, on the repeated circulation of this money among those who had received it as payment.

[4]Estimated to be 12/14 times the circulation of ordinary shillings, see Lietaer 2013, p. 153–155.

Fisher (1933) analyzed various examples of stamp scripts made during the Great Depression and identified a model he considered to be optimal for reactivating the economic cycle during periods of recession. During periods of economic uncertainty, brought about by negative economic trends or by low expectations for the future, money owners tend to favour the store-of-value function rather than that of exchange medium. Future earnings may seem uncertain and savings can be seen as a valuable tool for meeting future expenses. As is well known, this dynamic of low expectations and little investment triggers a vicious circle that aggravates the negative economic trend.[5] If the store-of-value function is removed from the currency, it is possible to enhance its function as an exchange medium and facilitate its circulation.

In line with Wörgl's experience, Fisher identified the application of an "ambulatory tax" on money as the key to multiplying the beneficial effects of stamp scripts (ibid., p. 8): a percentage of the value of the money should be paid periodically by the owner so as to discourage the accumulation of money and to favour its circulation. Those who have money will try to spend it as soon as possible so as to avoid paying the next value tax. A further positive effect of paying this tax in ordinary currency derives from the fact that over time the money would entirely "repay" itself. In Fisher's example, if the money had an ownership tax of 2% a week then, over the course of a year, its total value plus issuing costs (104%) would be repaid to the issuer. Unlike medieval coins, stamp scripts are a form of money that has no intrinsic value from precious metals or from reference to an external value (e.g. Gold Standard); they are best described as a form of debt of the issuer towards the holder which self-liquidates over a year. Unlike the production of other types of fiat money, the creation of this money from nothing does not cause inflation because, at the end of the year, the money collected from the applied weekly tax supports in full its real value based on ordinary money and on the capacity of the state to collect taxes (Fantacci 2013, p. 129).

Fisher's stamp script project can be seen as the first example of an intentionally constructed complementary currency capable of satisfying specific functions of the economic system that the ordinary currency is unable to satisfy. This example of complementarity between different forms of money also highlights the non-competitive nature of their coexistence: stamp scripts circulate money much more rapidly than ordinary money during recessions and, at the same time, they allow taxes to be collected and inflation avoided, thanks to the functions performed by the ordinary currency.

3.2.3 Wir

The stamp script experience demonstrated how it is possible to remove the store-of-value function from money by gradually depreciating it. Using money exclusively as a unit

[5]Keynes defined this situation as a "liquidity trap" (2007 [1936]).

of account and as an exchange medium is associated with the function performed by a clearing house. A clearing house records market sales and purchases between shareholders, offsetting debts and credits on their individual payment balances like a multilateral exchange system. Clearing houses are the system generally used for financial transactions and nowadays there are many that are also available for international trade exchanges (Amato and Fantacci 2013). There are also examples of complementary currencies operating on a local scale that adopt the clearing house principle: the most successful and longest-lasting one is that of the Swiss Wir (CHW).

The 1929 financial market collapse and the resulting liquidity and investment crises inspired entrepreneurs Werner Zimmermann and Paolo Enz to found Wir, a mutual aid cooperative, in Zurich in 1934. Wir is the abbreviation of the German word "Wirtschaftring", which means "us". Like stamp script, Wir was also influenced by the economist Silvio Gesell's "free money" theories (1958 [1916]) on monetary depreciation. The entrepreneurs who joined Wir could in fact sell and buy goods to each other without money changing hands, but their respective credits and debits were recorded by the Wir company. These credits and debits did not generate interest for member accounts but, until 1948, the positive balances underwent a gradual devaluation of their nominal value.

Wir became a bank in 1936 and since then its operating system has gradually moved closer to that of a traditional bank, combining the use of the ordinary currency with Wir and offering services for consumers, such as mortgages or loans, but it has always maintained the principle of mutual aid (Dubois 2014). To date, the bank has nine branches in Switzerland and 60,000 associates. The bank provides Wir loans to associates against collateral guarantees on a par with traditional banks but it can also provide Wir credit at much lower costs than ordinary money because it does not need to acquire money from central banks or other financial intermediaries. Credit, therefore, has much lower costs for associates but there is the limitation that it can only be spent on a local scale among other bank members. This limitation, however, does not seem to be an obstacle: it is frequently perceived by adherents as a chance to support the local economy (Fantacci 2013, p. 144).

The cost of the credit provided by Wir also has the advantage of not fluctuating with monetary exchange rates or the liquidity supply of financial institutions. Wir money is independent of international financial flows and remains based on mutual aid among members: it is a form of mutual credit between members whose value guarantee is linked only to the concrete possibility of having economic exchanges with other local economic actors.

The founders of Sardex studied, observed and endorsed many characteristics of the Wir *modus operandi* while they were developing a functioning model for Sardex.

3.3 A Brief History of Sardex

3.3.1 Project Development

The founders of Sardex, the brothers Giuseppe and Gabriele Littera, Piero Sanna, Carlo Mancosu and Franco Contu, all come from Serramanna, a town in the Sardinian hinterland where the principle economic activities are agriculture and sheep farming. The five friends, most of them born in the 1980s, have known each since they were children growing up in Serramanna. They moved to the Italian mainland and abroad during and after their university studies. Piero Sanna and Giuseppe Littera both studied at Leeds University from 2006 till 2008. In that period Gabriele Littera worked in marketing at Teramo. Despite the geographical distance, the friends kept in touch, exchanging ideas and discussing what they would do once they had all graduated, until, says Sanna:

> Peppe (Giuseppe Littera) and I almost "tripped over" the monetary issue and from that day on we have cultivated this interest, this passion and shared it with Gabriele and Carlo who in turn shared it with Franco. The first thing we tried to do was to understand how the present monetary system functions.

The previous chapter highlighted the fact that the nature of money and how it functions are still matters for debate among specialists. The approach the Sardex founders adopted for conceptualising money was influenced by the economy of conventions (Boltanski and Thévenot 2006 [1991]) which does not consider money as a commodity just like other commodities, but focuses instead on the socially constructed dimension of monetary value:

> We must then agree on the concept of money. I understand it as an agreement within a community that accepts a particular instrument as a means of payment. We could be three children playing at shop-keeping who decide they will be paid with chickpeas or stones, they are a community that decides to settle on a means of payment. Try explaining to the child that this is not a means of payment! Who are you to tell him? Then as adults we may forget this, but a community can always make decisions of this type. The community can also decide to pay taxes by agreeing to do so and it pays them; we record the information and animate the community (F. 1).

This point of view postulates that money has the role of facilitating exchanges: the Sardex founders consider a normative foundation that correctly defines the nature of money to be irrelevant, preferring to delegate to the social actors involved and allowing them to decide which mode of payment should be used.

This initial research phase was made fruitful by specific contributions from each of the five founders who came from different academic backgrounds, though interestingly none of them had studied Economics:

> At the beginning we were five friends with different passions and skills and we tried to combine them and make everyone's talents bear fruit. My brother, for example, was the geek of

> the computer science group. Piero had worked in brokerage and he still dedicates most of his time to managing and guiding this sector. I studied marketing and communications so I helped place this initiative on the market that existed here. I went away to study and I am putting into practice here what I learnt (F. 1).

The group were studying and working away from Sardinia while they were developing their ideas:

> We were all away from Sardinia communicating and exchanging ideas and documents via internet. After a period of studying "standard" money dynamics, we concentrated on existing alternative or complementary monetary systems. We came across many examples but the one that really impressed us, because of its longevity and the massive number of transactions it had generated and was still generating, was Wir. Gabriele, Giuseppe and Carlo did in-depth research to better understand how Wir functioned so as to ascertain what we could take directly from them and what we could adapt to our local situation, impacted by the dysfunctions that the ordinary currency was creating for the economy (F. 2).

The friends also visited Wir headquarters in Basel where they met the managers and received explanations on aspects of Wir operations.

Although the functioning basis of the Sardex system follows Wir operating principles, the group of friends soon realized that the Wir model had to be adapted to take into account the characteristics of the Sardinian economy and the economic actors involved. A possible innovation the Sardex project needed to take into account was the gradual emergence of a new technological scenario: *"At the beginning, when we started, there was still no ADSL, the web was still travelling at 56 kb, but we realized that [the web] would be our future and we tried to make ourselves ready to work in that space [on-line] in the immediate future"* (F. 1).

The founders began to ask themselves questions about how the Sardinian economic system actually functioned; they tried to ascertain the limits to and potential for development and how their idea could make a contribution:

> We tried to find answers to simple questions: for example why do Sardininan businesses import 80% of the food they sell when we should be able to export food stuffs? Why is there no cohesion in so many sectors? Why is there no networking? We tried to understand why and to find an apparently very effective solution: if you are a professional, for example, and you don't need to buy expensive raw materials, a fee paid in Sardex is compensation for your time and skills only. When a professional needs to buy a computer or a desk it makes no difference to him whether he pays one thousand euros or one thousand Sardex. The difference lies in the fact that accessing Sardex credit has a negligible cost compared to accessing bank credit. (F. 1).

In the eyes of the Sardex founders, one of the major problems of an economy made up of small businesses like those in Sardinia was not the lack of quality supplies, for example food and wine, but the difficulty of finding sales and collaboration channels that could offer stability and development possibilities for the economic system. Small companies often do not have the resources to develop the commercial channels needed to expand and develop their businesses. In times of crisis these structural limits combined with the disappearance of some customers and a few unpaid bills, can make it impossible for the business to remain open. The Sardex project tried to respond to the escalation of these structural difficulties in the Sardinian economy brought about by the economic crisis that began in 2008:

> The basic idea was to put together all the unsold items of Sardinian businesses: the un-expressed potential could not be expressed because the people who wanted those items could not afford them, it was not a demand that the market was ignoring. I always give the example of the beggar who is hungry even though he has no money and the restaurateur who has empty seats he would like to fill: there needs to be some mechanism for reaching an agreement. Until now an official mechanism [the euro] has kept us all in agreement [….] The market here only had small players, people the banks rarely saw before and never see now. We had to try to build tools and services based on the web, but we had to explain them in person—because I don't have to cheat anyone, honesty and ethics have never been lacking—and this orientation had to find the right way of expressing itself. A small company that is in difficulty does not have much money and entrepreneurs are often distrustful. (F. 1).

From the very beginning the founders were well aware that Sardex could not be an alternative currency to the euro but rather that it would play a complementary role:

> The euro and Sardex networks have to co-exist, neither of them can replace the other, in fact we have always told businesses to safeguard their euro market because if you don't have a euro market you can't have a complementary market, because there are taxes and other aspects that have to be taken into consideration … You use the euro for exchanges outside the network: buying abroad, buying in Germany, buying everything that is not available where you are now[6] (F. 1).

Once the general terms of the project had been defined, Franco Contu, the only partner with some business experience, played a decisive role in starting up the business. Accountants and legal advisors then clarified the framework within which the system should operate in order to comply with legal and fiscal obligations. The idea of doing something useful for Sardinia combined with the founders' desire to return to their place of origin so that their passion could become a job that provided a livelihood: *"We all wanted to return here and do something positive for ourselves and for others so we tried to invent an occupation that would provide us with a living"* (F. 1). *"For me after eleven years away from Sardinia in 'exile' in Leeds for study and then for work it was a great opportunity to return"* (F. 2).

---

[6] *For an explanation of how complementarity works see Sect. 3.4 Sardex at Work.*

3.3.2 Launching the Company and Seeking Out Members

The Sardex company was established in July 2009 and from December of that year the founders and five assistants began "knocking" on the doors of Sardininan businesses encouraging them to join the Sardex network.

> We spent part of our time calling businesses and asking them if they were interested in having new clients and new suppliers and part of our time going to visit them to get them to sign up. It was a period when businesses needed to look for new clients on a daily basis and we used that to make contact with them. The idea was simple: enter with nothing, buy and sell as much as you like, increase or decrease your budget and then leave with nothing. The more you exchange the better it is for you (F. 1).

In January 2010 a few businesses signed up and the first transactions using Sardex took place. During the first few months about 15/20 businesses signed up every month: about 2/3% of businesses that were contacted became members. It was not easy to overcome the initial distrust of entrepreneurs towards a new instrument, not readily understood by the man in the street, that offered them a very different way of doing business. Professionals and business consultants were also unprepared to assess the real effectiveness of Sardex: *"From the fiscal viewpoint many accountants suggested to their clients, potential Sardex members, that they should not join because it would not be to their advantage, while others suggested they should try Sardex for a year and then evaluate the return on their investment"* (F. 1).

The economic scenario for the Sardinian businesses contacted by the Sardex founders in 2010 was not encouraging: *"They all had payments that were blocked or delayed, they were all in the same situation"* (F. 1). The economic crisis in Italy initially caused payments to be delayed and this, combined with the simultaneous tightening of bank credit, caused many companies to default. For businesses that lacked the liquidity required to pay their suppliers, Sardex provided an opportunity to pay their debts and keep their business open: "[Some members] *tried with one business saying they would pay him a hundred euros in Sardex and they began to regulate part of their business activity in this way*" (F. 1).

When the founders were trying to increase the membership base they still adhered to their principles of correct, cooperative behaviour as the basis of their relationship with potential members: *"One characteristic has distinguished us right from the beginning: we met all the participants in person, we provided them with all the information necessary and we made sure members were aware of what they were about to do (we would also verify this in the first phone call we made to them once they were part of the network)"* (F. 1). All those who join Sardex have to pay an entrance fee to *"make it clear that membership entailed a small change in habits and that the member wished to deal with this"* (F. 1). The founders do not hide the uncertainty and the enthusiasm of this early period of Sardex activity: *"When someone you don't know trusts you and gives you the one hundred or two hundred euros [membership fee] it was a thrilling moment*" (F. 1).

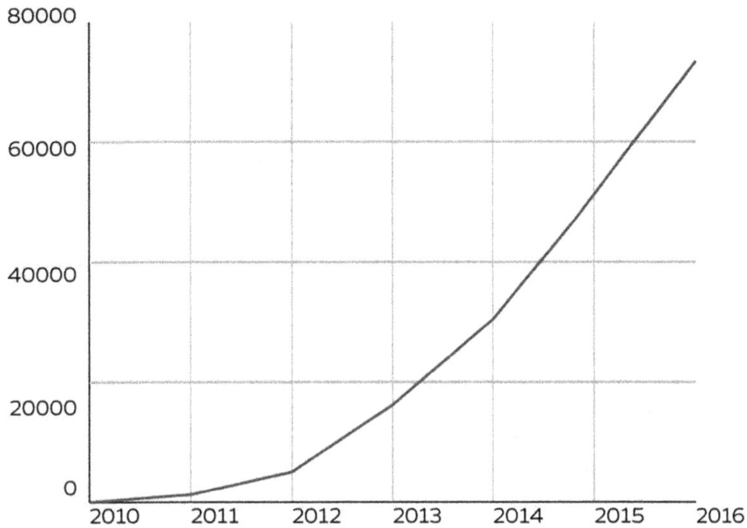

Fig. 3.1 Transaction volume in thousands of Sardex, historical series. (Source: Sardex Ltd, sardex.net)

After two years of operating and observing the Sardex network, the management decided to eliminate the commission charged on transactions so as to facilitate exchanges; the annual membership fee was maintained.

The Sardex network has been expanded rationally from the start: as soon as a membership was accepted the promoters would try to get other firms in the same sector to join so that members could easily find partners with whom to exchange products or services: *"So after two or three days we would return to the business with the first member in that sector and we would put them in contact with each other"* (F. 1). From its early development the self-expanding dynamic of the network was evident. This dynamic is due to the advantage that members have in bringing in other companies they deal with: *"Some members would introduce their suppliers, our first members were our best commercial agents and they have created their own network within the [Sardex] network. They realised that it was beneficial for them as well if their suppliers were members too"* (F. 2).

3.3.3 Development Phases

In the course of 2010, 200 Sardex members exchanged 300,000 Sardex credits. In 2011 the number of subscribers grew to 450 and 1,200,000 Sardex credits were traded. The increase in the exchange volume, twice that of the increased membership, strongly indicated to the founders that their project was valid and provided an incentive to continue. The increase in the number of transactions remains considerably higher than the increase in the number of members in the years that follow: F. 1 describes this phenomenon as a "network effect" created by the network[7] (Fig. 3.1).

Every year members who wish to remain in the network have to pay the annual membership fee in euros: this also means they have to decide if the benefits of the network exceed the membership costs or no. Over the years the average drop-out rate has been 3/4% per annum. The total membership is currently close to four thousand. Despite the encouraging results and economic success of Sardex the founders try to remain faithful to the principles that inspired this project and sustain the development of Sardinia:

> Over the years we have reduced our expenses as we have grown: if we had a two thousand euro surplus we engaged an extra broker rather than divide the money among ourselves. The mechanism was working well and it was more exciting to add another gear, to step on the accelerator. Unlike other web-based businesses we have fifty employees and an equal number of consultants because we believe that the service we offer is very important for a company like ours and it helps create wealth (F. 1).

From 2011 on media attention started to focus on the Sardex project: *"In that period an article appeared in the national pages of Repubblica; we also attracted the attention of the local media"* (F. 1). A little later the international media also began to take an interest in Sardex: see for instance an in-depth article published by the Financial Times in 2015 (Posnett). The echo generated by the media has aroused academic, institutional and business interest in the Sardex project.

> The 2012 article in Repubblica raised a lot of interest and a lot of people contacted us to ask if they could join Sardex but we told them they couldn't because they weren't in Sardinia or they were weren't as yet. People asked us if they could set up a network similar to Sardex in their area and we talked to them about this. Others have contacted us for information, some were just interested and others wanted to write a thesis or do research etc. We met so many people who wanted to set up a network, we learnt a lot, we made some errors too, but over a three year period eleven networks have been set up with 3500 to 4000 business members. These networks have more employees than we do now. Things have evolved here too: when we first set up we had no corporate participation but then we decided to enter into partnership with these colleagues. More recently we have become majority stakeholders in some companies and we have applied for leadership roles outside Sardinia also. We are confident we will soon be able to set up new networks to include the Italian regions that are currently without (F. 1).

To date the development of new regional networks covers twelve Italian regions thanks to the recent activation of the Val d'Aosta network (Fig. 3.2)

[7]For an analysis of the mechanisms at work here see Chap. 4.

Fig. 3.2 Expansion of the Sardex network to other Italian regions. (Source: Sardex.net)

In this process of expansion within and beyond Sardinia, Sardex management has noted the considerable interest displayed by local institutions and employers' associations although none of these seem to have played a significant role in promoting and developing networks. Although there are a number of agreements between Sardex and regional employers' associations which encourage their members to join the Sardex networks, so far none of these agreements has contributed to a real expansion of the Sardex network.

Among the statutory aims of the employers' associations is the promotion of initiatives for developing the businesses of their members; the Sardex project could be a driving force for the growth of company businesses. The experience of these years of project development, however, has shown how Sardex has played a complimentary and supplementary role in the traditional initiatives of employers' associations:

> We organised meetings with Sardex members right from the beginning: in 2016 we held 60/70 of these meetings, some days we held three meetings at the same time where we presented ourselves, members participated, people who were interested or simply curious came, we talked about the Sardex network and how it functions, in various towns of Sardinia. Even that provides the opportunity for building a single network for a small business whose owner does not have the resources to do anything more. Traditional employer associations no longer fill this role, the world has changed and many structures are not light enough to change rapidly (F. 1).

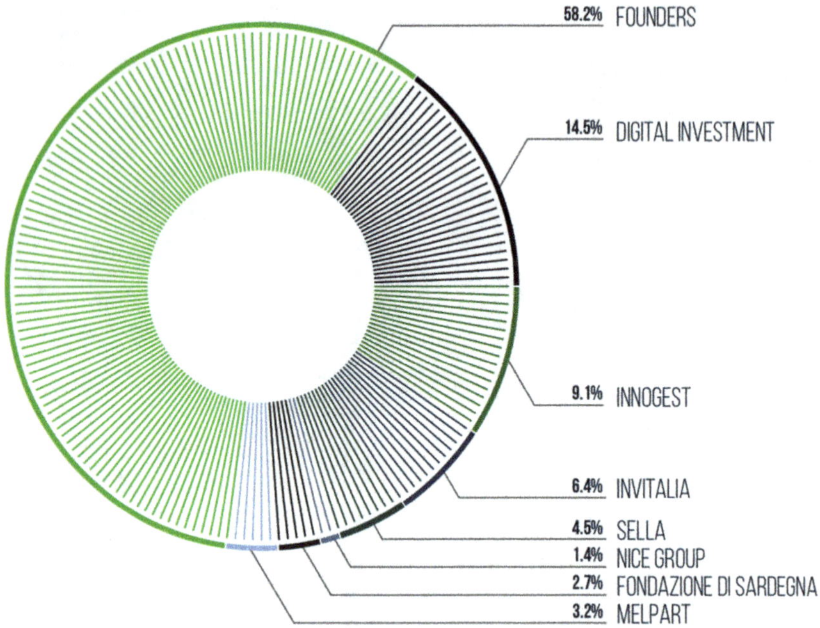

Fig. 3.3 Shareholdings in Sardex Ltd. (Source: Sardex.net)

3.3.4 The Current Configuration

Over the years the functional aspects of the company that manages Sardex have been gradually organised into different sectors of activity, each of which is coordinated by one or more members of the founding group. The present-day structure and functional organisation was consolidated in 2016 thanks to a three million euro capital increase introduced by new shareholders: Banca Sella, Innogest, Digital Investment and the investment company Invitalia, owned by the Economy Ministry. The founders, who own 58% of the capital, still control the company, but the capital introduced by these new shareholders has made it possible to develop new investment plans, recruit more personnel and undertake the legal transformation of the Sardex company to a public limited company (Ltd) (Fig. 3.3).

Currently Sardex Ltd has about fifty employees and fifty collaborators. The employees for the most part carry out internal functions at company headquarters, the collaborators are professional consultants or advisors who are involved in attracting new members.

The internal organisation of Sardex Ltd is divided into different sectors of activity. Management is entrusted to General Management and to Administration and Finance which is chaired by Gabriele Littera. Brokering activities, managed by Piero Sanna, include the management of members so as to optimise the alignment of supply and demand, sales supervision and customer care. The commercial sector, responsible for expanding the Sardex network, is directed by Stefania Campus. The marketing sector, directed by Carlo Mancosu, is responsible for internal and external communications relating to the Sardex project, for promoting Sardex and its member companies and organising promotional events around Sardinia. This sector includes Communities and Social Media Management, Content Management, Event Management, Graphic and Front-end Design, Public Relations and Press Office. A social media manager whose role is to manage how Sardex is presented on social media, has recently joined the marketing team, as has a story-teller, an ex-journalist, whose task it is to collect the stories told by Sardex members and load them onto the Sardex blog. The ICT sector, managed by Giuseppe Littera, is responsible for maintaining the Sardex IT systems and for developing and maintaining the platforms of the other regional complementary currency networks. The development sector, managed by Franco Contu, is responsible for opening new networks.

The Sardex project has received numerous awards for business innovation and ICT use; these awards have strengthened the public image of Sardex as an innovative and successful company. The following awards were particularly important in this regard: the 2012 IED Innovation Award from the European Institute of Design, the nomination for National Champion for Italy, which resulted in Sardex being nominated in the innovation category for the London-based European Business Awards, and being awarded third place among Italian start ups at Startup Italia 2014.

3.3.5 Future Scenarios

Over the years the Sardex company has developed new services for businesses, giving them the opportunity of paying part of their employee's salaries in Sardex (b2e) and also providing new opportunities for institutions to use Sardex. In 2016, for example, the Sardex payment system was trialled for monthly social benefit payments in Sassari. In this trial Sardex credit could only be used in Sardex-affiliated businesses so as to "direct" the money spent towards essential items and avoid it being spent on betting, lottery tickets and other non-essential goods and services where Sardex credit could not be used. Current research is working towards increasing Sardex involvement with consumers (b2c). A process is being developed that would enable companies with Sardex credits to pass on some of these credits to customers who have purchased goods as a bonus or loyalty reward, similar to the points systems used by large retailers. Extending Sardex credit to end consumers could represent a decisive qualitative leap in expanding the Sardex currency.

Payment of local taxes using Sardex credits would be another opportunity for further developing the Sardex system: this would force local government institutions to acquire some of their goods and services from local businesses, which would provide impetus to local development in much the same way as stamp scripts, the forerunners of Sardex.

The question of allowing local taxes to be paid in complementary currency has been raised several times with local government administrations but, even though the current level of Sardex IT infrastructure could easily handle payments of this kind, so far none have agreed to this proposal.

The World Bank and other international institutions dedicated to the economic development of poorer areas of the planet have shown interest in Sardex: *"Development overseas is the next step to take, we are collaborating with several countries and we have to decide where the conditions are best for carrying out trials"* (F. 1).

The founders try to keep faith with the principles of mutual aid and cooperation which animated the establishment of Sardex: *"Our ideal corporate model would be one in which members participate in the capital of the company that manages the network, in the future it wouldn't be a bad idea if a firm with 20%/30% of its turnover in Sardex wanted to join the company and participate in the responsibilities"* (F. 1). Sardex technological developments are oriented towards the creation of an IT infrastructure that will be in line with the project's guiding principles. To this end a block-chain model is used as a reference for horizontal ownership and content sharing.

3.3.6 Scientific Research on Sardex

The rapid entrepreneurial development of Sardex and the consequent attention from the media and institutions have been accompanied by increasing academic interest. The first studies and papers to be published were written by Paolo Dini of the London School of Economics (2012); studies carried out by Dini and other researchers followed (Dini et al. 2014; 2015; Littera et al. 2014). These studies explain how Sardex operates and describe the different development phases of the Sardex project. Yale University carried out a network analysis of Sardex transactions (Iosifidis et al. 2015, 2018); Dini's collaboration with Laura Sartori of the University of Bologna led to the publication of essays with a stronger sociological approach to the subject (Sartori and Dini 2016; Motta et al. 2017). Sartori and Dini were the first to study the role of trust as fundamental to the functioning of the Sardex currency. Their research was mostly based on interviews with entrepreneurs, which revealed the high levels of trust present in the Sardex network. The authors verified that most of the operating characteristics of an economic circuit as identified by Zelizer (2005), are present in the Sardex network (see Sartori and Dini 2016, pp. 283–284, 289–294). Melis et al. discussed the Sardex experience in two papers (2013; Melis and Guidici 2014). On the basis of these empirical studies, Sardex became a case study: economic historians Massimo Amato and Luca Fantacci from Bocconi University proposed Sardex as a reference model for responding to the economic crisis and as a possible form for developing capitalism (Amato and Fantacci 2013, 2015, 2016; Fantacci 2013, 2017; Doria and Fantacci 2018; Vallet 2016).

3.4 Sardex at Work

Although the Sardex currency has many of Wir's operating characteristics, it was designed for the Sardinian economic system which is made up of small businesses with low levels of technological innovation, mostly operating in the commercial sector. The founders quickly realized that the system had to appeal to entrepreneurs with low-level technological skills but it also had to be capable of exploiting the enormous innovative potential of the internet network that was expanding and being upgraded to high-speed networks in the early years of Sardex. The Sardex system is very innovative because it combines different technical and organisational factors. Although the basic principles of Sardex are derived from the idea of "free money" (Gesel 1958 [1916]) and Sardex operations are similar to those of a Wir-model clearing house, its success and its ability to expand can only be explained by the specific operating model the founders adopted and implemented in the Sardinian context.

To better understand how the Sardex device operates it is useful to identify three complementary system levels: the currency and its characteristics (Sardex currency), the members' network (Sardex network) and the company that owns and manages the Sardex working platform and develops its activities (Sardex Ltd).

3.4.1 Characteristics of the Sardex Currency: Interest-Free Mutual Credit

A Sardex (SRD) nominally has the same value as the euro, but it cannot be converted into any other currency. Sardex currency can only circulate within the network of companies that have joined Sardex and it cannot be spent outside this network nor can it be converted into other valuables. The currency does not exist in the traditional forms of bank-notes and metal coins but only as a credit or debit in the on-line personal accounts of Sardex members. A personal account, which can be accessed from a web platform or via a smart phone app, is assigned to every members of the Sardex network. Members can make payments using either the web platform or the smartphone app. Most payments are made using the smartphone app which allows simple, rapid payments for purchases in the same way as other payment apps.

Sardex credits held in personal accounts disappear after a year if they are not spent. Any Sardex debts that have not been re-paid within a year have to be reimbursed in euro to Sardex Ltd: the value of Sardex currency has a time limitation and it is also subject to real depreciation. Sardex, unlike Wörgl, is not subject to a nominal value depreciation, but the cost of the annual membership fee required by Sardex Ltd constitutes a real depreciation. This membership fee can be seen as the "cost" of Sardex credit. Bank credit has an annual cost that is usually expressed as a percentage of the amount of credit, the cost of Sardex credit can be equated with the annual Sardex membership fee. So even if Sardex credit has no nominal depreciation over time and no interest rates are applied, its value is discounted by the cost of the annual membership fee, without which the credit would be worthless. The contract binding Sardex Ltd and its members stipulates that Sardex credit is exposed to the risk of disappearing a year after it was generated if the credit has not been spent. This means that Sardex currency can only perform the store-of-value function in a very limited way over time: it was intended primarily as a means of exchange and a facilitator of exchanges between members of the Sardex network.

The Sardex currency can be considered a particular case of *fiat* money. Its value does not correspond to any objective material value (e.g. gold standard) and although its value is nominally linked to the euro it has none of the guarantees (validity, value protection) provided by sovereign states for their national currencies. Sardex is essentially a mutual credit provided by companies within the Sardex network to each other. The origin of this money lies in the trusting belief of member businesses that the debts contracted against them by other businesses will be repaid in the future with goods or services offered by the same businesses or by other network members.

The circulation of Sardex currency can be assimilated to the circulation of debt certificates issued by businesses in the Sardex network and exchanged as means of payment between the same businesses in exchange for goods and services. Sardex Ltd acts as a clearing house for exchanges between members in Sardex currency, recording debits and credits and guaranteeing the validity of the debts and credits for the stipulated time.

The mutualistic nature of Sardex credit becomes evident in the event that one of the businesses belonging to the Sardex network is declared bankrupt. If this happens, all the businesses that sold goods or services to the bankrupt company and received Sardex currency in exchange are obliged to register the loss of this money. If the payment had been made in euros, the money would not "disappear" in the event of the paying company being declared bankrupt, because its validity would be guaranteed by the state or, in the case of a payment in euros, by the European Central Bank. When a business receives payment in Sardex from a bankrupt business it loses its money because the bankrupt business will not be able to repay its debt, unless traditional bankruptcy procedures provide the means of paying the creditors.[8]

To ensure the continued viability of the Sardex currency it is essential that the member companies belonging to the Sardex network continue to exchange goods and

[8]Sardex Ltd has no contractual obligation to respond jointly in the event of member businesses being declared bankrupt and their creditors losing the credit owed to them. Interviews with Sardex members, though, have brought to light a case where a member company was declared bankrupt and Sardex Ltd paid off the debts this company had contracted in Sardex with other companies. Members see this decision as an indicator of the trustworthiness and reliability of the Sardex project and its management.

services. The Sardex currency only has value and validity within this resilient economic network which has further potential for development.

3.4.2 Sardex Members Network

The Sardex currency can only be exchanged within the Sardex member network. At present only businesses based in Sardinia can join the Sardex network (b2b).[9] Businesses can join the network by applying directly to Sardex Ltd or they may be contacted by an advisor. Sardex Ltd has a group of advisors who promote the Sardex network to Sardinian businesses. These advisors act as sales representatives for Sardex Ltd visiting companies to explain the Sardex currency, the services offered by Sardex Ltd and how to join the network.

Only six of the entrepreneurs interviewed had learnt about the Sardex currency from these advisors; most of the others had learnt about it from friends and colleagues and a few had heard about Sardex from the media. When companies contact Sardex Ltd directly to obtain information on the network or to join up, this first contact is always followed by a visit from the advisor to company head-quarters to explain how the network operates and, if the company is still interested, commence membership procedures.

When a company asks to join the Sardex network the advisor helps it put together a "buying list" and a "selling list" which list the products or services acquired and sold by the business in the course of a year. These lists are forwarded to the broker management of Sardex Ltd which assesses whether or not to accept the request for membership. The assessment evaluates the compatibility of the goods and services bought and sold by the potential member with the supply of and demand for these goods and services within the membership network at that point in time. This type of evaluation and selection procedure is necessary to ensure that the network functions effectively (see the next sub-section) and that the potential member does actually benefit from joining the network. New members must be immediately able to buy the goods and services they require from the network and to find potential buyers for their goods and services to ensure their membership brings them economic benefits.

> Right from the start the commercial investigation process has followed the same steps: I get to know your business and I analyse the products and the outlay you want to put into the network. This way I create your commercial identikit and I'm able to tell you if there is market potential for your company (F. 2).

[9] Employees of member companies can receive part of their salaries in Sardex (b2e), subject to agreements with the companies involved, and a new experiment allows customers of member companies to use Sardex (b2c).

Once the broker management has agreed that the company can enter the Sardex network the would-be member signs the membership contract, pays the annual membership fee and starts using the Sardex currency. The contract describes how the currency and the membership network operate and regulates their use: members can be excluded from the network for serious mis-conduct. The annual membership fee for joining the network is paid to Sardex Ltd in euros: the amount varies from two hundred euros for small non-profit associations to three thousand euros for large companies. The amount payable for this annual fee is decided by the broker management on the basis of the information obtained by the advisor from the company. Every year the company can choose whether or not to renew its membership: once the membership fee has been paid the member can continue to use all the services offered by Sardex Ltd for another year with no further costs.

The broker management assesses how much credit should be offered to the new member once it has decided whether or not the business meets membership requirements. The Sardex currency is not purchased in exchange for other currency but rather the initial credit is assigned to the member's account for "free" when they first join the network.[10] This Sardex credit is not accredited to the member's account; rather it is granted as a possibility for that account to be overdrawn for that amount. Given the complementarity of the Sardex market to the euro market for the member companies, the broker management grants an initial credit to members that is approximately equal to 10% of the company's annual turnover in euro. The limited amount of credit that can be used in Sardex performs the dual function of not exposing the network to excessive indebtedness of a new member whose reliability has yet to be ascertained, and of avoiding that member businesses use the Sardex network as a shelter from the competition present in the euro market. The business conducted using Sardex is only a small portion of a company's annual turnover and this means the company has to be competitive on the euro market if it is to remain competitive and viable. The initial credit granted by Sardex Ltd allows businesses to immediately spend their Sardex on current expenses or investments for their business. Many of the entrepreneurs interviewed were either not eligible for bank credit or could only obtain it at very high rates of interest. In an ordinary bank, the credit granted by Sardex would be considered an overdraft or a credit line thereby attracting interest rates in excess of 10%.

The debt contracted in Sardex by using the credit granted is repaid by members through the sale of their goods and services to other members. Debits (purchases) and credits (sales) in Sardex in members' personal accounts offset each other and create a credit or debit position for each member with regard to the network. These positions do not generate negative or positive interest. The zero-cost of Sardex credit makes

[10]Although there are no direct costs or interest payments associated with Sardex credit, the annual membership fee that companies pay to remain in the network and use this credit needs to be discounted.

it advantageous for members to keep their Sardex accounts overdrawn and to use Sardex-generated income and the credit granted by Sardex Ltd for current company expenses or for investing in the company.

Each company has a page on the on-line members' platform where it can customise the company's profile or publicise special discounts or offers. Once a company joins the Sardex network it appears on the list of Sardex members which all members can consult to look for suppliers of goods and services. Members are contractually obliged to sell products in Sardex for the same price they sell them in euro. Thanks to this price-parity rule the competitive advantage of belonging to the Sardex network does not lead to an increase in prices on the Sardex market compared to the euro market.

Members can apply to the broker management for special credit lines for investments or for business development projects. Many of the entrepreneurs interviewed have used these special credit lines to invest in machinery or real estate. A Sardex credit line financed one-third of the construction of a new studio for a professional that cost over one million euro: an important example. The broker management evaluates the sustainability of the credit lines requested; the criterion used is not debtor solvency expressed through the demand for collateral, the method used by traditional banks, but rather the sustainability of the debt is assessed on the company's capacity to trade within the Sardex network. A high level of trade, both buying and selling, within the network is the best guarantee for Sardex Ltd and other network members that the company will be able to repay its debt. The broker management knows all the transactions, sales and acquisitions of every business belonging to the Sardex network and this makes it possible to accurately estimate a company's future capacity to repay a new debt.

3.4.3 The Role Played by Sardex Ltd

The internal organisation of Sardex Ltd is similar to that of a business services company which provides a commercial trading platform. Management, marketing, commercial and ICT sectors are standard for a business that provides online services. The brokering services and the methods adopted to expand the membership network are unique to the Sardex project and probably explain much of its success.

Brokerage and Consultancy Services

The brokerage team has a call centre service for members and it supervises trading between members; credit management is entrusted to broker management.

The main functions performed by the call centre are:

- providing free advice to members to help them identify suppliers for the goods or services they require; obtaining quotes for members;

- directly seeking out customers within the network who may wish to buy the products of member companies;
- calling members to alert them to the presence of new members in the network who might be useful clients;
- collecting reports of problems or difficulties encountered by members and trying to resolve them.

Brokerage management responsibilities:

- evaluating whether it is in the best interest of the companies nominated by the advisors to join the Sardex network and assessing the appropriate line of credit to disburse;
- evaluating proposals for special lines of credit for businesses with development projects;
- monitoring the accounts of members with fewer transactions in Sardex and suggesting member businesses with whom they could trade.

The Sardex broker team performs the function of a buying and selling office for members at no cost: the services are included as part of the annual membership fee. The brokers' in-depth knowledge of the purchases and the expenses of each member (the "shopping lists" prepared prior to joining Sardex and the transactions between members) allows them to facilitate a balance between demand and supply within the network:

> They put me in a position to choose, they suggest two or three companies and in the end it is always me who chooses. It's a very good brokerage service. There are people like me who are not used to using the computer properly so it is useful (E. 15).
>
> I use the brokerage service all the time because I have a person who works for me. For example I needed to do periodic checks on fire extinguishers, so I called my broker who sent me three quotes from different companies. I did the same thing for special waste and for everything else I needed. The broker asks companies for quotes, the companies contact you if they need more information on the work to be carried out and then they send you the quotes. It's like having a buying office available. It provides a service which would waste a lot of time, it's like having a human search engine, but more reliable! Because the broker knows the reliability of the members and advises you (E. 21).

The added value of this service is clearly perceived by Sardex members: entrepreneurs appreciate having free access to a sales and acquisitions office which knows every aspect of all exchanges in the market. The brokerage service facilitates exchanges in the Sardex market because it works towards balancing supply and demand; it reduces transaction costs and it facilitates comparison and competition between companies, even when they are far apart.

> I often call the brokerage service, sometimes for advice on strategic choices for my business. For example, ahead of Christmas I call for suggestions on what type of promotions I

> should offer or when I have to make an important purchase. But not only that, sometimes my broker calls me and says: "Look, such-and-such a company has joined Sardex, have you noticed?" This means working together and offering me great service. I am an attentive entrepreneur, but I cannot monitor the 4000 member companies to see who has joined and who has left. Knowing you can count on a person who calls you and tells you for example, "Do you know that such-and-such stationery wholesaler has joined up?", is a great service. Or: "Do you know you could rent this service?" This allows me to save time, expand my knowledge network, save money. If I don't have time to look through the list of members, I call my broker who gives me, say, six names: I get six quotes and I choose the cheapest one. This means saving time and money. The brokerage service is crucial and fundamental within the network. Everyone works with passion and determination. There is an air of positivity. Today in a period of crisis, where everything seems to be going wrong, seeing enthusiastic people connecting companies creates a climate that brings out the best in companies (E. 19).

The Sardinian economic fabric is made up of small businesses almost none of which can afford the expense of internal acquisitions and sales departments or of paying another company for these services. Business owners normally do this work which is very time-consuming. The possibility of using the free brokerage service offered by Sardex Ltd is seen by entrepreneurs as an important extra benefit of joining the network.

The quality of the Sardex Ltd brokerage service is enhanced by total access to the database of Sardex transactions. The brokerage office can access all transactions taking place within the Sardex market and it also receives constant feedback from members through the broker's call centre to which members report their positive or negative opinions on the exchanges transacted with other member companies.

A computer platform for currency operations and Sardex Ltd's development and implementation of specific brokerage functions has made this in-depth market knowledge possible. The information available allows the brokerage service to offer a very effective business advisory service to any members requiring it. The operators observing the trend of Sardex transactions can ascertain whether the demand for any given product or service is up or down. The buying lists completed by participating companies, compared with the transactions actually carried out in the network, provides useful information as to which sectors or products have unsatisfied demand in the Sardex market and which already have a supply surplus with strong competition among producers. The brokerage area can also provide members with this type of consultancy for business strategies, at no additional cost. The service is particularly appreciated by the most dynamic and innovative companies. This type of market analysis would be very expensive and hard to implement, and therefore not accessible to Sardinian companies, without the Sardex database and members' daily feedback to broker team.

Network Expansion Strategies

The brokerage and consulting activity carried out by the broker team facilitates exchanges within the network. The positive experience of Sardex members plays a fundamental role in increasing Sardex membership. Information provided by the advisor is sometimes seen by potential members as a marketing strategy that highlights the positive effects of membership, but direct feedback collected from participating entrepreneurs is perceived as reliable and trustworthy. The interviews conducted reveal that the stories of other Sardex members were one of the main elements for convincing them to join Sardex. The expansion of the network often follows a "snowball" structure, where a new member generates further new members among his or her direct contacts. This mechanism is particularly useful for the geographical expansion of the Sardex network because it ensures that even a single new member in an area where the network is not present can generate its expansion thanks to the direct contacts the member has with other local companies.

Sardex Ltd has been equipped with a communications area since 2016. Its role is to promote an understanding of how Sardex works and its image in the media and on social media. The Sardex blog presents weekly stories of member companies, interviewed by the Sardex storyteller, who describe their positive entrepreneurial experiences associated with using Sardex. The stories are particularly convincing because the entrepreneurs, also present with photographs, talk first-hand of their own experience—and the article also helps promote their company within the Sardex network.

Sardex Ltd organises membership promotion initiatives called "AperiSardex" to increase awareness of Sardex in areas of Sardinia where it is not yet present. These gatherings are usually held in rooms or public spaces in small urban centres: local entrepreneurs are invited through a media campaign and direct contacts to learn about the complementary Sardex currency. The appointments take place in the late afternoon and the entrepreneurs are offered an aperitif; Sardex operations are presented and explained by a representative of Sardex Ltd. If some businesses in the area are already Sardex members they may be invited to present their products during the evening and to make themselves known to the other entrepreneurs present. Some of the entrepreneurs who attend the AperiSardex are not familiar with the functioning of the Sardex currency, others have already acquired some information from acquaintances or advisors and want to learn more about the project.

Sardex Ltd organises small fairs among local producers to encourage its members to get to know each other. These fairs are held in small provincial centres to which local producers or those from neighbouring areas are invited. On these occasions, each manufacturer has a small stand for presenting his/her products and establishing relationships with visitors. Such marketing opportunities in the small towns of Sardinia are only possible thanks to the Sardex network that can easily set into motion the contacts and organisational structure required for promoting such events. Local administrations and trade associations present in these small towns do not seem to have the resources required to offer this type of services to local businesses.

Within the Sardex network, customers of a business often become suppliers of the same business. Apart from suppliers of specific-sector products, the goods offered by most Sardinian businesses target the consumption requirements of the local population. It is therefore common for a Sardex business that buys goods from another

Sardex business to also supply that business with products or services for the business or perhaps for the personal consumption requirements of the business owner and his family. These small fairs are therefore particularly profitable for local businesses because they help them to find suppliers and customers for their products at the same time.

The entrepreneurs' appreciation of these market fairs emerges clearly in the interviews. These fairs are usually held at the weekend and they combine commercial activity and socialising, with a communal lunch or dinner for the entrepreneurs and their families once the fair is over. Some Sardex-member social dinners are organised independently of the town fair as exclusively social events. Sardex members say that some dinners are organised by Sardex members without the involvement of Sardex Ltd. These dinners are primarily organised for getting to know and socialising with other local entrepreneurs, even though the entrepreneurs themselves recognise that these social occasions can also lead to commercial opportunities.

Rational Network Expansion: A Local Market with no Excess Supply or Demand

Not all businesses applying for Sardex membership are accepted. A business is chosen and accepted only if, there are strong indications at the time that the goods it produces can find a market within the Sardex network and that it can source the goods and services it requires within the Sardex network. The business's so-called annual "buying list" and "selling list", compiled by the Sardex Ltd advisor and the business owner, are analysed by broker management to ascertain whether or not the business has the potential to buy and sell goods and services, at that time, within the Sardex network. To verify whether the activity of the business is complementary with the Sardex network the supply of and demand for the goods and services of that business are cross-referenced with those of other businesses already members of the Sardex network.

> We have rejected thousands of membership requests because they came at the wrong time and because we decided not to "sell" credits to potential members. Members pay to enter [the Sardex network] so they expect a lot from us and 365 days of the year we do our best for them. If we realise there is no balance between purchases and sales, because, for example a business can sell all its goods but wants to buy goods that are not available [within the Sardex network], we don't accept accept that business as a member of Sardex because its balance sheet would not be balanced (F. 1).

This "rational" growth of the Sardex market tries to avoid imbalances within the Sardex network, for example an excessive supply of some products and an inadequate supply of others. Situations like these would mean some Sardex members would have a Sardex credit they were unable to spend whilst others would be in debt and unable to sell their products through the Sardex network. This type of commercial stalemate would not be beneficial for individual firms or for the network as a whole, because it would slow down currency circulation. If a business has little chance of trading its products within the network it will develop a negative opinion of the Sardex network; this opinion will spread to the member's contacts and reinforce a negative attitude to Sardex, making it less attractive to potential new members. Uncontrolled expansion of the Sardex network could result in commercial imbalances within the network and negatively impact network growth in the medium term.

The entry procedure for an aspiring Sardex member always follows this evaluation process but only rarely is it necessary to refuse a request to join the network. When the Sardex network was first expanding there was a limited supply of and demand for goods from the few businesses within the network and the risk of commercial imbalances was real. For example, there might have been a risk in the early days of Sardex that there were a lot of restaurants in the Sardex network but not many suppliers of primary produce. If such a situation had arisen it would have benefited the network to delay adding further restaurants to the network until there were more suppliers of primary produce to avoid the restaurants not being able to spend their Sardex credits. Any such delays to entering the network would have been temporary and soon removed thanks to the network's rapid expansion.

The Sardex network currently includes almost four thousand businesses distributed throughout the entire region and covering every productive sector of the Sardinian economy (Fig. 3.4) so it is unlikely that demand and supply for the goods and services of any business will be incompatible with the network. Even if a business were unable to source customers or suppliers for its products in the immediate vicinity, the brokerage expertise provided by Sardex Ltd makes it easy to buy or sell products from network businesses further afield. This makes it unlikely that a business could be incompatible with the demand for and the supply of goods and services present within the network.

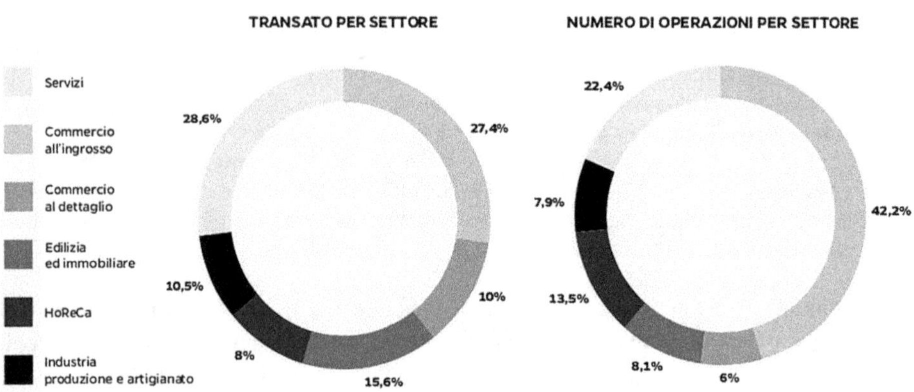

Fig. 3.4 The value and the number of transactions in Sardex per economic sector 2010–2016. (Source: Sardex Ltd, Sardex.net)

The rational expansion of the network pursues the objective of horizontal and vertical expansion of the Sardex market. The horizontal expansion of the network seeks to expand the range of Sardex products to all sectors of production in every part of Sardinia. The vertical expansion attempts to complete all the production chains so that all members can find suppliers and customers within the Sardex network.

The network cannot always expand vertically, especially in sectors with no raw materials or no producers in Sardinia. In these cases the Sardex credits, a complementary part of the business that on average does not exceed 10% of the annual turnover, can be used to buy other goods and services (e.g. rent, capital goods, business services, payment of salaries).

> In the meantime we have gradually understood our territory better. When a construction company entered the Sardex network we asked the owner what goods he required, then we took the list and went around our island to ascertain who produced these goods, who sold them and who distributed them. This gave us an understanding of this particular economic network: we know what will never be in short supply, what will always be difficult to procure for the company and the network because it is not part of the present-day economic DNA of Sardinia. The network has an abundant supply of well-being, health, culture, events, shows, food, tourism etc. but it will always difficult to supply Chinese technology: having two [currencies] means you use one for the things it does best and the other for everything else where at present Sardinia is still unable to compete (F. 1).

During the interviews many entrepreneurs expressed interest in trading with networks in other regions of Italy, using their regional currencies that are based on the Sardex model. This inter-network trading could be extremely useful for businesses in the tourism sector: it would attract tourists from other Italian regions who could pay using complementary currencies; it would also be very useful for those retailers/businessmen whose suppliers for the most part are not in Sardinia. The Sardex Ltd management has assessed the viability of opening up the Sardex network to exchanges with other networks several times: such a move would satisfy the pressing requests from network members and it could have a strong positive impact on the number of members and the number of transactions, given the enhanced commercial potential for networks in the tourism and retail sectors. The option of inter-network exchanges has, however, been avoided thus far by Sardex Ltd management because it might be counter-productive for their vision of the Sardex project. Opening the Sardex network to exchanges with other similar networks would risk replicating the commercial imbalance currently existing between the richer, more competitive regions (Northern Italy) and the poorer regions with a less competitive economic system. The Sardex project was set up to help improve the competitiveness of the Sardinian economic system in the face of global competition. Opening the Sardex network to trade with more competitive economic systems would risk fuelling the flow of money and investment in euros that are already leaving Sardinia for more competitive regions of Italy.

The founders of Sardex conceived it as an instrument for local development that would help small to medium local businesses become more competitive. So although Sardex management recognises the economic potential of inter-network trading it will not be adopted until the regional network covers all production chains and has consolidated trading. Otherwise in economic sectors where there is little or no supply in Sardex in the regional network, buyers would tend to buy from other regional networks instead of seeking or creating supply of these goods and services from Sardinian companies. Once the Sardex network has been developed in all production chains it would be feasible to allow inter-network trading for production chains which utilise raw materials or supply products that are not available in Sardinia.

At the current stage of development of the Sardinian economy and the Sardex network, the catering sector has the best developed Sardex supply chain which extends from producers to consumers. Food and wine have long been among the best developed sectors in Sardinia and nearly all Sardex entrepreneurs are also frequent consumers of these products and services.

Member companies are located throughout Sardinia with their geographical distribution broadly matching that of the population: Sardex-member firms are heavily concentrated around the city of Cagliari in the south and scattered among the small urban centres in the north (see Fig. 3.5 and Iosifidis et al. 2018, p. 2).

Fig. 3.5 Distribution of Sardex transactions in each province 2010–2016. (Source: Sardex Ltd, Sardex.net)

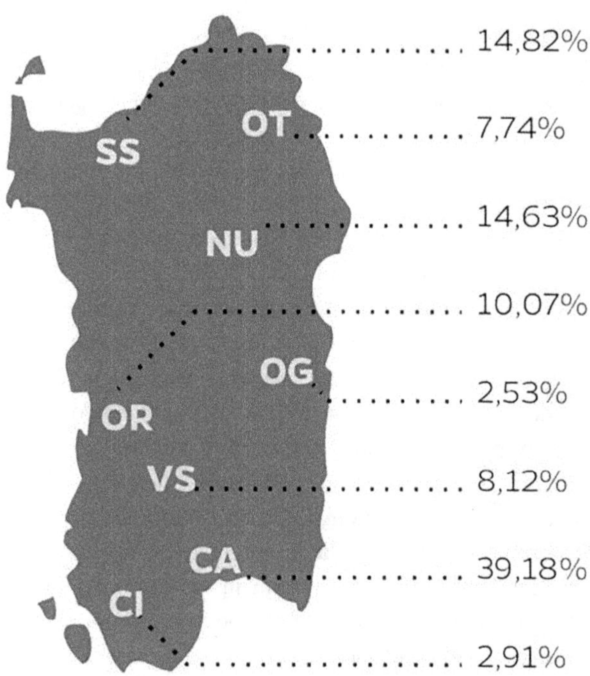

3.5 A Summary of How Sardex Works

Sardex is the name given to a credit unit which is assigned a constant value equal to one euro. This credit is primarily intended for trade between businesses (b2b), but the use of Sardex to partially pay salaries (b2e) and to reward customer loyalty (b2c) is also developing. The Sardex Company (Sardex Ltd) was founded in 2009 and manages the credit service with about hundred employees. Credit in Sardex currency is paid to member companies; they spend it buying goods and services from other member companies. Companies that have bought goods and services from other member companies acquire a debt with the entire network, not with Sardex Ltd. Their debt is repaid when they sell goods and services to other member companies. Companies pay an annual fee to belong to the Sardex network. This fee varies from three hundred euros for small no-profit organisations to three thousand euros for large companies. Debts and credits contracted within the network do not attract interest. Although the Sardex currency nominally has the same value as the euro (1 = 1) it cannot be exchanged for euros.

The Sardex Ltd statute has a clause that states that all profits have to be reinvested in the company (Dini et al. 2015, p. 27). Sardex Ltd operates as a commercial consultancy promoting membership of the Sardex network to non-member companies and helping members use the network to obtain maximum benefits for their businesses. The Sardex brokerage service facilitates supply-demand equilibrium within the network although members are free to choose their suppliers and buyers.

Almost four thousand companies belong to the Sardex network at present with a significant rate of membership increase. Members are contractually obliged to use Sardex currency to pay for transactions that do not exceed one thousand euros. Where transactions exceed this figure the companies involved decide how they will divide up any quota in euros. All transactions adhere to the total fiscal transparency rule: they are completely trackable and VAT is applied to all transactions independently of whether the values are expressed in euros or in Sardex.

The Sardex device is made up of four fundamental elements (Littera et al. 2014, p. 5):

1. Sardex.net (Sardinian Exchange Network): the network of companies, sole proprietorships and employees that makes commercial transactions between members possible without using euros.
2. Sardex.net is the network website. It is also the virtual space where commercial transactions between members take place and where long-distance relationships are maintained.
3. Sardex (SRD) is a unit of credit created by the founders of Sardex Ltd and used by network members for commercial transactions. The Sardex cannot be exchanged for other currencies and can only be spent within the Sardex network. There are no Sardex notes or coins; the Sardex is only exchanged on the Sardex.net on-line platform and it does not generate active or passive interest.

4. Sardex Ltd is the company which set up and manages the network. It develops and maintains the online platform, promotes opportunities for its members, seeks out new members as well as developing and implementing network operations. The company is financed by the network members who all pay an annual fee which varies according to the size and type of their business.

Thanks to the Sardex experience, a functioning model known as the "Commercial credit network" has been developed and the founders are replicating this model in other regions of Italy and similar versions of it are spreading to other countries (France, Great Britain, Spain).

Sardex currency cannot be accumulated and this acts as an incentive to the circulation of goods and stimulates spending. Companies have no advantage in keeping their Sardex balance sheets active. There are also contractual rules that encourage currency circulation: unspent Sardex credits are cancelled after a year, similarly Sardex debts not repaid through sales have to be reimbursed in euros after a year. The optimal condition is for budgets to be balanced with an equal number of Sardex spent and collected, or alternatively to have opened a budget deficit for investment expenses, a form of credit with very low costs for member companies.

References

Amato, M., & Fantacci, L. (2013). *Saving the market from capitalism.* Cambridge: Polity.

Amato, M., & Fantacci, L. (2015). *Moneta complementare.* Milano: Bruno Mondadori.

Amato, M., & Fantacci, L. (2016). Failures on the market and market failures: A complementary currency for bankruptcy procedures. *Cambridge Journal of Economics, 40*(5), 1377–1395.

Blanc, J. (2013). Community and complementary currencies, practices and research: State of the art. In: Unrisd conference international symposium on potential and limits of social and solidarity economy—Special session on alternative finance and complementary currencies, 6th, 7th and 8th of May 2013. Geneva. Presentation. Geneva: International Labour Organization, 2013. http://www.unrisd.org/sseconf.

Bloch, M. (1954) [1936]. *Esquisse d'une histoire monétaire de l'Europe*. Paris: Armand Colin.

Bloch, M. (1962). *Feudal society*. London: Routledge and Kcgan Paul.

Boltanski, L., & Thévenot, L. (2006) [1991]. *On justification. The economies of worth.* Princeton: Princeton University Press

Day, J. (1999). *Money and finance in the age of merchant capitalism.* Oxford: Blackwell.

Dini, P., (2012). *Community currencies and the quantification of social value in the digital economy.* The London School of Economics and Political Science, London. http://eprints.lse.ac.uk/47349/.

Dini, P., & Kioupkiolis, A. (2014). *Community currencies as laboratories of institutional learning: Emergence of governance through the mediation of social value.* In Inaugural WINIR Conference, London. http://eprints.lse.ac.uk/59307/. Accessed 11–14 Sept. 2014.

Dini, P., van der Graaf, S., & Passani, A. (2015). *Socio-economic framework for BOLD stakeholders*, OpenLaws.eu Deliverable D2.3.d1, European Commission. http://eprints.lse.ac.uk/62819/.

Doria, L., & Fantacci, L. (2018). Evaluating complementary currencies: From the assessment of multiple social qualities to the discovery of a unique monetary sociality. *Quality & Quantity, 52*(3), 1291–1314.

Dubois, H. (2014). *Faszination WIR – Resistent gegen Krisen, Spekulation und Profitgier*. Lenzburg: Faro Verlag.

Einaudi, L. (1937). The medieval practice of managed currency. In A. D. Gayer (Ed.), *The lessons of monetary experience: Essays in honor of Irving Fisher, presented to him on the occasion of his seventieth birthday* (pp. 259–68). New York: Farrar & Rinehart.

Einaudi, L. (1953) [1936]. The theory of imaginary money from Charlemagne to the French revolution. In F. C. Lane & J. C. Riemersma (Eds.), Enterprise and secular change (pp. 229–61). London: Allen and Unwin.

Fantacci, L. (2013). Reforming money to exit the crisis: Examples of non-capitalist monetary systems in theory and practice. In J. Pixley & G. C. Harcourt (Eds.), *Financial crises and the nature of capitalist money* (pp. 124–147). London: Palgrave Macmillan.

Fantacci, L. (2017). Resocialising finance to exit the crisis. In M. Magatti (Ed.), *The crisis conundrum* (pp. 111–129). Cham: Palgrave Macmillan.

Fisher, I. (1933). *Stamp scrip*. New York: Adelphi.

Gesell, S. (1958) [1916]. *The natural economic order*. London: Peter Owen Ltd.

Goldsmith, R. (1987). *Premodern financial systems*. Cambridge: Cambridge University Press.

Ingham, G. (2004). *The nature of money*. Cambridge: Polity.

Iosifidis, G., Charette, Y., Littera, G., Tassiulas, L., & Christakis, N. (2015). *Network analysis of the sardex community currency*. Yale Day of Data. Paper 4. http://elischolar.library.yale.edu/dayofdata/2015/Posters/4.

Iosifidis, G., Charette, Y., Littera, G., Tassiulas, L., & Christakis, N. (2018). Cyclic motifs in the Sardex monetary network. *Nature Human Behaviour, 2*(11), 822.

Keynes, J. M. (2007) [1936]. *The general theory of employment, interest and money*, UK: Palgrave Macmillan.

Lietaer, B. (2013). *The future of money*. New York, NY: Random House.

Littera, G., Sartori, L., Dini, P. & Antoniadis, P. (2014). *From an idea to a scalable working model: Merging economic benefits with social values in Sardex*. In: Inaugural WINIR Conference, Greenwich, London. http://eprints.lse.ac.uk/59406/.

Melis, C., & Guidici, E. (2014). Is Barter a Strategic Response to the Global Capitalist Crisis?. In H. Kazeroony & A. Stachowicz-Stanusch (Eds.) *Capitalism and the social relationship* (pp. 265–277). London: Palgrave Macmillan.

Melis, C., Giudici, E., & Dettori, A. (2013). Revitalizing the barter: The case of Sardex. Net. In P. Spagnoletti (Ed.) *Organizational Change and Information Systems* (pp. 129–136). Berlin Heidelberg: Springer.

Motta, W., Dini, P., & Sartori, L. (2017). Self-funded social impact investment: An interdisciplinary analysis of the Sardex mutual credit system. *Journal of Social Entrepreneurship, 8*(2), 149–164.

Place, C., & Bindewald, L. (2015). Validating and improving the impact of complementary currency systems through impact assessment frameworks. *International Journal of Community Currency Research, 19*(D), 152–164.

Posnett, E. (2015). The Sardex factor. *Financial Time Magazine*. https://www.ft.com/content/cf875d9a-5be6-11e5-a28b-50226830d644.

Sartori, L., & Dini, P. (2016). From complementary currency to institution: A micro-macro study of the Sardex mutual credit system. *Stato e Mercato, 36*(2), 273–304.

Schroeder, R. F., Miyazaki, Y., & Fare, M. (2011). Community currency research: An analysis of the literature. *International Journal of Community Currency Research, 15*(A), 31–41.

Servet, J.-M. (2013) Monnaie complémentaire versus microcredit solidaire et tontines: contribution compare à un développement solidaire local [Complementary currency versus solidarity microcredit and tontines: comparing contributions to local solidarity-based development]. In: Unrisd conference international symposium on potential and limits of social and solidarity economY, 6th, 7th and 8th of May 2013. Geneva. Draft paper. Geneva: International Labour Organization, 2013. http://www.unrisd.org/sseconf.

Vallet, G. (2016). A local money to stabilize capitalism: The underestimated case of the WIR. *Economy and Society, 45*(3–4), 479–504.

Zelizer, V. (2005). *Circuits in economic life*, Working Paper, University of Milan, http://www.socpol.unimi.it/papers/2009-06-26_Viviana%20Zelizer%20.pdf.

Social Mechanisms Influenced by Sardex 4

This chapter proposes to explain how a series of social effects associated with the use of Sardex are generated. Research carried out in 2017 sustains the thesis that specific social mechanisms that are explained in this chapter produce the observed economic effects. The first three sections open with a description of trust, cooperation and solidarity, the three principle social effects of using Sardex. Trust and solidarity are treated as the effects of a pool of mechanisms. Trust is the effect of selection, signalling, reciprocity, monitoring and sanctioning mechanisms; Solidarity is the effect of mechanisms of opportunities, desires, beliefs and collective action. Cooperation is treated as a single mechanism even though it originates from different processes. The general working principles of each social mechanism are described, followed by an analysis of how the mechanism works within the Sardex network. The chapter concludes with a fourth section, which summaries the relationships between the social mechanisms described.[1]

4.1 Trust

Sociological research on trust covers a very wide field and, over time, has adopted different forms for conceptualising trust and different hypotheses regarding its social role. The description below concentrates on some of the conceptualisations and characteristics of trust that will help to explain the role of trust in Sardex currency operations.

Simmel (1990 [1907]) identified three different conceptual models for studying trust and explaining how it functions. The first model addresses the expectation that, in the future, life and the world will proceed in a similar way to the past. This expectation is

[1]Thanks are due to Prof. Andrea Maurer for her constant support and rigorous approach in identifying the social mechanisms operating within the Sardex experience.

G. Bazzani, *When Money Changes Society*, Wirtschaft + Gesellschaft,
https://doi.org/10.1007/978-3-658-28533-3_4

based on an inductive logic that hypothesises the emergence of future conditions on the basis of past observations. This form of trust is the basis of ontological security regarding the stability of one's existence: it enables individuals to trust the future and make long-term plans for their life. The second conceptual form of trust identified by Simmel concerns the spontaneous trust that is placed in other individuals, even if they are not known to us. This form of trust has the characteristics of a socio-psychological trait, rather than a specifically sociological form of trust (Simmel 1990, p. 179), and can be classified as a generic tendency to be trusting towards others. The third conceptual form of trust lies in the ability of individuals to hypothesise "future behaviours" (ibid.) of others, albeit with limited or scarce information, that may help predict their future effective behaviours (Simmel 2010, p. 413). In this conceptual form, trust comes closer to its most common and recent use in the sociological field. This use highlights the relational character of trust and describes it as a willingness to put oneself in a position of vulnerability with respect to others, with the expectation that others will not exploit this situation and that the decision to be trusting will result in more or less direct benefits (Cook and Gerbasi 2009, pp. 219–220).

Simmel's conceptualisation of trust includes expectations of stability for the future, faith in the positive intentions of others and explanatory hypotheses of future social behaviours developed on the basis of the information available. Each of these three elements is usually present when social relationships based on trust are observed, but the relevance of each element is subject to debate, as are the specific social mechanisms and situations that generate trust.

Luhmann (1979, 1988) adopts a functionalist perspective, defining the problem of creating trust as a cognitive and practical strategy for reducing the ever-increasing social complexity of modernity. A complex society renders individual actions less predictable while interpersonal trust helps reduce uncertainty and stabilises expectations towards *alter*. Coleman (1990) emphasises the decision-making role played by individuals in promoting relationships based on trust: the decision to trust another person is taken on the basis of the information available about that person's reliability and on considerations of the possible expected benefits that might come from this fiduciary relationship. Assessing the reliability of another person and evaluating the possible advantages offered by the relationship are always complex operations based on scarce information the predictability of which is always subject to a margin of uncertainty that varies according to the specific situation.

Hardin (2004) notes that trust, reliability and fiduciary behaviour are processes that must be analytically distinguished. Assessing the reliability of an individual (trustee) requires a process of rational evaluation of the available information. The individual who assesses the reliability (truster) will base his decision to trust on this process. The transition from the decision to trust, which is a cognitive process, to fiduciary behaviour towards other subjects involves an assessment of the risk that this action entails. The evaluation of reliability and fiduciary behaviour both contain an "encapsulated interest" (Cook et al. 2005) which binds and benefits the partners in the relationship: trusters expect a positive return on the risk they are running, while it is in the trustee's interest to repay this trust and demonstrate his or her reliability to maintain the bond and its benefits for the future. This form of bonding occurs mainly when the relationship has its own intrinsic value (love, friendship) or when it has reputational effects.

The concept of *encapsulated interest* has been criticized for using the term "interest" because it hints at an economistic analysis of social action. Cook (2001, p. XV) suggests that in reality the concept effectively describes many fiduciary relationships, including the mother-child relationship and intimate relationships. Only trust relations based on pure altruism with no expectation of direct or indirect benefit can be excluded from the concept of encapsulated interest. So the validity of this concept, need not be limited to a utilitarian theory of action but can include different forms of rationality in social action. Cook and Gerbasi (2009, pp. 223–224), for example, distinguish, between *cognitive* trust and *affective* trust. On the basis of past experiences cognitive trust assumes future behaviours will be positive; emotional trust is based on the *feeling* generated by the interlocutor when there is no previous experience of reliability. These two types of trust are interrelated and often support each other: this can starting reverse causation processes (McAllister 1995, p. 30). What distinguishes a trust-based relationship from other forms of direct and immediate reciprocity is the particularly advantageous position enjoyed by the trustee who might have a short-term advantage in not reciprocating the trust received. In the long run, though, the trustee would suffer reputational damage or some other disadvantage. The classic example of this is the used car dealer whose comments on the quality of the cars for sale are trusted by the buyer; the dealer can decide whether to repay this trust and provide accurate information and fair prices, or to abuse this trust by selling cars that do not correspond to the description given (Akerlof 1970). The dealer would have a short-term advantage if he did not repay the trust received but instead provided false information about the quality of the cars and sold them at prices that exceeded their real value. If there were no advantage associated with not reciprocating the trust received, there would be no fiduciary relationship and the relationship would not require trust. The immediate advantage obtained by betraying the trust received would, however, have negative reputational negative effects in the longer term.

Hardin (2004) criticises overly general conceptions of trust and emphasises its situational nature: to trust means trusting a specific person in a specific context and with reference to the specific reason for the relationship. From this perspective, common measurements of trust based on aptitude surveys are not necessarily reliable predictors of fiduciary behaviours. General questions about the degree of trust placed in strangers, or in the general population, reveal generic attitudes that are potentially disconnected from real choices as to whether or not to be trusting in specific contexts (Rotter 1980; Kosugi and Yamagishi 1998).

Zucker (1986) notes that contextual reliability assessment cannot be considered as entirely within the domain of the actors involved, nor can it be totally a function of their interests, as the utilitarian approach affirms, but rather, it needs to be assessed within the institutional context that influences the norms and rules of interaction. In this way

Zucker identifies three-forms of trust, distinguishing them by the elements from which they are generated: process-based trust, characteristics-based trust and institutional-based trust. Process-based trust is generated when the relationship is based on strong social ties or on reputation; characteristics-based trust depends on the effect of personal similarities (sex, age, origin, etc.) to develop. Neither form of trust is easily generalised and Zucker argues that wider forms of trust need the third type of trust, which is created by formalised institutional structures that sustain it, such as laws, professional associations and bureaucracies.

Trust is therefore both an effect of modern social differentiation and one of the essential elements of a complex network of social interdependencies. Encapsulated interests, repeated interactions (family, friends or professionals), personal characteristics and supportive institutions are the elements that allow us to describe the social processes that create fiduciary relationships. These elements provide the basis for the positive expectations of future behaviour identified by Simmel as necessary for relational trust. The trust found in the Sardex network, in general terms, is process-based and institutional-based (the support of Sardex Ltd) as well as containing an encapsulated interest for all those involved.

The combination of these elements, their specific characteristics and the social mechanisms that govern the relationship between them have the situational characteristics determined by the configuration of the Sardex device. Understanding their form and functioning requires an empirical description of the elements and an analytical breakdown of the social mechanisms that generate trust.

The role played by Sardex in facilitating trust-based relationships among network members has already been described in the preliminary analyses conducted by Sartori and Dini (2016), Littera et al. (2014) and Dini and Kioupkiolis (2014). Research has shown that trust is essential for network functioning, both for companies joining the network (Sartori and Dini 2016, pp. 286–289; Dini and Kioupkiolis 2014, p. 13) and as a facilitator of exchanges among members (Sartori and Dini 2016, pp. 292–293; Littera et al. 2014, pp. 12–14).

The Sardex device generates trust by using all three forms of trust described by Zucker. These three forms of trust creation (see Table 4.1) operate in the Sardex case through known social mechanisms: characteristics-based trust uses selection and signalling mechanisms; process-based trust uses reciprocity and monitoring mechanisms as well as horizontal sanctioning; institution-based trust primarily uses monitoring and

Table 4.1 The generative mechanisms and the nature of trust in Sardex. (Source: own presentation)

	The nature of trust		
	Characteristics	Processes	Institutions
The trust-generative mechanisms in Sardex	• Selection • Signalling	• Reciprocity • Monitoring and reputational sanctioning	• Hierarchical monitoring and sanctioning

hierarchical sanctioning mechanisms. The ways in which the Sardex device creates the different forms of trust and the role played by social mechanisms are described in this section.

4.1.1 Selection

Selection Mechanism

The Sardex currency circulates within a closed member network. The selection of members is partly endogenous, an effect of the interest that Sardex inspires in member companies and entrepreneurs, and partly exogenous, through the rational expansion of the market carried out by the Sardex broker management. Despite Sardex Ltd's constant efforts to expand the network, the member companies still represent a very small proportion of Sardinian companies and they constitute a group with precise rules of interaction between members. The process of selecting which companies will become members is the most basic social mechanism involved in the functioning of the Sardex device.

The effects of selection have been widely studied in various areas of sociology: ranging from studies on urban social segregation to the reproduction of inequalities in schools and work. The Sardex experience can be compared to studies that examine how selection affects competition and the creation of monopolies. Elias (2000) studied how competition affected selection in terms of power accumulation and monopoly creation. The competition mechanism is based on a theory of action in which conflicting interests drive individuals to compete for the acquisition of scarce resources. Elias uses the example of medieval feudal lords competing against each other to acquire more territory. Initially they all possess small fiefdoms, so no-one can easily dominate anyone else, but subsequent wars and peace agreements result in some lords acquiring the territories and resources of others. When there are further battles for land and resources, the fiefdoms that were victorious previously have a competitive advantage over the smaller ones, which makes it easier for them to acquire yet more land and be further advantaged. The outcome of this mechanism is the formation of monopolies which, in the case of medieval wars in Europe, led to the formation of nation states.

The competition mechanism dictates that all actors use every possible opportunity to obtain greater benefits at the expense of others. Competition has no form of hierarchical regulation and it is not possible to opt out *(exit)* or criticise *(voice)* it (Hirschman 1970). Participants cannot avoid the competition; losses are real and have tangible effects. Every advantage obtained through competition is obtained at the expense of someone else; further resources and privileges are accumulated which increases the likelihood of yet more success in the competition in the future (Maurer 2016, p. 32). The effect at the aggregate level is an unequal distribution of opportunities and social and material resources which, over time, thanks to the progressive accumulation of resources, results in the successful actors dominating the competition and monopolising the scarce resources. The monopoly mechanism described by Elias continues its dynamics for as long as scarce resources are available to be acquired.

The process of gradually selecting participants, envisaged by the monopoly mechanism, redefines the boundaries between in-group and out-group at every turn and, with the formation of a monopoly, generates long-term effects that cannot be modified by individual actors, and are not the fruit of their direct intentionality. The enlargement of the feud modifies the quality of the relationships among the individuals who are associated with it (peasants, artisans, servants, knights, etc.). These individuals, depending on the selection made by the competition and the new boundaries of the social group, may adopt collaborative, rather than competitive, forms of relationship. Finally, those who lose cannot compete again, so the network of relationships within the competition is constantly being redefined by the selection process.

The process of selecting companies to join Sardex activates a mechanism that influences the form and quality of the network of actors involved.

Selection in Sardex

The endogenous selection of Sardex network members is based on the characteristics of entrepreneur members that best conform to the characteristics of the network. Almost all the entrepreneurs interviewed report that joining the Sardex network is in line with their company's development needs in periods of economic difficulty: finding customers and having sufficient liquidity to meet current expenses and make investments.[2]

> We decided to join because of the economic crisis; we thought Sardex could bring us new customers and that is what happened (E. 10).

Some companies urgently needed more customers and liquidity because they were in serious difficulties:

> I was thinking of closing because there was very little work and I couldn't pay my taxes and go forward (E. 4).
>
> We were badly hit by the crisis and Sardex arrived when our pockets were empty and gave us the opportunity to move forward (E. 3).

Some entrepreneurs based their decision to join Sardex on characteristics and beliefs not necessarily linked to the economic aspects of their company. The novelty represented by Sardex for the local economic scenario was considered by many entrepreneurs as a disadvantage and a source of entrepreneurial risk that advised against membership. Some entrepreneurs though, were curious and attracted to the novelty of the Sardex project. This, together with the increasingly good reputation that Sardex enjoyed, was an incentive to join:

[2]For an analysis of the reasons for joining the network see Sub-sect. 4.3.2.

> Other local companies had told me about Sardex Then I got more information and joined up, partly out of curiosity, but also because all the members were talking about Sardex so enthusiastically: turnover increases, you meet new people, learn about new niche products … So, I said let's try it and see how it goes. Using Sardex our expectations were confirmed (E. 32).

There were some entrepreneurs whose motivation for joining Sardex were not primarily economic: their personal beliefs about the functioning of the local and global economic system were an important factor in their decision to join. A certain distrust and dissatisfaction with the banking system is part of the experience of many members and Sardex appears as a possible way out of a problematic relationship:

> I fell in love with Sardex after I discovered it because of my anarchist attitude towards the banks (E. 2).
>
> One of the reasons you might enter Sardex is that you hate banks (E. 21)

For some members, the characteristics of the Sardex network coincide with their own political convictions and ideas as to how the economy should be regulated. In recent years Sardinia, like the rest of Italy, has seen the rapid development of shopping centres, managed by large retailers, which have undermined traditional local production, distribution and trade systems.

> We decided to join Sardex because we liked the philosophy of excluding shopping malls, of accepting local companies, of having economic transactions not dominated by finance. It wasn't the economic aspects that made us decide to join (E. 7).

The challenge, unequal in many respects, between small Sardinian businesses and large-scale international retail is experienced by some companies as a threat to survival. The economic project associated with the Sardex currency appears as a tool capable of counteracting this competitive disparity:

> I joined Sardex to save myself and counteract globalisation. I was losing customers who were buying on the internet and I didn't know what to do. Since I am unable to counteract globalisation, I entered Sardex (E. 15).

For these entrepreneurs, Sardex represents an important economic resource for their companies offering general value orientations as well as immediate economic returns. In some cases, the Sardex selection process was based primarily on value orientations that prevailed over economic calculations:

> The values are those of a solidarity network: it also gives companies that are in difficulty the opportunity to obtain a little credit which for them could be very important. For us the values of the project were more important than any economic interest in entering the network, if we had only considered our company's objective economic data, at the beginning we probably would not have taken this road (E. 37).

For these entrepreneurs, joining the network is consistent with their own system of expectations about how the local economy functions and the relationships that should be made between local companies to develop together.

> For me, the fact that the fundamental principles of Sardex are combined with the principles of my activity, was fundamental to my joining up. I have been studying local tourism systems since 2008 because of my business. Sardex is an instrument that pays attention to environmental and social sustainability. The globalisation of large retailers has been moving into tourism since the 2000s. Ever since then it has been necessary for my small tourist business to cooperate with other small local businesses so we can all grow together (E. 9)

Mutual help between local actors is an idea that coincides with the nature of the Sardex currency as mutual credit between companies. For these entrepreneurs, joining Sardex, is not only an innovative form of business support, as it is for most interviewees, but it is also coherent with their system of values and convictions. The Sardex device in these cases operates an endogenous selection of members, conveying a system of values and relationships that is coherent with that of the member entrepreneurs.

Endogenous selection for entry into the Sardex network operates in both an economic and a cognitive direction. The founders, when interviewed, underlined how the decision to charge an annual membership fee ensured Sardex Ltd's economic survival, but that this fee was also a request to the entrepreneur members for an economic, cognitive and emotional investment in Sardex: *"If you enter, it is because you believe in it"* (F. 2). The founders wanted members to feel the Sardex project was important so that they would dedicate effort and energy to optimising the Sardex resources made available to them, to ensure the network functioned well and everyone could benefit from it. Joining the network is seen by entrepreneurs as a demanding choice: there is an annual membership fee (economic investment) and business habits have to change (new customers and new suppliers have to be sourced from within the Sardex network). This means that only entrepreneurs with the right character for managing this type of change, or those who were forced by the economic crisis to seek out new business opportunities, will join up:

> Now the network has become a virtuously positive market because all the member companies have made a good choice (E. 26).

In addition to the endogenous selection of members, which mainly concerns economic benefits and/or value orientations, there is an intentional selection process carried out by Sardex Ltd. This selection follows a logic of progressive vertical and horizontal expansion of the production chains present in Sardinia which aims to cover all supply chains and provide competitive supplies of all products. The rejection of a company's application to join Sardex is never final and depends mainly on the contingent situation of the network's expansion in a specific production sector. The entry of a new company might result in a supply surplus that the network cannot absorb, or the products or services requested by the company for its operation may be lacking. Some of the entrepreneurs interviewed had been denied entry at first or were aware of these temporary blocks to membership:

> I learned about Sardex through a Sardinian newspaper in 2012 and I immediately decided to join. But at the time the advisors told me they didn't believe in my business and they didn't let me join. In 2015, though, an advisor let me enter and since then I have made some progress because I have gone from being a C framework to being an A framework so I now have a larger credit line (E. 11).

This entrepreneur is not among those who associate ethical values with the Sardex currency, but he sees it as a valid instrument for economic growth for his own business activity, started a few years before he joined Sardex. The rejection of his membership application did not deter him from taking an interest in the network and, some years later, he managed to get his broker to accept his entry.

Conclusions

The selection mechanism for network membership used by the Sardex device, offers a competitive advantage to those selected, which operates in a somewhat similar way to the monopoly mechanism described by Elias. Thanks to the endogenous entry selection and the Sardex Ltd selection process described above, network members have the competitive advantage of being able to exchange goods and services in Sardex exclusively with other members. Those who are not network members cannot do this. The selection process described by Elias is based on competition while the selection process for joining Sardex is based on other elements, not necessarily of a competitive nature (e.g., the type of products sold or requested). Both selection processes, however, generate a competitive advantage over future competitors. The selection made by Sardex, though, unlike the selection between feudal lords described by Elias, will never result in one company monopolising an entire economic sector because the broker management intentionally operates to provide multiple offers in each sector, to ensure members have freedom of choice.

It is theoretically possible that a monopoly might be created if the Sardex network were to expand to the point where a significant share of Sardinian companies were members. In that case entrepreneurs might find that entering the network was no longer an option but had become a necessity. Most of the company's suppliers and customers at that point would have part of their business in Sardex and not being able to make and receive payments in Sardex might be considered a handicap by the market. The dynamics triggered by the competitive advantage of being selected for membership could lead to the Sardex network monopolising the complementary, but now virtually obligatory, medium of exchange for Sardinian companies. This possibility is unlikely, however, because, although Sardex could potentially reach all Sardinian companies, it is not possible for companies that do not have their headquarters in Sardinia to join the Sardex network. Sardex was, in fact, conceived as a support tool for the Sardinian economy to help it confront the competitive pressure of much larger, well-structured and competitive external companies; for this reason, membership is limited to Sardinian companies. Even if all the Sardinian companies were network members, non-Sardinian companies could still continue to operate in Sardinia and put Sardinian companies out of business if they sought shelter within the Sardex network.

The effect of selection, though, does create a competitive advantage for companies that are network members, compared to those that are not. Network members who have collected Sardex and accumulated a positive surplus in their Sardex account have to seek out suppliers so they can spend their Sardex surplus.

> Being able to barter makes you interested in wanting to know which products to trade with. I need to know how to spend Sardex. Sardex customers come to me and I earn Sardex which I then need to know how to spend. You can do many things, for example buy a computer, renovate your home, buy car tyres, buy something for the shop, spend them at a restaurant (E. 7)

The search for suppliers necessarily takes place within the network, sometimes with the support of the broker team and sometimes by consulting the list of members. In this phase members enjoy the competitive advantage given by their entrance selection because non-members cannot receive payments in Sardex. This competitive advantage, entirely due to the entrance selection mechanism, is documented in the research results of Iosifidis et al. (2018). A network analysis of exchanges in Sardex confirms the presence of long exchange networks that cross Sardinia from one side to the other (Ibid.). It is very unlikely that such long exchange networks, sometimes two hundred kilometres long, would be used outside the Sardex network, especially for small quantities of supplies. If they were used, the companies involved would face high promotional and transactional costs. The interviews confirmed that it is common to look for a supplier in Sardex by consulting the list of members or the broker team and to choose one independently of previous business relationships or physical proximity.

The competitive advantage of joining the network also manifests itself in terms of customer loyalty. Faced with a local offer of comparable quality, the entrepreneur who has Sardex to spend may find it advantageous to repeatedly opt for the same supplier in Sardex. An entrepreneur who works with numerous commercial and catering companies has clearly found Sardex customers to be much more loyal than his euro customers:

> Sardex has produced customer loyalty in the catering sector; they found a good product and because they can pay in Sardex they have become regular customers (E. 14).

The economic and cognitive investment required for joining the network has important effects on how members use Sardex. If access to the network were free, there would probably be many more member companies but the level of transactions would be lower than at present. Entrepreneurs would have a passive attitude towards the network and would wait for some promising economic opportunities to arise. A network in which entrepreneurs do not risk anything and can afford to wait for an economic opportunity without any specific deadlines would be less dynamic than the current one. The founders of Sardex in fact, after the first experiences of the network and various experimental trials, decided to charge a fixed annual membership fee and made transactions free (Littera et al. 2014).

> The euro is part of people's life in an obligatory manner, Sardex members, though, choose to be part of this network: you use the euro because you have to, you use Sardex credits because you choose to do so. From that moment on, they begin to change customers and that changes your social circle. The euro cannot be chosen (F. 2).

The decision to join the network and pay the annual membership fee puts the entrepreneurs in the position of investors who pursue an economic return on their investment. Members know that to ensure that their investment in the annual membership fee is fruitful, they have to maintain a high level of economic transactions. They soon realise (or are reminded by the broker team) that only their direct commitment to using the Sardex currency will bring them the economic benefits they expect.

> We are bound by the economic mechanism of money that restricts spending to within the network. You have to get a move on to spend and earn (E. 7).

Although Sardex Ltd makes available many services that favour transactions within the network, even the passive use of these services cannot happen unless the entrepreneur members are directly engaged with the network and undertaking economic transactions. The obstacles to entering the network (membership fee and changing business habits) means the entrepreneurs selected for membership are averagely motivated to engage with the Sardex network. However, the psychological mechanism of cognitive coherence, relative to the investment decision taken, and the need for an economic return on the same investment, push these entrepreneurs to be an active part of the success of the project. The selection mechanism adopted by the Sardex device, transforms potentially passive network users into members who feel they are an active part of the success of their company within the network and, as an aggregate effect, of the good functioning of the Sardex network in general.

Like the selection process described by Elias, the types of social relationships within Sardex network also change (see Fig. 4.1): the entrance selection creates two distinct groups: those who are inside (members) and those who are outside (non members). The following sub-sections will present the social mechanisms that generate the specific form of interaction that develops among network members.

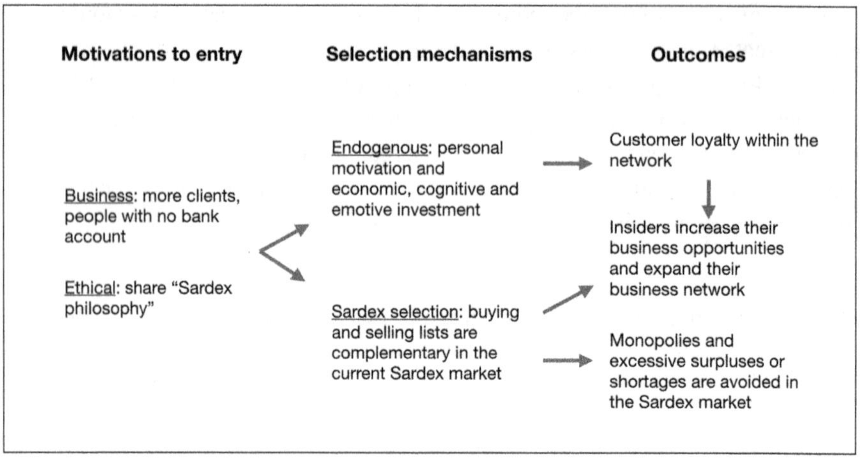

Fig. 4.1 Sardex selection mechanisms. (Source: own figure)

4.1.2 Signalling

Signalling Mechanism

The decision to trust is based on a variable level of uncertainty about a partner's future behaviour that cannot be completely eliminated. If the uncertainty were eliminated the relationship would no longer be based on trust but would be a different form of social relationship. In economic market relations, the need for trust between partners grows exponentially compared to more traditional forms of social bonding. An increase in uncertainty is required to make the market more dynamic and open, but at the same time, this uncertainty makes the actors more unpredictable, increases the need to resort to relational trust increases and also exposes the truster to the risk that this will not be reciprocated.

> Especially market relations in modern societies demand that risky advance concessions must be made without precise knowledge of the exchange partner, without relying on long-term relations, and despite only incomplete observation of his action with others, as in situations that are not extensively guaranteed by power or norms. The core of the problem of trust consists precisely in this "middle condition between knowing and not knowing" (Simmel 1992: 393), even when institutions, social norms, power and calculations of interest contribute to forming expectations (Beckert 2005, p. 14).

The initial problem for the construction of relational trust is to identify the degree of interlocutor reliability in relation to the object of the relationship. The partner of the relationship that must give confidence suffers uncertainty about the real reliability of the partner in the relationship (Bacharach and Gambetta 2001, p. 148). The partner's real characteristics, which would literally make the relationship "reliable", that is with results certainly in line with expectations, are not actually accessible: honesty and goodness are not clearly identifiable qualities and, even if they were identified in the partner, would not guarantee stability over time. The identification of honesty and goodness is problematic: they are often subjectively interpreted and both characteristics require context-related assessments; they are also changeable so they can manifest themselves differently in the same subjects. Uncertainty is therefore an ineliminable and more or less extensive part of the relationship of trust that the truster seeks to reduce by identifying the degree of trustee reliability. There are contingent situations where the truster, despite not knowing the real reliability of the interlocutor, needs to decide whether or not to trust the trustee.

The choice to give trust can be interpreted both as a rational orientation in the pursuit of one's own interest, given the expected advantage (Spence 1973), and as a necessity imposed by the interaction process in which the truster is involved (Goffman 1969). Due to the radical uncertainty of the decision-making process, neither interpretation provides a clear generalisable explanation of the elements in play, nor can they reliably predict the truster's decision. Identifying the degree of reliability depends on identifying characteristics of the trustee that can act as indicators of future reliability (Molm et al. 2000; Malhotra and Murnighan 2002). These signs do not eliminate the uncertainty of trust, but are used by the truster to reduce his or her uncertainty and guide decision making.

> Trust can be described as the social mechanism that expresses the shutdown of the latent uncertainty of the trust-giver: trust works as a tranquilizer in social relations enabling the trust-giver to remain calm despite the uncontrollable freedom of action of the trust-taker (Beckert 2005, p. 18).

The signs that should act as indicators of personal reliability multiply and become more difficult to interpret with the increase in social complexity. If the family name or profession could be considered a clear indicator of reliability in pre-modern times, the subsequent increase in social mobility and the end of traditional belonging made the traditional indicators less reliable and saw the emergence of new ones.

The classic example of the signalling mechanism being linked to personal integrity is Weber's description of American entrepreneurs' strategic membership of sects and clubs (Weber 1946, pp. 309–311). Membership of prestigious clubs signals moral integrity and guarantees trustee reliability thanks to a mechanism which functions in a similar way to to Sardex membership.

> He who wished to be fully recognised in this [US] democracy, in whatever position, had not only to conform to the conventions of bourgeois society, the very strict men's fashions included, but as a rule he had to be able to show that he had succeeded in gaining admission by ballot to one of the sects, clubs, or fraternal societies, no matter what kind, were it only recognised as sufficiently legitimate. And he had to maintain himself in the society by proving himself to be a gentleman (Weber 1946, p. 311)

Trustees can have a high degree of reflexivity about the signs of reliability they provide to the trusters and can try to control and orient them according to their own interests (Offe 1999). Bacharach and Gambetta (2001) clarify this distinction by introducing the concepts of *kripta* and *manifesta* reliability. Kripta reliability is the real reliability that is known only to the trustees: only they know their real intentions about their future behaviour. Manifest reliability is that which trustees make visible with the signs they emit towards trusters ranging from their own biological signs (e.g. skin colour, stature, facial features, age, etc.) to more or less manipulable elements (e.g. clothing, verbal and non-verbal communication, etc.). Emitting manifest signs of reliability, intentionally or unintentionally, and their decoding and acceptance are therefore indispensable elements for the construction of the relationship of trust.

Signalling in Sardex

Being a member of the Sardex network is perceived by entrepreneurs as a guarantee of high reliability. Network membership offers sufficient guarantees of reliability to the point that it replaces the usual reliability assessments and signals adopted in commercial exchanges. The reliability signal is so effective that entrepreneurs report how, from the very first meeting, the relationship with other members is "different". They perceive the characteristics of this difference quite clearly:

> The relationship with other Sardex members is different. There are many more topics for chatting and at some point you start talking more (E. 21).
>
> When you see yourself with customers, it's like a family. You hug and greet each other warmly (E. 4).

Joining the Sardex network immediately creates a sense of familiarity and closeness among entrepreneurs, relationships are easier and the quality of relationships is different from ordinary commercial relationships.

> We have made many friends with Sardex customers who have also come from far away, such as from Sassari or Olbia. Ours is an exclusive, high-end, non-commercial product, Sardex has given us the opportunity to make ourselves known. These friendships that are born in euros occur more rarely and take longer. Sardex unites us and this creates a closer relationship from the first meeting. Even with euro customers we have a wonderful relationship but in Sardex we have formed a "clan", let's call it that: a new way of approaching. This was created by the fact that Sardex allowed us to create new work and new opportunities (E. 10).

The initial "diversity" of relationships is subsequently transformed into a greater ease in forging friendly relations than in the euro market. The rievocation of "clan" relationships provides a good idea of how much network membership transforms the nature of relations between entrepreneurs. Normal commercial relations are characterised by strong competition and sometimes by opportunistic behaviour which means entrepreneurs tend to be very detached and distrustful in commercial relations. The "clan" relationship avoids the initial distrust and places the "enemy" outside the group to which they belong: the other members are natural "allies" within the market.

Although the entrepreneurs are clearly aware of this "difference", even in the initial phase of their relations within the Sardex network, they cannot precisely identify the causes. When asked about their relationship with other members, entrepreneurs report their "diversity" but provide different reasons to explain this. Entrepreneurs clearly perceive this "difference" and appreciate it very much but find it difficult to clearly identify the determining causes. It is however possible to identify at least four elements of the Sardex network which are crucial in making network membership a sign of high reliability for entrepreneurs. The selection mechanism described above is the first process that guarantees the reliability of the members.

> The first impression of exchanges in Sardex was very positive because it gave me the opportunity to meet many entrepreneurs. Meeting each other was facilitated by the fact that we belong to the same network. If you and I meet on the street and you want me to offer insurance, it's hard for me to trust you without knowing you. If, on the other hand, you come from a network whose back office has examined your credentials, this gives me greater confidence. This is one of the elements that makes the difference (E. 13).

The selection process prior to entering the network operated by Sardex Ltd and the daily monitoring activity carried out by the broker area are perceived as elements that guarantee the reliability of network members. The ordinary reliability assessment processes that are carried out between entrepreneurs on the market are substituted, in the perception of the members, by the selection and monitoring processes carried out by Sardex Ltd. The "knowledge" evoked by the interviewee as necessary for creating trust is delegated completely to Sardex Ltd as reliability assessor and the relationship can start from the beginning with a high degree of mutual trust.

In addition to the guarantee of selection and monitoring carried out by Sardex, word of mouth among adherents is also perceived as a source of reliability. The high level of initial trust in the relationships between members allows their business relationships to acquire confidential features that are usually not present in economic exchanges. The exchange of opinions and advice on other members with whom to have commercial relationships is the first topic of conversation between entrepreneurs: this goes beyond mere economic exchange and is also a common interest.

> In Sardex like in many other categories you exchange information about colleagues. It's like a big group where things come to light sooner or later. When you meet another member you chat, talk and share experiences. The first question is: "What company are you from?", The second question is: "Who are you buying from?", So opinions are exchanged. Let's say that with Sardex patients there are plenty of chat topics (E. 21).

Members share their experiences in the network and pass on comments made by other members (word of mouth): this provides an element of guarantee regarding the reliability of other members. Entrepreneurs believe that misconduct would soon be known around the network and would be punished with expulsion.

The third reason which entrepreneurs cite for the "difference" in Sardex relations with respect to those in euros, is linked to the expectations of utility that entrepreneurs place in relations with other members. The Sardex currency can only be used within the network and credits obtained through selling goods or services can only be spent in the network so entrepreneurs need to find suppliers of goods or services inside the network.

> I ask the client in Sardex immediately what kind of work he does because he could be my supplier. For example, if he produces LED bulbs I am very interested (E. 26).

Entrepreneurs also use the Sardex currency for specific investments not made in euros (see Sub-sect. 4.3.1). The meeting with a customer who supplies a specific product can be an opportunity for an investment until then postponed: compared to the euro, Sardex spending "weighs" less on the budget, suppliers do not need to be researched and selected and their reliability is guaranteed by their network membership. This greater willingness to cooperate can extend beyond traditional commercial exchanges and facilitate the truster's availability for more demanding economic collaborations:

> When a "Sardex" comes here, I ask him who he is and what he does, and find out if I can interact with him and start new relationships, not only commercial but also collaborative, for example, if we can organise an event together to promote our activities. These are possibilities that you do not use with the customer in euros, while in Sardex it becomes natural … It is important to know the people who come to your shop to see if they can give you an address for where you can spend Sardex. We made letterheads, envelopes, tags, etc., it becomes a currency of exchange that is closer to barter than to real money (E. 7).

Relations in Sardex thus acquire different characteristics from the ordinary ones thanks to the signalling effect of network membership which becomes a guarantee of reliability and a facilitator of economic initiatives. The continuity with which this type of relationship is established in the network can be considered an indicator of its independence from specific contexts or actors. The specific characteristics of the relationship are maintained by the association of actors, the technological network, and the activated social mechanisms that go beyond individual intentions.

> I see Sardex as a social network that keeps us in touch. When someone calls you or comes here to buy, you are curious enough to ask: "What are you doing in Sardex? What services do you offer?". There is not the coldness of an economic exchange that ends with the exchange of services for money, there is the curiosity to know what the other person does, which comes from wanting to know if the service offered by the other person, who has contacted me, may be of use to me. From there comes a relationship that pushes you to know who is in the network, if it can be useful for your business or your personal needs. This extra social relationship in the course of economic transactions is always activated in my experience of Sardex transactions (E. 30).

The fourth element that favours the link between perception of reliability and the signalling mechanism concerns the shared values that entrepreneurs ascribe to network members:

> When you meet a member, you immediately address each other informally. This happens because we are both in agreement on at least one thing [network membership A/N]. In Sardex we have both subscribed to a different vision of the world of work (E. 13).

The diversity of the type of relationships established is in this case ascribed to a communion of values that binds members. Joining the network acquires an ethical connotation that favours a common sense of belonging. The positive expectations of members' behaviour seem to find confirmation in the repetition of positive experiences within the network: the experiences confirm the expectations and consolidate them for subsequent interactions.

> I have made about fifty new friends over time thanks to Sardex, some are very close relationships where these friends have been invited to weddings or baptisms. With Sardex you belong to the same club. When you meet two people you always look for an element in common, it can be the same jacket or a common acquaintance. The first question that is asked is: "How are you? How are things going?", which aims to acquire general information. Then each of us works on these little pieces of information to find common elements. Sardex is certainly an element in common. Then, if the interlocutor were to [engage in misconduct with me], the relationship would be interrupted, even if we have Sardex in common. But the incidence of [misconduct] in Sardex is really low (E. 34).

Conclusions

Market studies identify four main strategies where the signalling mechanism establishes trusting relationships: commitment, congruence of expectations, competence and integrity (Beckert 2005, pp. 23–24). The Sardex case can be considered a specific case of integrity strategy: network membership signals the integrity and fairness of member behaviour to the truster, thanks to the specific network characteristics described above. Network membership is considered a guarantee of correct behaviour, adherence to values and a business opportunity.

The guarantee of integrity provided by joining Sardex also refers to the signal given by the "good" family name in the pre-modern era: individuals' behaviour conformed to stable and recognised social expectations and norms, making it more predictable. The modern increase in uncertainty about the behaviour of *alter* is reduced by the signalling mechanism activated by the Sardex device. Entrepreneurs who join the Sardex network signal a high level of partner reliability to other members.

In the eyes of members, the reliability expected of Sardex depends on four elements: entrance selection and monitoring carried out by Sardex Ltd, reputation and word of mouth among members, the advantages expected from good relations within the network

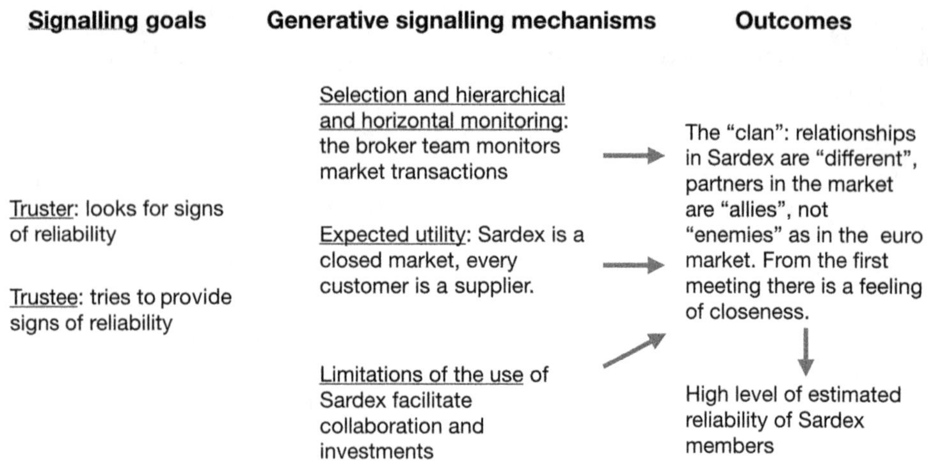

Fig. 4.2 Sardex signalling mechanisms. (Source: own figure)

and the ethical values associated with network membership. The signalling mechanism in Sardex as a whole (see Fig. 4.2) can be considered as a facilitator of relations and market transactions: entrepreneurs who have never met each other, at their first meeting, already consider each other worthy of a high level of trust. Outside the Sardex network such high levels of trust are conceivable only after repeated positive interactions, extended waiting times and possible failures, all of which are drastically reduced by the Sardex device as a whole and conveyed through the signalling mechanism.

4.1.3 Reciprocity

Reciprocity Mechanism and Norm of Reciprocity

The signalling mechanism demonstrates how expectations regarding *alter* behaviour play a decisive role in building trust and increasing the likelihood of cooperation. Trust will not be established if trustees do not signal their reliability; in the case of market transactions, a lack of trust means exchanges will not take place. Signalling is essential in the case of one-shot interactions between people who do not know each other; where there are repeated interactions, stable expectations of reliability can also arise independently of, or in addition to, those generated by signalling. Repeated interaction favours the creation of strong ties of interdependence between those involved, permitting the stabilisation of expectations regarding *alter* behaviour. Although the utilitarian model may consider free-rider behaviour advantageous, in the case of one-shot interactions, it recognises that a pattern of repeated interaction favours cooperation and makes the free-rider model disadvantageous (Gouldner 1960). The free-rider who betrays the trust given by the truster precludes the possibility of further interactions and exchanges:

the utility derived from such behaviour is greatly inferior to that obtained from a series of exchanges based on mutual trust.

> Individuals with whom one has a continuing relation have an economic motivation to be trustworthy, so as not to discourage future transactions; and departing from pure economic motives, continuing economic relations often become overlaid with social content that carries strong expectations of trust and abstention from opportunism (Granovetter 1985, p. 490).

Conditions of repeated interaction can also favour cooperative behaviour in selfish individuals who are completely disinterested in the destinies of *alter* (Dasgupta 1988). The effect of repeated interaction on cooperation has been demonstrated experimentally by repeating the prisoner's dilemma (Axelrod 1984; Kreps et al. 1982), by increasing number of repeated games (Gibbons 2001) and by adopting specific vignette experiments (Buskens and Raub 2002). Cook et al. (2005) created a version of the prisoner's dilemma which allowed the participants to decide how much to invest on the basis of the level of cooperation they expected from their partner. The results showed that both the initial trust investment of the *truster* and previous experiences of positive interactions increased the level of cooperation between the participants and reduced free-rider behaviour. The mechanism of reciprocity can thus emerge through repeated interaction "*since communication could enable individuals to coordinate, persuade, precommit, and signal trustworthiness*" (Baldassarri 2015, p. 360; Ostrom 1990).

A pattern of social reciprocity can also emerge through repeated interaction outside the mechanism of reciprocity. Fehr and Gachter (2000) used experimental research on group dynamics to demonstrate how group membership can promote in-group reciprocity, sanction controls on rule compliance and prompt individuals to face significant costs for enforcing group rules. In one-shot interactions, the trust shown by the truster and the consequent reciprocity-based behaviour of the trustee demonstrate that there are reciprocity rules which cannot be explained in utilitarian or reputational terms (Berg et al. 1995). The pattern of reciprocity that emerges from one-shot interactions in experimental contexts is explained by the existence of social norms which inspire the participants' behaviour. Numerous versions of social dilemmas: prisoner dilemmas, public good games (Marwell and Ames 1979) and gift games (Fehr et al. 1997) were used to verify the presence of reciprocity norms. Research results consistently demonstrate the existence of reciprocity norms, although contextual variables influence how these norms perform and how they are interpreted. For instance, studies carried out in developing countries, where economic exchanges are permanently intertwined with reciprocity rules, reveal the prevalence of a "balanced" form of reciprocity, where the amount the trustee returns to the truster is proportional to the sum invested (1:1) (Greig and Bohnet 2008). Conversely, the experiments carried out in wealthy countries (the majority), are characterised by "conditional" reciprocity, where the amount the trustee returns to the truster increases with the level of trust given (Camerer and Fehr 2004).

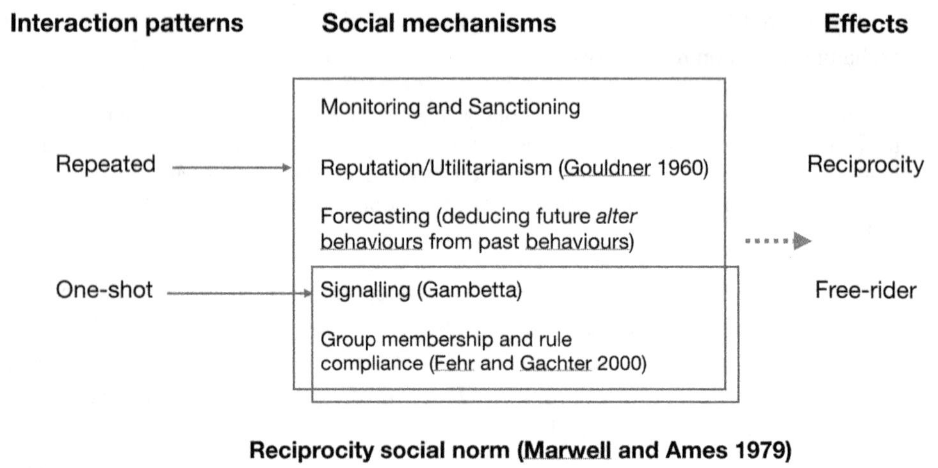

Fig. 4.3 Reciprocity social mechanisms. (Source: own figure)

The presence of reciprocity norms in one-shot interactions unrelated to repetition and reputation is due to social norms; unlike the reciprocity engendered by repeated interactions it cannot be considered a social mechanism, see Fig. 4.3.

Reciprocity in Sardex

The selection mechanism reduces the number of economic partners within the Sardex network and the signalling mechanism generates a high degree of trust in others. These mechanisms encourage repeated interactions and exchanges between members of the network.

> We usually have a relatively abstract view of money. With Sardex, the money I earn is the justification for my work which involves a person who is part of my own network, unlike euros which everyone is involved in. As a consequence, you establish a different relationship with that person, because it is as if Sardex is bringing you a little closer. A euro customer may be just a temporary customer, who passes by once and then departs. A Sardex customer comes back to you because he knows that you are in the network: if he has a coffee here, he will definitely come and have another one. A relationship is established with this person because he comes back daily, unlike someone who may just be passing through. Seeing someone regularly leads to a relationship with the manager or with employees. This brings you a little closer and pushes you to create a different relationship than the one you have with an occasional customer. Among the people in Sardex there is a little more humanity because you start with a simple purchase that then becomes a part of your everyday life (E. 11).

The entrepreneur observes how the network's entry selection facilitates the development of a daily relationship between members. This closeness creates a different relationship with the customer compared to customers paying in euros.

The entry selection affects consumer behaviour by favouring economic exchanges within the network. Members cannot use the internet to buy on-line from large-scale retail stores; they can only buy from medium-small firms that mostly operate in the local market. This limitation of the Sardex network has the secondary effect of encouraging local economic networks and personal relationships with local entrepreneurs. The network "disconnects" economic exchanges with large retailers and e-commerce so as to trigger local exchanges that often involve direct personal contact.

> From a sociological perspective, Sardex is a brilliant idea. With Amazon Prime we have the goods at home in 24 hours without saying: "Good morning, good evening, thank you" to anyone, shopping is going to be dehumanised. Everybody buys from the other side of the world, without having any personal interaction. With Sardex, instead of going on the internet to look for goods, you go to the local store. First you look among Sardex members–who are all like the shop next to your home–and if you don't find anything, then you look on the internet. It's a way to get back to creating social interactions (E. 21).

Entrepreneurs are very much aware that Sardex modifies their social relationships within economic exchanges. They describe interactions within the Sardex network in terms of repeated interactions, trust in exchanges and personal relationships. The network rules favour patterns of social relations based on direct and repeated interaction within economic exchanges.

> After the first exchanges in Sardex, I changed the way I look at this currency because you create a personal relationship with other members. I don't just look at the economic aspects as an entrepreneur anymore, but at the relationships with people. I think that the main purpose of Sardex is to re-establish communications between everyone. Basically Sardex is a form of bartering to which we must add that we become friends with some people or go out to dinner together, there are exchanges of ideas and advice, some related to Sardex and some not. Above all there is a return to personal relationships. Sardex has an influence on this, because you no longer have the gap that usually exists between customers and sellers. Usually, I order the goods, I pay you, you deliver the goods, thank you and goodbye. With Sardex, on the contrary, a friendship can arise, not only economic exchanges take place. Sardex makes people a little more human, it brings you closer (E. 11).

Entrepreneurs attribute Sardex with a capacity for allowing them to communicate directly with each other. They perceive the ordinary economic system to be deeply imbued with opportunism and are highly distrustful of interacting with it. Sardex encourages closer relations which facilitate strong social ties as well as economic ones. This type of relationship and its repetition favour a relationship pattern based on shared norms and reciprocity. Reciprocity norms develop through the creation of strong bonds between members and through simpler and more immediate reflections on the expected utility of future economic exchanges:

> I don't know the jobs of most of my patients. When a patient in Sardex arrives, the first question is: "Which company do you work with?" Because then, the next step is reciprocity

> because I know you, I know that you are within the network and if I know that you sell goods and services that I need, I will come to you. That's how reciprocity is created (E. 21).

Repeated interactions, driven by the economic utility expected from these exchanges and by the creation of strong ties between members, promote mutual trust and reciprocity. Reciprocity also emerges in relationships between members and between members and Sardex Ltd where there is no repeated interaction. For entrepreneurs who recognise that the Sardex project has an ethical trait that they share (half of the sample), reciprocity rules emerge without repeated interaction. The reciprocity rules in the Sardex network also include reciprocity towards the Sardex project as a whole and to Sardex Ltd. While these reciprocity rules are experienced by all interviewees, their specific interpretation depends on the personal experience of the individual entrepreneur, on the firm's history and on how their relationship with Sardex Ltd developed.

The strongest form of norm-based reciprocity in the Sardex network can be found in entrepreneurs who attribute the Sardex project with a strong ethical nature which requires a collective commitment. This ethical feature of Sardex is related to ideals of social justice, local development and mutual aid. For these entrepreneurs, the strong ethical connotation they see in the Sardex project creates reciprocity ties to the extent that they themselves (i) promote the Sardex project image and encourage new membership; (ii) are strongly committed to facilitating the correct and efficient functioning of the network, both for ethical reasons as well as for their own benefit; (iii) defend the internal rules of the network in discussions with other members. For these entrepreneurs, joining Sardex is an ethical as well as an economic choice and it requires conduct ethically compatible with the Sardex project. For some entrepreneurs joining Sardex is a project for developing their business and the local economy, which also requires the involvement of their employees:

> I want to spread the idea that Sardex is a network within which you can find relationships based on reciprocity: the Sardex network is a great resource not only for companies but also for consumers. This firm has 50 employees, if I can pay 5.000 € per month of salaries in Sardex at the end of the year that will be 60.000 € saved for other projects. It is an opportunity for the company to grow, in which the workers also participate (E. 37).

The Sardex project is seen as a collective project that adheres to reciprocity norms, from which all stakeholders can benefit, which requires the convinced participation of all participants.

The first truster to activate this type of reciprocal relationship was Sardex Ltd. All members expressed their appreciation for the correct behaviour of Sardex and for the company's substantial initial "investment" in them. The trust Sardex gives to its new members is perceived by many as an "investment" in their person which requires a return of equal value, both in economic and ethical terms and in their commitment to the network. This trust investment by Sardex Ltd in its new members is also evident in the way the founders of Sardex Ltd describe the relationship they have sought to develop with their members:

> We have a good relationship with our members, we have never called them customers. We do not call them customers, not even in the administration services among those who prepare the invoices. We didn't grow up with that idea. Of course we need to balance the budget, but the challenge is to do it with a bit of originality, without contradicting our principles (F. 1).

The founders are aware that if membership and network use were driven by purely economic reasons, Sardex would probably not function well, nor would it have its current growth rates. When the network first started operating relatively few companies were involved and the possibilities of exchange were limited. If entrepreneurs had decided to limit themselves to purely short-term economic considerations, they would not have chosen to enter or remain. The founders still clearly remember how exciting it was when, after many refusals, some progressive and visionary entrepreneurs signed up to Sardex. The first members were not motivated by expectations of high sales and profits in the short term, given the embryonic nature of the network and the limited number of suppliers and trading opportunities available.

It is reasonable to think that, in the early phases of the Sardex project, the participating entrepreneurs considered their participation in the project to be more important than obtaining short-term economic benefits.[3] This ethically motivated investment in the Sardex project is associated with expectations of fairness and reciprocity from all involved. Even though network membership and use now have to be economically viable there is still reciprocity among the entrepreneurs who attribute strong ethical connotations to the Sardex project and in some cases this reciprocity exists independently of economic reasons:

> Last week we hosted a professional course for dentists in my dentistry office, which was attended by ten colleagues, each of whom brought a patient to try out the new product presented. I decided to invite a patient in Sardex to offer a benefit to a member of the network. I chose a Sardex patient because Sardex is giving me something extra and so, as a result, I want to give back everything I can (E. 21).

In this case, the decision to invite the patient adhering to Sardex instead of inviting a patient who pays in euro does not have any specific economic returns. The patient invited for the free trial is likely to be more grateful and satisfied than patients who were not invited. But a euro-paying patient would probably have been equally appreciative. The decision to invite the patient who is part of Sardex is based on a rule of reciprocity towards Sardex Ltd which is more about ethical criteria of fairness than about economic interests.

[3]The founders of Sardex had the same priorities in the early stages of the Sardex project.

Entrepreneurs offered a variety of reasons for their reciprocities towards Sardex Ltd most of which originated in the specific history of their companies and in their relationship with Sardex Ltd. A common element, however, was their difficult relationship with banks and fact that Sardex Ltd proved to be a viable alternative.

> Sardex is so peaceful. The bank has a thousand problems, a thousand bureaucracies. With the bank it would have been easier for me to invest all my savings in the firm than it would have been to obtain a loan from them because they wanted all my savings as collateral. With Sardex instead, we asked and we received. I will ask Sardex to increase my line of credit so I can renovate my restaurant. I think that if I can repay my debt of 4,000 Sardex over one summer then my credit line might be extended to 10,000 Sardex (E. 28).
>
> When I changed my company from VAT number to Ltd I opened an account in Sardex first and then a bank account. The Sardex account was much easier (E. 21).

Entrepreneurs describe Sardex procedures for obtaining credit as very simple and fast and often compare them favourably with previous dealings with ordinary banks where procedures took longer and were more bureaucratic. Easy access to credit is in itself an incentive for new investments.

The performance gap with ordinary banks is even greater for so-called "non-bankable" entrepreneurs, i.e. those to whom banks refuse to give credit. There are four reasons for classifying entrepreneurs as "non-bankable": (i) the company has been set up recently and has no previous balance sheets or collateral to provide for borrowing; (ii) the company's balance sheets are not robust and the entrepreneur has no collateral to provide for borrowing; (iii) the entrepreneur has not repaid previous debts on time; (iv) macro-economic changes lead to tighter credit conditions and previous levels of indebtedness are no longer accepted by the banks. In our sample, 62% of the entrepreneurs polled were considered either "non-bankable" or had problems with accessing ordinary credit. Entrepreneurs who had been rejected by ordinary banks but given credit by Sardex rated the economic and ethical value of the Sardex project very highly. Some companies would not even exist if they had not received credit from Sardex:

> At the beginning, when I was joining Sardex, the advisor asked me what kind of projects I had in mind for my company and what kind of investments I was planning on making. I needed a website to start my business as a business marketing consultant and so they gave me a credit line to do this. The banks did not give me any credit to start my business but only the possibility of opening a bank account. Without Sardex and the possibility of creating my website I would not have been able to start my own business (E. 30).

This businesswoman is currently promoting membership of the Sardex network among other companies in her town. The trust given by Sardex Ltd to her business project created a strong reciprocity obligation for the Sardex project:

> I became a promoter of Sardex. If there is a chance to talk to someone about Sardex, I always ask people why they are still not a member! I talked for a whole year with

> the restauranteur next door to bring him into the network and we managed to overcome his distrust (E. 30).

Sardex members often think that Sardex Ltd assesses their business differently to the banks:

> Sardex is considered more credible than the banks: they look at the personal aspect and maybe they can give you a credit line. Banks, on the other hand, look at the numbers. Sardex, rather than evaluating, "believes" in people and entrepreneurship (E. 11).
>
> At this point, I do not ask for certain things at the bank, but I ask for them at Sardex. I do things in Sardex or I don't do them at all. I don't think the banks have people capable of evaluating my projects. When I come to ask for something, it's because I've evaluated what can be done, if you tell me no, I will not deal with you anymore. Sardex has always evaluated my proposals positively (E. 15).

This perception of a differently functioning economic system, connected to "believing" in people as opposed to "calculating" numbers, makes the entrepreneur feel invested with a high degree of personal trust that he feels he must return. The *modus operandi* of Sardex credit creates a strong commitment to the Sardex project which impacts desires (see Sub-sect. 4.3.2) and reciprocity constraints.

> I went to the bank to ask for a credit line and they told me that I was too young, even though we have a company we are only youngsters, so we are not credible because if we have a dispute we might dissolve the company. Then Sardex appears, you develop your project and they fully approve it, some merit must be given to them. They financed my project. The repayment of the debt was planned for one year and, in fact, we will repay it within 11 months because we prefer, by personal choice, to repay the debt as soon as possible even if there is nothing in it for us. Entrepreneurship cannot be done on debts. We pay all our suppliers and then if something remains we take it for ourselves, otherwise we take nothing. We have seen how Italy has been damaged by years of being in debt. Debts generate further debt, it's a vortex (E. 11).

Many entrepreneurs associate their experience with Sardex with a different type of relationship which involves reciprocity.

A similar credit system based on a high level of trust is also used to grant special credit lines for investments. Ease-of-operation and investment based on personal trust are the basis of this credit:

> Banks, even for ridiculous amounts, pose enormous problems and act as though they are donating money to you, even though they are selling money at a very high price. On the contrary, the guys from Sardex came, they looked, they liked my idea, they liked the project and there was a handshake. There are no payback times and no interest. It is up to each of us, of course, to make repayments as soon as possible. I think they evaluate the turnover of the company in Sardex, they saw how many Sardex I exchanged, then they trusted me and accepted my project. Unlike what happens in the bank, where you have to put 200,000 signatures, one after the other, because you're signing unfair terms; with Sardex there was a handshake, nothing else, and it's much more valuable (E. 21).

Many entrepreneurs feel that Sardex has revived the "handshake" and they welcome this as a reassertion of past relationship modes. A "handshake" signifies strong trust based on reciprocity.

A final sign of reciprocity emerged during the collection of interviews. It is well known that entrepreneurs are often reluctant to give interviews to avoid subtracting time from business. During preliminary phone calls to schedule interviews, entrepreneurs were often more willing to accept once they knew the interview would be about Sardex. Some entrepreneurs specified that they were only agreeing to be interviewed because of the gratitude that binds them to Sardex.

Conclusions

The reciprocity mechanism generated by repeated interaction among members and the reciprocity norm among members and towards Sardex Ltd are both evident in the way Sardex functions. Both forms of reciprocity are closely tied to how Sardex functions, its limits and modes of circulation, and also to the social mechanisms of selection and signalling. Reciprocity towards Sardex, on the other hand, originates in the initial trust and interest free credit that Sardex provides to its members. This initial credit is granted mainly on the basis of a "handshake" which creates the expectation that the entrepreneur will repay the debt. Members sign contractual obligations when they join the network but, given the absence of collateral to guarantee the debt and the well-known difficulties of the Italian judiciary in resolving credit issues, it is reasonable to argue that, if there were no strong ties of reciprocity, many debts would probably not be repaid by members and the network would not be so dynamic. These ties of reciprocity can therefore be considered as a form of social bond which underpins the functioning of the Sardex device, see Fig. 4.4.

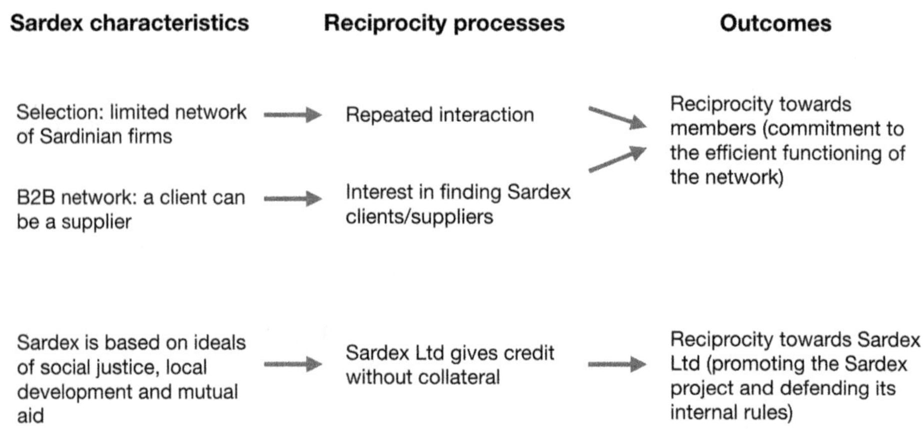

Fig. 4.4 Sardex reciprocity processes. (Source: own figure)

4.1.4 Monitoring and Sanctioning

Monitoring and Sanctioning Mechanisms

Repeated interaction creates the basis for operating and implementing other social mechanisms such as "learning, monitoring, dyadic sanctioning and increasing mutual dependence which reinforces the basis for trust" (Cook and Gerbasi 2009, p. 229). The presence of strong social ties favours the establishment of social control systems that monitor members' behaviour. Where such conditions exist the trusting relationship is no longer a dyadic, two-way relationship but it includes wider social networks. Within these networks the level of trust used and the level of reliability assessed are no longer just the effects of the quality of the protagonists in the dyadic relation, and of their relationship, but they are also the effects of their relationship with third parties (ibid. p. 221).

The influence of third parties or organisations in determining the degree of trust and reliability in a relationship is a situational characteristic whose importance ranges from minimal to decisive. For example, when people first interact with policemen or doctors, they tend to expect a high level of reliability from their interlocutors: this reliable, stable behaviour is borrowed from the social perception of the profession or organisation to which their interlocutors belong. In contrast, interlocutor membership of organisations such as the Chamber of Commerce or the simple presence of the judicial system is sometimes perceived as insufficient for guaranteeing a high degree of reliability in present-day economic transactions. In these situations the economic protagonists seek further elements to better evaluate the level of reliability (signalling) or they adopt more stringent contractual conditions in an attempt to limit the costs of a possible defection.

In fiduciary relationships the presence of third parties (organisations or individuals) can, therefore, play an important role in determining the degree of trust and the corresponding cooperative behaviour. Burt and Knez (1995) studied the effects of ties with third parties on dyadic trust within organisations. High levels of trust between interlocutors are more likely when there are large numbers of people who know them both and less likely when there are fewer such people. The relevance of relations with third parties in trust relations is confirmed by the fact that the nature of these bonds also affects the influence exerted. Strong ties to third parties who are known to both interlocutors increase the degree of trust in the relationship. Strong ties with third parties that are not shared by both interlocutors have no particular effect on the degree of trust in the relationship. These social effects on trust relations with third parties can be explained as effects of the reputational risk associated with betraying a fiduciary relationship. It is reasonable to expect—and social actors expect it regularly, and with performative effects—that the truster, betrayed by the trustee in a fiduciary relationship, will utilise sanctioning tools available against the trustee.

When the protagonists share strong social bonds with third parties, the truster can inform these third parties of the trustee's low level of reliability, damaging his/her reputation and, consequently, his level of socially perceived reliability. The same third parties who have observed or become aware of the betrayal of the fiduciary relationship can signal this behaviour to other protagonists or simply refrain from assuming the role of truster in future relations with the trust betrayer. Studies related to games theory show that the presence of third parties and the reputational effects of betraying trust make the betrayal of trust disadvantageous from the first interaction (Dasgupta 1988). This social mechanism that influences the degree of trust in relations can be identified as "monitoring".

When the monitoring role allows third parties to administer real sanctions for behaviours that betray the fiduciary relationship, the monitoring mechanism becomes a sanctioning mechanism. This mechanism's influence is well known for facilitating cooperation among people accessing public resources, where free-rider behaviours would probably be more advantageous. In the experimental context of public-good games Ostrom notes how *"the rate of contribution to a public good is affected by various contextual factors including the framing of the situation and the rules used for assigning participants, increasing competition among them, allowing communication, authorising sanctioning mechanisms, or allocating benefits"* (Ostrom 2000, p. 140–141).

Sanctions can be administered horizontally among peers or by a central hierarchical authority which has power to control. The modern state is the most common example of a central authority whose real and potential power to administer penal and administrative sanctions fosters cooperative relations among citizens. The presence of a central hierarchical authority capable of administering sanctions following incorrect behaviour is also seen as a valid tool for reducing transaction costs in economic market relations (Williamson 1975).

The horizontal sanctioning mechanism can be described mainly in terms of reputational sanctioning. In such cases cooperative behaviour can be supported by (i) the presence of social norms or group rules whose violation by *ego* generate punitive desires in *alter*; (ii) relational patterns that facilitate feedback exchange among participants. Social norms and relational patterns influence subjects' behaviour but, from a utilitarian point of view, they *"can also influence the trust-taker's utility function so that he attaches a higher utility to cooperation (value rational action)"* (Beckert 2005. p. 11).

There is debate as to whether horizontal or vertical sanctioning systems are more effective in promoting cooperative behaviour. Hierarchical sanctions are advantageous for sanction management because sanctions are administered in a coordinated and stable manner. Horizontal sanction mechanisms are based on sanctions administered spontaneously by individual participants with obvious risks of irregularities in administering the sanction and in the choice of sanction (O'Gorman et al. 2009). The distance separating the hierarchical institution from the sanctionable behaviour, however, makes it more difficult for the institution to actually administer the sanction. Local monitoring and sanctioning systems tend to sanction more effectively than the centralised state (Erikson and Parent 2007). Subjects feel stronger ties to norms and rules promoted by local institutions and groups, for which they feel a stronger identity bond than they do for norms implemented by large institutions which they perceive to be more distant and which involve many more subjects. The perceived degree of legitimacy of the institution appointed to administer sanctions influences that institution's ability to actually implement sanctions and effective deterrents against future violations (Baldassarri and Grossman 2011).

Monitoring and Sanctioning in Sardex

Hierarchical and horizontal forms of monitoring and sanctioning mechanisms are present in Sardex, both independently and in hybrid forms which reinforce each other. Exclusion is the most radical sanction for inappropriate behaviour within the member network. Sardex Ltd decides whether a member charged with serious misconduct against other members should be excluded from the network and, if necessary, expels him/her. Members know Sardex Ltd has the right to do this because it is part of the contract they signed when they joined the Sardex network. Relations between Sardex Ltd and individual members are, however, private and Sardex Ltd cannot violate the confidentiality of any sanctions they administer. Members, though, are aware that sanctions are administered for misconduct:

> The price in Sardex is the same in euros. It happened that someone wanted to cheat and apply different prices. I reported it to Sardex and I understand that someone who misbehaved was rightly excluded from the network (E. 25).

The sanctioning mechanism is more effective because it discourages misconduct. The effects of monitoring and sanctioning are felt at first encounters and isolated one-off interactions. The effectiveness of this mechanism depends principally on members being aware that they are "monitored" and "sanctionable": this awareness fosters appropriate behaviour. Conversely the sanctioning mechanism's primary role is not meting out sanctions so that the person sanctioned subsequently learns the right behaviour.

Group members need to desire that misconduct be punished if a horizontal monitoring and sanctioning system is to develop. The presence of reciprocal constraints, developed in the course of repeated interactions and laid down by norms within the Sardex network, described in the previous sub-section, creates the conditions which foster the desire for misconduct within the network to be punished:

> It happened that I went to a Sardex shop and when I went to pay they told me that for Christmas Eve they were not accepting payments in Sardex. What does that mean? You are either part of Sardex or you aren't. I spoke to the Sardex managers about this (E. 18).

Members recognise the positive goals of the Sardex network and this reinforces their strong reciprocal bonds with the network and their desire to punish those who damage it by violating norms:

> We should return to a code of ethical behaviour in economics. A customer who paid in Sardex came to me. I asked him what he produced and if he could supply me with goods. He replied that he could, but not with payment in Sardex. I was a bit annoyed because it

> seemed to me poor behaviour, so he then agreed immediately to accept Sardex. This person should be immediately reported and excluded from the network. The principle of reciprocity should be at the base of our transactions (E. 15).

Faced with behaviour they deem unfair, members develop different strategies to deal with the problem. The most common is to try and resolve the problem directly themselves and if this does not work they contact Sardex Ltd to report the matter:

> It should be noted that if a member has been in the network for many years this means he is not a cheat. If he were, it would have been common knowledge immediately in Sardex. When I have found someone in the network who cheated me I have called my broker immediately and reported the matter. The brokers thanked me for the report. (E. 13).

Members consider the presence of brokers, who supervise all transactions, to be important for the network. The fact that the brokers monitor the network significantly influences the way in which members relate to each other and the way in which they deal with possible defections. Broker supervision of all transactions acts as a deterrent for possible attempts to defraud other members and it can also play an active role in mediating conflict within the network:

> My first experiences in the network were positive because everyone I met was honest, we trusted each other a lot. Something similar to a closed network is created in which people behave well because they are monitored by Sardex. They reprimanded me once because I had a customer who wanted to cheat me, he wanted to take other people's money and then pay everything in Sardex, and I got really angry, but this sort of thing normally never happens. He then went to [Sardex Ltd] management to complain, but his version was not right and we clarified with Sardex (E. 1).

Hierarchical sanctions imposed by Sardex Ltd for misconduct are one result of horizontal monitoring of member behaviour; peer reputational sanctions are another. As was seen for the signalling mechanism, network membership activates forms of interaction that are characterised by familiarity and highly collaborative attitudes. Members frequently exchange information about their respective Sardex suppliers and their opinions on past transactions:

> I changed my accountant after asking one of my patients for advice. Now when we see each other we exchange opinions on the services he offers us. There are fewer discussions with euro-paying patients (E. 21).

When an entrepreneur is looking for specific goods or services in Sardex, opportunities for meeting with other members can be used to ask for advice and opinions. The advice of another member may well be preferred to the members' list available online or to a broker's advice. Although there is general confidence in the goods and services offered by companies within the network, faced with a long list of members supplying a certain item, entrepreneurs can find it difficult to decide how to choose a supplier. The list itself does not provide the sort of specific information required for comparing different offers and the broker service, which has to be neutral with respect to all members, can hardly come down in favour of a particular firm when comparing offers from similar firms. The Sardex customer who comes to the shop however, is free to express his personal opinion and talk about the impressions he received while exchanging with other members. This type of qualitatively dense information on goods and services provided by other members, is greatly appreciated by entrepreneurs because it simplifies the selection of suppliers and reduces the time required to start new business relations.

The network's limited size facilitates occasions for repeated interaction and reduces the number of single interactions. Every Sardex customer knows their supplier could become their customer and that it is very likely they will meet again. These expectations, together with the monitoring systems, create the conditions whereby the advice exchanged by members is as genuine as possible: given the rapid circulation of information within the Sardex network, false or misleading information would probably be more costly than any immediate benefit. Horizontal monitoring carried out by members can lead to reputational sanctioning through word of mouth or through the Sardex members' Facebook page. Reputational sanctioning on the Facebook page can shatter a firm's credibility and as a result its business within the Sardex network. The Facebook page, in fact, is followed daily by many members who use it to publicise or search for discounts or special offers for goods and services in Sardex. A post or a comment that raises doubts as to whether a member has behaved correctly, combined with the consequent word of mouth among members, can rapidly destroy, in a relatively stable way, that member's chance of transacting within the network. Negative comments on other members' business dealings are used sparingly and limited to cases of real necessity; for minor problems members prefer to use other ways of sanctioning so as not to irrevocably damage the business involved:

> If a company cheats me, I write it down, obviously with the proofs, and it loses all its clients. Except in extreme cases such as in the case of bankruptcy where you write it on Facebook, because it is good for everyone to know, in other cases you report it to Sardex, who then calls the person involved. It may happen that you go to a firm and ask for the price. The answer might be: "1,000 euros or 2,000 Sardex". They are the "smart" ones. They are extremely few, very few. You signal them to Sardex Ltd, with the proofs and they are contacted. If they continue, they are excluded (E. 19).

The Sardex network accelerates reputational sanctioning mechanisms that are also present in the euro market. Word of mouth and Facebook groups are social dynamics that also exist outside the Sardex network but the selection, signalling and reciprocity mechanisms reinforce and accelerate the impact of these dynamics. The beneficial effects on market functioning of this increase in information circulation are much appreciated by member entrepreneurs, so much so that members hypothesise possible enhancements in line with the possibilities offered by other social platforms:

> The network is a way of selecting members, as is normal life, but the network is more selective. For example, I reported on the Sardex Facebook page the rare presence of some members who apply different prices and discounts in Sardex than in euros. A slew of comments came from other members in response to my post and we started to think about what could be done to stop member misconduct. The initiative started spontaneously from members, it was not promoted by Sardex Ltd. We made a series of proposals that will be examined by Sardex Ltd and put into practice. One of these is the possibility of providing some sort of feedback on behaviour between members (E. 7).

The need for Sardex Ltd to administer sanctions to discipline members' behaviour seems to belong to the early stages of the network's existence:

> When the network was first set up some firms engaged in misconduct offering higher prices for buyers in Sardex than for buyers in euro. I reported what happened to the network managers and some companies were excluded from the network. Now the network is mature and these things no longer happen (E. 37).

Standardised practices and behaviour within the network, horizontal and broker monitoring and the threat of reputational sanctions from Sardex Ltd all act as effective deterrents to misconduct within the network.

Conclusions

The monitoring and sanctioning mechanisms present in the Sardex network operate in a similar way to those of organisations in which third party control is added to dyadic monitoring. Network members and Sardex Ltd, the managers, assume the role of third parties in the Sardex device. The monitoring and sanctioning mechanisms are present in both the horizontal and the hierarchical forms. Horizontal monitoring is carried out by members and may result in reputational horizontal sanctions (word of mouth and the Facebook group) or hierarchical sanctions, where misconduct is reported to Sardex Ltd so it will administer the appropriate sanctions. The hierarchical monitoring carried out by the Sardex Ltd brokers is primarily based on the horizontal monitoring undertaken by members who report misconduct in much the same way as they would if they were to suffer damage and seek redress in the courts. The monitoring and sanctioning activities undertaken by Sardex Ltd, though, are seen as more efficient at enforcing the rules than the justice system because the Sardex Ltd response is immediate and effective because of the shattering effect of the sanctions. Information is rapidly circulated by word of mouth and using the social tools available to members; this reinforces the impact of the reputational sanctions, also present in the euro market, amplifying their power to deter.

Thanks to the selection and reciprocity mechanisms the Sardex sanctioning system enjoys a high level of legitimacy among members. Members make a deliberate choice to join Sardex: membership requires an economic and cognitive investment and the reciprocal ties with Sardex create the basis for strong economic and identity commitment to the project. The desire for the network to function properly is widespread among members

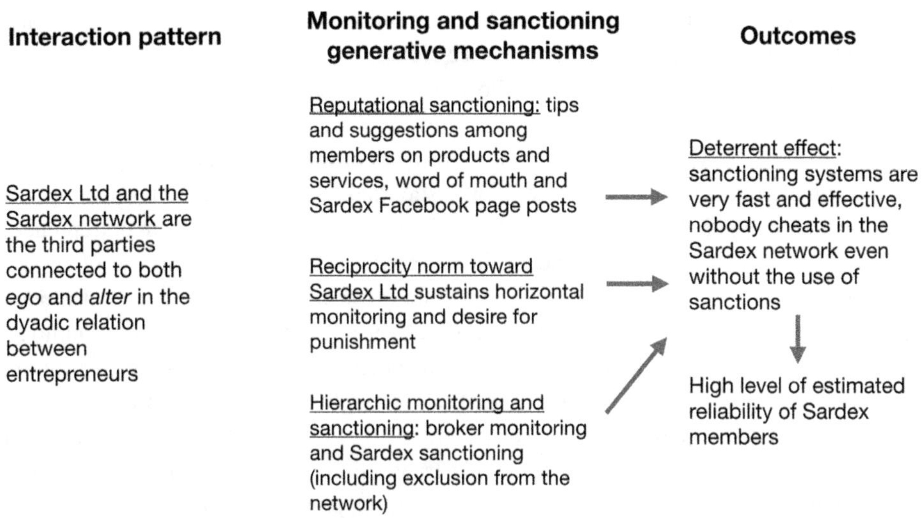

Fig. 4.5 Sardex monitoring and sanctioning mechanisms. (Source: own figure)

and this activates a corresponding desire to punish opportunistic behaviour. In this context the sanctioning role of Sardex Ltd is well accepted and supported by the members.

The Sardex network is now in a relatively mature phase of its operation; the deterrent power of the monitoring activity, combined with the risk of sanctions for misconduct, is so effective that it seems sufficient to ensure there is very little misconduct that requires sanctioning by Sardex. In this context the truster has numerous, effective sanctioning tools at his disposal which tend to make any defections disadvantageous. Together with the other social mechanisms described, monitoring and sanctioning create an interactional context useful for developing relationships based on a high level of trust (Fig. 4.5).

4.1.5 Conclusions: Trust in Sardex

Luhmann (1979, 1988) argues that low levels of familiarity between individuals and low levels of trust are a modern day characteristic. The lack of repeated interactions and familiarity in relationships would, in fact, be the cause of the lack of trust in others. While the presence of trust is a way of reducing social complexity, its lack exposes individuals to more risky relationships, where high levels of assessment, calculation and monitoring are required. The modern state has partially taken on this reduced level of interpersonal trust: state apparatus is used to control and suppress deviant behaviour and this fosters cooperation among its citizens. Trust in the institutions of the modern state should be sufficiently robust to ensure a level of interpersonal trust that enables collaborative relationships to develop and avoids free-riding.

Economic relations, though, have followed a particular development path. Although administrative and judicial control and sanction apparatus are developed in this area, as in other areas of social life, economic development in a free market requires a high level of indeterminacy to ensure that capitalistic "animal spirits" can develop and the economy can prosper (Keynes 2007 [1936]). The increase in uncertainty in entrepreneurial initiative, in labour relations and in the economic system in general are often seen as a driving force capable of fostering economic growth. In the "iron cage" of modern bureaucracy (Weber 2013 [1905]), interpersonal trust has never disappeared, although many of its social coordination functions have been replaced by trust in institutions. The increased uncertainty in economic relations, brought about by recent developments in capitalism, can be partially offset, especially at the local level, by trust-based interpersonal relations. For large-scale economic transactions (and also for those involving large companies), contractual rules and the control apparatus are almost the only instruments for reducing uncertainty. For small transactions on a local scale, though, interpersonal trust facilitates transactions, making them faster and reducing transaction costs. Buyers, therefore, do not need to write complex contracts that cover all possible situations (Macaulay 1963): the costs of negotiating and writing contracts are reduced and the transaction is more efficient.

The effects on interpersonal trust of the Sardex device are aligned with the need to reduce complexity for small businesses that cannot allocate large sums for regulating and controlling economic transactions. This increase in trustee reliability does not reduce the uncertainty of future market dynamics but it increases the chances of successfully concluding the transaction by reassuring the entrepreneur. Opportunistic behaviours and misconduct are discouraged by the social mechanisms described: selection, signalling, reciprocity, monitoring and sanctioning. These social mechanisms ensure it is highly likely that economic transactions have a positive outcome.

The high level of trust in interpersonal relationships in Sardex is also supported by a high level of institutional trust in the Sardex Ltd network manager: trust in money is always an effect of institutions also. Simmel (1990) noted that trust in money surpassed, in the common sense, trust in other important modern institutions such as professional orders or politics. Modern money in the form of *fiat* money has no intrinsic value corresponding to the goods or services for which it is exchanged. Its value lies only in the recipient's trust that it can be exchanged again with third parties for goods and services of equal value. The stability of money's real value and its future exchangeability with any other goods or services are characteristics of money open to uncertainty, but in the common sense these aspects are only brought to light and questioned during crises: for example during periods of great upheaval of the social and political order such as wars or hyperinflation. Trust in the stability and exchangeability of money is widespread and stable: this is explained by its political nature, its ease of circulation and the material use of banknotes and coins. Every day individuals exchange money several times and this ease of circulation supports an image of reliability and durability. Unlike other modern institutions that are associated with the current holder of the top office, money is identified with the banknotes that everyone is able to use, control and hold with ease every day. Money, in its modern form, seems "usable" unlike other political or administrative institutions which seem more remote and tied to their own functioning logics. In reality, the stable value and exchangeability of money also depend on traditional modern institutions. Ingham (2004) convincingly explains how the value of modern currencies depends on the capacity of modern states to maintain their exclusive rights to use violence and to collect taxes.

Although money shares actors and *modus operandi* with other modern political institutions, it is widely considered as more reliable than other political and administrative institutions. The Sardex device "borrows" this high level of institutional trust in money, transforming the principle of credit between companies into a form of payment that can easily circulate and whose stability and legitimacy are guaranteed by Sardex Ltd through the social mechanisms described above. The Sardex currency, although it does not have a material form with banknotes and coins, is easy to quantify, accumulate and move, thanks to on-line accounts that can be managed with a smartphone app. The perception of Sardex liquidity is comparable to that of an on-line bank account, although Sardex Ltd's operating and management characteristics increase the circulation speed of the Sardex currency to well beyond that of ordinary money. Interpersonal trust among Sardex network members and institutional trust in the stability and exchangeability of the Sardex currency feed each other: the currency circulates readily because the interpersonal trust among members is high; this ease of circulation, in turn, reinforces interpersonal trust among members. The Sardex case confirms Sztompka's (1999) interpretation of institutional trust: the role played by those who operate the institutions and the institutions themselves, considered as a set of norms and procedures, cannot be separated when determining the overall level of trust accorded to the institution. The Sardex device renders the membership network and the Sardex Ltd management highly reliable and extends this reliability to the currency's abstract value and operating system.

The Sardex trust-enhancement system is therefore attributable to (i) social mechanisms traditionally associated with interpersonal trust (signalling, repeated interaction reciprocity, horizontal monitoring and reputation) and (ii) social mechanisms (selection, monitoring and hierarchical sanctioning) and interaction mediators (money) traditionally associated with institutional trust. The effects of the Sardex device, therefore, can be identified in the high level of interpersonal and institutional trust but, from the theoretical viewpoint, it is possible to observe the presence an intermediate level of trust, not yet described in the reference literature. Although the functioning of monitoring and sanctioning mechanisms through the presence of third parties can be traced back to the mechanisms observed by Burt and Knez (1995), the trustees involved in the Sardex case cannot just be defined as members of the organisation. When the network was first established and only a relatively small number of businesses were members, the operating system of the Sardex device could have been considered an organisation but, with the rapid increase in the number of companies belonging to the network, amplified by the fact that the Sardex device only operates in a single region, the Sardex device has assumed different characteristics which make it impossible to classify it as an organisation. The Sardex network activates economic relations that often extend beyond the traditional economic sphere, creating strong social ties; the coordination capacity of the social protagonists also exceeds that of an organisation. Sardex, according to the Sardex Ltd motto, aspires to put "an island on the net". In this sense the role of Sardex is very similar to that of ordinary money: from a sociological viewpoint it creates specific interaction patterns and establishes a form of social tie. Unlike traditional formal institutions, the role of the Sardex device goes beyond the direct coordination of resources in view of a common goal; in a less hierarchical but nonetheless incisive way, it manages to provide the economic actors of an entire region with a tool for economic transactions and social interaction that uses social mechanisms to modify this form of the social tie.

The Sardex device channels the geographical limitations and the expanding ambitions of the network and aspires to becoming a form of social interaction available to an entire region. Its goal is to facilitate strong social ties characterised by a high level of interpersonal trust. The development of strong social ties within a limited geographical area echoes, in some respects, the pre-modern community form of social tie (Tönnies 1887). Taking into account the different historical periods and the diversity of contexts between the strong social tie promoted by Sardex and the tie associated with traditional communities, the intermediate level of trust between interpersonal trust and the institutional trust promoted by the Sardex device, can be described as a form of "community trust".[4]

In Weber's interpretation (1978 [1922]) of the form taken by corporate relations, as against relations within a pre-modern community, the commercial contract would be a typical example of a corporate relationship. In commercial contracts the impersonal relationship, mediated by the contract itself, is objectively defined and tends to reduce the part that is interpreted subjectively. The forced implementation of commercial contracts is entrusted to administrative authorities outside the contractual relationship (administrative and judicial systems). Parts of commercial contracts cannot be negotiated between the parties: the formal rules underlying the contracts, previous contractual models and the language used to write these contracts are all non-contractual elements that are part of commercial contracts (Durkheim 1984 [1893]).

The basis for the transactions carried out in Sardex among entrepreneur network members is contractual. The way the network functions is laid down in the contract signed by the entrepreneurs when they join the network. As was noted when describing the social

[4]Thanks are due to Jens Beckert for this description of the different forms of trust in Sardex. To compare community forms of trust with trust in the industrial district see Sub-sect. 5.1.2 Transaction costs and brokerage.

mechanisms at work in Sardex, the results obtained by the Sardex device exceed those laid down in contractual norms by activating denser forms of social interaction. Signalling, reciprocity, horizontal monitoring and sanctioning are all social mechanisms not directly attributable to contractual norms: They are the effect of characteristics of the Sardex currency and the way it is regulated by Sardex Ltd. The forms of relationship developed by the social mechanisms described above take on the characteristics of strong social relations: relationships between members are "different" from other commercial relationships, there is always something to talk about, members exchange advice and opinions, they become friends and there is a strong bond of reciprocity towards other members and towards the Sardex project in general. Strong personal relationships and non-contractual reciprocal bonds are relationship characteristics at variance with the traditional form of corporate relations, more oriented towards community relationships.

The high level of trust found in network transactions is only partly attributable to the selection mechanisms and the hierarchical monitoring and sanctioning mechanisms put into place by Sardex Ltd. If trust depended entirely on Sardex Ltd's hierarchical activity and on members' trust of Sardex Ltd, the trust present within the network could be characterised as institutional trust and its principal promoter would be Sardex Ltd. However, the trust found in relations between members cannot be considered entirely interpersonal: trust is placed in the interlocutor's future behaviour but it is also placed in the functions carried out by Sardex Ltd and in the behaviour of all possible members of the network. The trust present in the Sardex network is a synthesis of interpersonal trust, institutional trust and trust towards a group characterised by their membership of the Sardex network. The particular configuration of the Sardex device generates another form of trust in addition to the interpersonal and institutional forms. The form of trust present in Sardex has characteristics that go beyond a simple intermediate characterisation of trust that takes aspects from both traditional forms; the community trust present in the Sardex case presents characteristics that can be considered unique.

Interpersonal trust is usually divided into two main forms: *thick* trust and *thin* trust. Thick trust is the one referred to by Luhmann in his analyses and nowadays it is mainly concerned with family relationships; thin trust refers to all other forms of interpersonal trust that do not involve family or couple relationships. Thick trust is linked to stable expectations of cooperative behaviour from the interlocutor for most aspects of the relationship, for example affective reciprocity, the use of money, sharing important choices (Cook and Gerbasi 2009, pp. 219–220). Thin trust, on the other hand, is often linked to a specific reason that initiated the relationship; thin trust is placed in the correct performance of the interlocutor with respect to the purpose of the interaction; for example the good care expected from a doctor, a bureaucrat's administrative rectitude or a mechanic's technical ability to repair one's car. Given the predominantly economic relations within the Sardex network it would be logical to expect prevalently thin forms of trust, with respect to the quality of the goods traded and the certainty of payment being made (Beckert 2009). This trust relationship should, therefore, end with the delivery of the goods and their payment, a relationship in which the roles of truster and trustee alternate between the interlocutors. In the case of the Sardex network, as a result of the mechanisms described above, the fiduciary relationship also encompasses other aspects of the relationship which are not strictly related to the economic transaction: opinions and advice are exchanged between network members, it is easy to become friends and share a code of behaviour and ideals.[5] The presence of these strong social bonds among network members gives this trust a dense connotation which goes beyond the simple thin trust which characterises economic transactions.

The thick trust found within the Sardex network, therefore, is different from ordinary forms of thick trust because it does not refer to members of one's own family or to persons linked by emotional ties, but to subjects whose relationship is principally economic. Using the mechanisms described above, the operation of the Sardex device generates both institutional trust towards Sardex Ltd and interpersonal trust towards other members; this thick interpersonal trust exceeds that of the dyadic relationship with which it is often associated, by addressing a social group (all the members of the Sardex network) which exceeds the size of an organisation and lacks most organisational characteristics. Thick interpersonal trust within the network is ordinarily directed to all members independently of previous interpersonal relations.[6] Given the geographically restricted dimension of the Sardex network and its gradual internal expansion, both vertically and horizontally, along all the production chains, the network is establishing a relationship pattern that has the potential to be shared among many of the individuals who live in the same geographical area. The Sardex device establishes thick social bonds within a social group originating from the same geographical area; this group is increasing and has the potential to involve all Sardinian entrepreneurs. This process also generates a value orientation towards the geographical region to which it belongs (see Sect. 4.3). Thick interpersonal trust, the trend towards territorial saturation and value orientation towards the region to which the group belongs are characteristics of the social bond attributable to the community form. Despite the significant contextual differences with respect to the community social bond,[7] the thick form of trust present in the Sardex network exceeds the interpersonal form but cannot be attributed to a purely institutional form. Its operation activates the characteristics of the community social tie and this makes it possible to describe it as orientated towards community trust, see Fig. 4.6.

[5]For the shared ideals see Sect. 4.3.

[6]Although thick trust enhances the effects in some cases, it is also present in the network independently of any repeated interaction.

[7]Although these social effects are similar to those observed in community relationships, the origin of this form of social bonding is radically different: strong community social bonds are the result of tradition oriented action and of ascribed status, while the thick social bonds present in the Sardex network emerge from within an economic network freely chosen by the participants who can leave the network if they so desire.

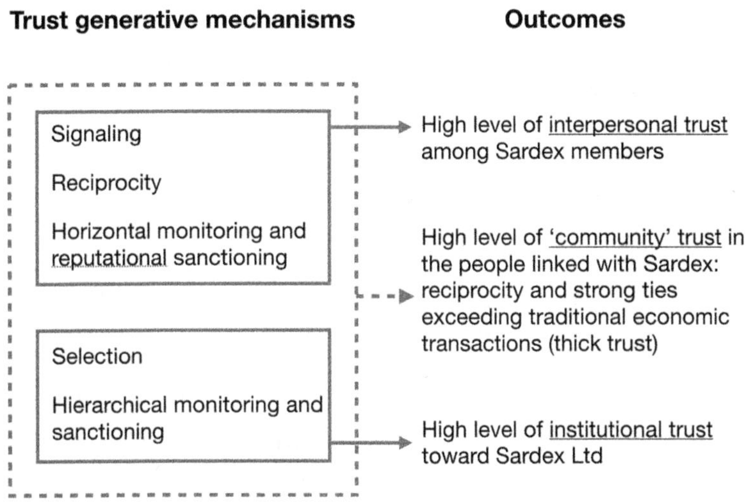

Fig. 4.6 Sardex trust generative mechanisms. (Source: own figure)

4.2 Cooperation

4.2.1 Cooperation Mechanisms

The trust that exists among members of the Sardex network facilitates their economic transactions and social relations. The correct behaviour of members is partly the effect of contractual and legal constraints and the presence of hierarchical sanctioning in the network and partly the effect of the horizontal social mechanisms, described above, which develop among members. The moment in which the truster's trust is reciprocated by the trustee doing that which is expected of him/her, can be considered the basic element of cooperative behaviour. However, cooperation cannot be reduced to a consequence of trust because cooperative behaviour can also emerge when there is no trust between the interacting partners (Cook et al. 2005). For example, the presence of stringent contractual rules makes cooperation possible even when there is no interpersonal trust or direct interaction. Broadly speaking cooperation can be considered as the capacity of individuals to coordinate their behaviours in order to achieve a shared goal (Bowles and Gintis 2011).

Cooperation has been studied in the social science field mostly in relation to the issue of trust (Gambetta 1988; Fukuyama 1995; Bacharach and Gambetta 2001; Cook 2001; Yamagishi 2011), to the use of common goods (Olson 1965; Ostrom 1990, 2000) and to social networks (Granovetter 1985; Gould 1993; Baldassarri and Grossman 2013). The (lack of) ability to cooperate is seen as a central problem in complex societies where often the most advantageous behavioural option is free-riding. In societies characterised by weak social ties, free-riding is usually seen as undermining the likelihood of achieving common goals.[8] Management of common goods is particularly vulnerable to free-riding which can render the coordination efforts of many citizens ineffective (Ostrom 1990). This highlights *"the disparity between individual optimisation and collective optimality"* (Coleman 1989, p. 5). Lack of cooperation can also make the ordinary functioning of complex systems difficult, inducing, in the case of markets, for example, a low level of trust among the actors and disadvantaging economic transactions, productivity and economic growth (Fukuyama 1995; Zak and Knack 2001).

The conceptualisation of trust as an "encapsulated interest" highlights the mutual interdependence of protagonists in social relations: where there is repeated interaction, horizontal monitoring or reputational sanctioning, the positive effects of cooperation over time should exceed the benefits of free-riding. Although this assumption may be valid in specific contexts, it does not means that cooperative behaviour emerges spontaneously as an effect of the greater utility expected (Marx 1963 [1852]; see also Pizzorno 1983). For example, as the Sardex case demonstrates, the level of trust estimated in *alter* influences the propensity to trust and consequently to cooperate. Dirks and Ferrin (2001) note that incentives to cooperate are not sufficient to produce cooperation within a group either. In a group situation, individuals with a low level of trust are more likely to free-ride than others with a high level of trust who are more committed to common goals. Trust and cooperation are usually positively correlated personal characteristics (Kimmel et al. 1980).

Trust, however, is not the only mechanism generating cooperation. In the context of economic transactions, for example, prices and the role of the authorities are other cooperation governance mechanisms (Arrow 1974). Cooperation cannot be reduced to the role played by institutions, norms and long-term relationships either, but *"the performative production of the willingness to trust must be examined as an independent dimension in the explanation of stable market relations"* (Beckert 2005, p. 26). The factors that sustain the desire to cooperate in conditions of uncertainty need to be studied *"as a problem always to be solved in the situation"* (Beckert 2005, p. 25). Like cooperation, social mechanisms often have a situational-type, limited explicative validity (Manzo 2014) but the complexity of the social processes that generate cooperation makes it hard to reduce them to a single social mechanism. Usually, a pool di mechanisms contribute to achieving cooperative behaviours, and the same cooperative behaviours can result from different social mechanisms.

[8]Attempts to orientate both top-down and horizontal behaviours leave room for the possibility of free-riding: even in the most stringent social systems the possibility of free-riding cannot be completely eliminated. The possibility of escaping from the existing social order, or of opposing it, is hard to eliminate even from totalitarian regimes, though they are capable of ensuring such behaviour is extremely costly and disadvantageous. Free-riding can have a positive connotation as an area of individual freedom that may offer possibilities for changing the existing social order (Arendt 1973).

The literature describes both cognitive and interactional factors that influence cooperation. The cognitive aspects range from pure individual utility to altruism. Individual incentives are, in fact, one of the most common solutions to the problem of cooperation (Olson 1965) and are widely used in various areas of social life, from bureaucratic bodies to organisations. The presence of pure altruism in individuals also facilitates cooperation (Fehr and Gachter 2002). These two seemingly opposite motivations for cooperative behaviour are not mutually exclusive: in specific situations a balance between egotistical motivations and altruistic motivations in individuals' behaviour is possible (Fehr and Gintis 2007). The intermediate cognitive collocations between entirely selfish and entirely altruistic motivations for cooperation can have many different forms: they can, for example, consider their own level of injustice considered admissible towards others (Fehr and Schmidt 1999) or they can also be influenced by social norms which inspire their conduct (Durkheim 1984 [1893]; Elster 1989).

Generally, though, social closeness and group membership facilitate cooperative relations. The effect of group membership is noticeable when the membership refers to ascribed categories, such as religion, and also for randomly assigned memberships (Goette et al. 2010). Although the effect on cooperation for social groups linked by ascribed status could be attributed to their shared status which determines their belonging to the group, the case of random social groups demonstrates that it is the presence of the group itself that has cognitive effects on the propensity to cooperation: *"group attachment derives from a process of categorisation in which individuals generalise their interpersonal experiences to a broader class of alters and relate to others even in the absence of a personal relationship"* (Baldassarri 2015, p. 359).

In addition to the cognitive dimension that motivates subjects to cooperate, cooperation can also be encouraged or discouraged by specific interactional situations. Not even the clear presence of purely selfish or purely altruistic motivations is a sufficient condition for the emergence of cooperative behaviours in the absence of *alter* and contexts that favour cooperation. The social mechanisms that create trust (signalling, repeated-interaction reciprocity, monitoring and sanctioning) reduce uncertainty about *alter* behaviour by favouring trust and, consequently, the activation of cooperative behaviours.

The possibility of direct contact has shown that communication can be a decisive element for initiating forms of cooperation (Ostrom et al. 1992; Sally 1995; Baldassarri 2015). Communication enables the activation of social norms that create cooperation (Bohnet and Frey 1999a, 1999b). The activated norms, however, do not exclude the possibility of sanctions and subsequently they can be replaced by specific agreements thanks to communication. Among the horizontal sanctions that support cooperation, it is significant to note how individuals are willing to personally bear the costs of sanctions against those who violate the rules of the group (altruistic punishment) (Fehr and Gachter 2002).

These mechanisms often work together to support cooperation and they reinforce each other. Just how effective they are in fostering cooperation depends largely on the type of problem and the size of the group that has to cooperate (Van den Assem et al. 2012). A system of sanctions seems to be the most effective in supporting cooperation in large public and private institutions (Scholz and Gray 1997). Where public resources are used it is considered necessary to deploy hierarchical sanctioning mechanisms in order to avoid free-riding (Fehr and Gachter 2002); for smaller groups, where interaction and direct communication are feasible, the horizontal mechanisms of reciprocity, monitoring and horizontal sanctioning are very effective (Poteete et al. 2010).

In economic relations within markets, the need to cooperate emerges in the face of uncertainty as to the real intentions of *alter* regarding the quality of the products sold and respect for the conditions agreed to (Bacharach and Gambetta 2001), but also about the subsequent uncertainty of *alter* as to whether he will receive from *ego* the payment agreed for the goods sold (Beckert 2009, p. 259). In commercial exchanges between companies, it is common for payment to be deferred for an agreed period of time with respect to the delivery of the goods. The quality of the goods received is not always completely verifiable: this would often require measuring instruments, technical skills and time, none of which are available to the purchaser (Akerlof 1970). Market exchanges only take place when trading partners achieve a sufficient degree of trust in the correctness of future reciprocal behaviour.

Finally, social networks influence cooperative behaviour in the economic sphere with effects similar to those they have on trust: positive interactions in the past and close social networks make it more likely that the protagonists will be cooperative. (Granovetter 1985, p. 490).[9]

4.2.2 Cooperation in Sardex

If a willingness to cooperate in economic relations indicates a capacity for carrying out economic transactions, the main objective for developing the Sardex project was precisely that of encouraging economic transactions among Sardinian businesses. The overriding objective of Sardex currency operations is to foster economic transactions among network members, so the number of transactions concluded is a key element for evaluating member usage of Sardex. In order to establish the actual influence of network membership on members' business transactions, economic performance indicators were collected for member businesses for the previous ten years.[10] The trends for the number of employees, suppliers and customers and for revenue were analysed for the period since the companies became members of the Sardex network. Data for the trends in customer numbers and revenue proved to be the most significant for assessing the effects on the participating entrepreneurs' willingness to cooperate.

---

[9]For an interpretation of these effects on transaction costs, compared to the industrial district see Sub-sect. 5.1.2 Transaction costs and brokerage.

[10]In the case of companies founded less than ten years ago, only the years of business activity were taken into account.

The general theory of economic equilibrium (Walras 2013 [1877]) considers preferences as exogenous to the economic system, so it postulates that the presence of a complementary currency, such as Sardex, should not have any effect on trade. If money is only a means for achieving predetermined goals then being able to exchange goods and services in either Sardex or euros should not affect the total number of transactions carried out. It could be argued, therefore, that the only effect of a complementary currency would be that it replaces exchanges that could have been made using ordinary currency with exchanges made using the new currency. The economic impact of the complementary currency would, therefore, be zero or even negative, because the existence of two circulating currencies might reduce market exchangeability of goods and services denominated in one or the other currency and increase transaction costs. Less exchangeability would also mean less competition and consequently an increase in prices.

To assess whether member companies' business transactions in Sardex are only the result of a substitution effect of their ordinary business transacted in euros, historical data on the companies' business performance of the sample was recorded separately for both currencies. The year each company joined the Sardex network was taken as a reference for observing both their overall business performance and their business performance in euros and in Sardex. The entrepreneurs were explicitly asked how many of their new customers and revenues in Sardex were already acquired customers and revenues that had changed from paying in euros to paying in Sardex.[11] The incidence of the increase in business is very variable: it reaches peaks of 200% for small, recently opened companies, with no employees, but stabilises at values between 5 and 15% for more established companies. The substitution effect of euro clients and revenue passing to the Sardex system is 13% of customers and 11% of revenues of the total increase recorded from when these companies joined Sardex. The average increase in business following Sardex membership is 23% for the number of customers and 26% for revenue: both values are net of the estimated euro-to-Sardex substitution effect. It is important to take into account the fact that the complementary currency Sardex was developed in the years following the 2008 economic crisis, when Sardinia's GDP shrank by 9.1% (Banca d'Italia 2018, p. 13). The average performance of the euro business of the companies sampled was stable or down in the years following the crisis. The increase in business brought about by the Sardex currency appears to be very significant for the member companies, especially in the light of the widespread economic recession and the weak performance of their parallel euro market.

The data is consistent with interviewee perceptions regarding the performance of their business after becoming members of the Sardex network. As soon as they joined

[11]Where the entrepreneurs had not made this distinction in their accounts it was decided that any reduction in euro revenue and euro customers would be considered as an effect of substitution by Sardex business although this estimate could potentially exceed the effective substitutions because some of the fall in euro business may have been due to other uncontrollable factors.

Sardex the brokers would signal their presence to other member companies potentially interested in the goods or services supplied by the new member. For small artisanal businesses employing only the business owner, joining the Sardex network was often a turning point for their business. The promotional activity carried out by the brokers, together with the social trust mechanisms described above in Sect. 4.1, could result in a new member receiving numerous requests from Sardex clients within a few days. These small companies do not have resources to invest in promoting their business and customer growth is often due to word of mouth among personal contacts on a local scale. Phone calls from geographically distant customers amaze the entrepreneurs and strengthen their confidence in the Sardex project:

> Already from the day after I entered Sardex I received five calls from new clients who asked me for appointments (E. 18).

The Sardex network very effectively promotes small businesses. Sardex provides these micro-companies with free access to the services of a buying and selling office which works to promote their businesses:

> In Sardex I have a very long waiting list, I program jobs for clients seven months ahead because I have so much work. I have several clients who are waiting for very nice furnishings of a certain quality. My first customer was a jeweller in a nearby town for whom I did 5,000 Sardex of work and he is still waiting for me for other work he has commissioned [….] Sardex has turbo-charged my business! It has given me a heap of work. Before I used to hope clients would call me now I hope they won't because I am behind in deliveries, I have to ask them to wait (E. 4).

For commercial businesses that interact daily with dozens of end customers the impact of becoming a member of the Sardex network, although certainly less radical than it would be for small artisanal companies, is nonetheless tangible:

> There are new customers who have come to us only because we are part of the Sardex network. This surprised us, especially as some new clients were not local (E. 3).

In periods of economic down-turn the arrival of new customers generates enthusiasm for the Sardex project. Customers with Sardex to spend create new opportunities for consumption and they change family habits:

> We do all our grocery shopping in Sardex. My husband also changed his car tyres, we buy from the chemist, etc. In my house the Sardex has replaced the euro and I think it would be a good thing if it replaced the euro [everywhere] because the Sardex inspires more confidence than the euro. We lost confidence in the euro a long time ago but Sardex has given it back to us. It has also given us a little serenity. Before that I was always in financial difficulties, I was always close to going under even though I work well, but I have mortgage payments of 900 euros a month for this building. Sardex gave me some peace and I have even managed to put some money aside. Sardex increased my customers by 30% and these

> customers have made the difference. I don't care whether they pay in euro or in Sardex – it is the 30% increase which counts for me (E. 18).

A 30% increase in customers during a period of widespread economic crisis changes entrepreneurs' perceptions of their work and, in the case of entrepreneur n°18, has created a strong attachment to the Sardex project to the point where she has become a convinced promoter of the network among her personal acquaintances.

The widespread perception among entrepreneurs that their business has increased between 10 and 20% of their total business thanks to the Sardex network, is in line with the assessments made using the business data on business trends:

> With Sardex I was able to contain the crisis, I was able to increase my turnover by 10% to compensate for the crisis (E. 15).

Entrepreneurs are also aware that the costs required to increase customers and turnover are very low. Joining the Sardex network and using the services it makes available has a very low investment cost, unlike bank interest or investments in very expensive promotional activities that aim to increase business:

> No interest is charged on Sardex money. Credit from a local bank costs 8.5% per annum for € 5,000.00; the effective interest rate at the end of the year needs to be multiplied by 1.85 to cover the extra expenses. For small business owners, Sardex collects an annual tax of between three hundred and four hundred euros which can be amortised in many ways. If an entrepreneur doesn't "move" in the network his business increases by 10%. I, in my experience, have to decide how much I want [my business] to increase, because people phone me. It sometimes happens that I put the brakes on requests from Sardex members (E. 34).

The extra receipts in Sardex soon become a source of structural revenue for companies that allows them to consolidate and expand. This source of revenue also allows some companies to pay part of their salaries in Sardex or to put their euros aside to pay salaries and keep staff on even during times of economic crisis:

> The Sardex gives you a surplus: the customers who came to me in Sardex, are customers who would not have come otherwise. The 8 to 9% increase in turnover that I have had, is extra turnover, I haven't had Sardex replacing euros. People spend more readily because they know this money is extra … I have got so used to Sardex that I could no longer do without it, I would feel limited. I take 4,000 Sardex a month, the equivalent of paying two salaries (E. 35).
>
> In this period of crisis Sardex brings us a lot of customers and gives us a big helping hand. Without Sardex we would have had less work and fewer employees. Sardex helps us endure the crisis we are passing through and really helps us to keep going forward (E. 16).
>
> Of course if I have to choose between euros and Sardex I prefer euros, but the choice here is between Sardex and nothing. These [restaurant] tables, are empty today, so the choice is not between the Sardex and euros but between Sardex and nothing (E. 2).

Small commercial or restaurant businesses are able to directly control how much of their new turnover in Sardex is a substitution of transactions that would have been carried out in euros. Owners of catering firms or small shops often know their customers personally and, if a known euro customer asks to pay in Sardex, they easily classify that payment in Sardex as a replacement of a probably equal payment in euros:

> Only two of our customers were already euro customers and we discovered that they were able to pay in Sardex too, all the other customers were new, we enlarged our customer base (E. 10).

This increase in economic transactions is highlighted by the data collected and by the entrepreneurs' own perceptions: it can be explained as the effect of the social mechanisms that generate interpersonal and institutional trust among members, the low cost of Sardex money and the intentional broker activity aimed at fostering transactions within the network.

Entrepreneurs maintain that the ease of transacting in Sardex is due to the ethical code of conduct of Sardex members. The mechanisms of selection, reciprocity, monitoring and sanctioning create the conditions for affirming an "ethical code" of behaviour among members:

> We are very protected, because, worst case scenario, you can call your broker and then everyone knows that someone took you for a ride and that is not good publicity for them. There is an ethical code. You don't enter Sardex like that, just applying and entering. There is an ethical code, otherwise it would become a jumble of companies that don't benefit anyone (E. 19).

The perceived presence of an ethical code of conduct among members stabilises the behavioural expectations of *alter* and makes it easier to strike economic deals and carry out transactions. The ethical code of conduct is perceived as a sufficient guarantee of the quality of the goods exchanged and of compliance with the stipulated payment agreement. The high level of reliability accorded to *alter* within the Sardex network allows entrepreneurs to accept terms of payment that would normally be considered too risky to be accepted within the euro market. For example, for retailers who make dozens of small sales every day it would be unthinkable to delay payments in euros because it would entail unsustainable management costs. For small daily expenses immediate payment is in fact the recognised rule of conduct. The presence of an ethical code of behaviour within the Sardex network allows entrepreneurs to waive the rule relating to immediate payment of purchases, with the relative certainty that the payment will be made without having to check or recall within the established terms:

> A trusting relationship develops between network members. It sometimes happens that a buyer does not immediately conclude the Sardex transaction but does it later from home: That isn't a problem. This trust comes from the fact that we have brokers behind us who can manage any problems that occur, but also from the fact that network members generally

> behave correctly. This depends on the members themselves, because those who choose to enter Sardex usually have a positive attitude towards the network which has created opportunities for meeting and getting to know each other [Aperisardex, etc., A/N], and on the positive word of mouth which develops among those who have dealt with other members. Those with positive experiences provide feedback that is passed onto others and circulated amongst members (E. 6).

The high level of reliability accorded to *alter* also involves certainty regarding the quality of the goods exchanged and the successful completion of the transaction. In this situation too, endogenous selection mechanisms (Sardex selection process, monitoring and sanctioning) seem to be the guarantee of trustee reliability and the successful completion of the agreement made.

> If you go wrong once, there are 4000 of us, everyone knows who you are. If you pay for a car and the car is never delivered to you, the event is reported and the car salesman doesn't look good. As well as reputation there is also a question of attitude. It is the attitude of a person who associates, who identifies with the ethical code, who becomes a member to grow, not to try and cheat others. The guarantee depends on the fact that to enter [Sardex network] you are chosen. You can't just apply and join. You apply and then you have an interview to assess your possible potential within the network. Those who join want to create a network (E. 19).

In this case, the intention to create a network is interpreted as the desire to expand one's business and to cooperate with other members: business expansion and willingness to cooperate among economic protagonists are seen as closely related aspects of economic activity.

Thanks to the social mechanisms described above and to the characteristics of the currency, the Sardex device affects the propensity to collaborate of its members. Forms of cooperation emerge which, even to members, appear unrealistic for the euro market. The propensity to collaborate in some cases is so strong that it is able to modify traditional working habits even when there is no particular immediate advantage. The entrepreneurs interviewed provided anecdotes that, in their eyes, showed differences in the willingness to cooperate between the euro market and the Sardex market:

> It is hard to understand why, it is as if you entered a different dimension, of total trust, we all belong to the same club. Reliable interlocutors means that usually economic operators are wary with one another. You are dealing with people who manage their own interests, carry out economic operations, it means finding a balance that is in everyone's interest, a purely economic balance. In the Sardex network you find entrepreneurs with whom it is easy to have social goals. I'll give you an example: yesterday evening I was looking for a car electrician at seven in the evening, around closing time. Since I didn't know who to contact I took the list of Sardex members to find one as I always do. At seven o'clock in the evening I found a car electrician from a small town about forty kilometres from Cagliari. I rang and asked him to do some work on a car that was in Cagliari. I explained that I needed the car to be fixed by this morning. The car electrician replied: "There are problems because I have family problems, I can't understand how you found me at this time of day".

> I replied that I had found him in the Sardex network. When he heard that I was a Sardex member, he changed his mind without hesitating and said he would look at the car for me. I would never have gone to the car electrician in that small town by myself (E. 34).

A willingness to cooperate is perceived by some entrepreneurs, even more explicitly, as an aptitude for mutual assistance that emerges from within the network. Significantly, this perception that relations within the Sardex network are different, emerges soon after the entrepreneurs become members:

> I entered the network three months ago and I have seen that what we talked about with the broker or with friends is really true. [Sardex] is a sort of group where everyone embraces this philosophy. Belonging to the network is a way of helping yourself. I have spoken to customers who have been with Sardex for a long time and they talk about it really enthusiastically because they have had excellent results (E. 12).

As the literature suggests (Ostrom et al. 1992; Sally 1995; Baldassarri 2015), one of the determining factors for fostering cooperation among members is being able to communicate directly: this is often part of economic transactions in Sardex. When the Sardex network was first established, the founders set up an online platform for transactions among Sardex members but the results were disappointing:

> We avoided creating a tool based only on the web, in the first version of the platform there was a marketplace and members could list their products. In the first two years only three products were bought online. This means members want to see each other, get to know each other and meet each other (F. 1).

Sardex Ltd management soon realised that direct interaction among members had much more potential for development than on-line contacts. Although the on-line platform remains a fundamental part of how the Sardex device functions, its overall operational strategy has been oriented to foster direct interaction among members. Aperisardex and the small fairs were introduced so members and their products could make themselves known and meet each other. As the network has consolidated some events are organised by members themselves in addition to those organised by Sardex Ltd:

> Members hold meetings and dinners they have organised themselves. They have lunch together, they hold company presentation banquets and then maybe some deals are made but here it is the social aspect which generates the economic transactions (F. 2).

The presence of an ethical code of behaviour and strong reciprocal constraints also creates the conditions where members desire horizontal sanctioning for those who violate behavioural norms. Reputational sanctioning and hierarchical horizontal sanctioning are social mechanisms fostered and directly encouraged by Sardex members:

> I told the Sardex president as well, that whoever joins the network has to embrace the Sardex mentality or get kicked out of the network (E. 18).

4.2.3 Conclusions

The research results show that a willingness to cooperate can impact positively on economic transactions and business development. A willingness to cooperate in the economic sphere reduces transaction costs because it reduces the need for contractual agreements between the parties. Where the partner's reliability is assessed as high or where there are monitoring and sanctioning mechanisms, it is easy to make verbal agreements or loose contractual solutions that do not consider every possible situation. In these cases the successful conclusion of transactions is ensured by the parties' ability to cooperate independently or in excess of the contractual obligations. The willingness of Sardex entrepreneurs to cooperate facilitates transactions and fosters economic development.

> A strange vibe is created in Sardex, it is all about demolishing walls and it works towards that. The walls don't get demolished because the system works, but the system works because the walls are demolished. It is a reversal of cause and effect. In a normal economy, relationships are usually good because the economy is working well, here it is the opposite: the economy works because relationships are good. In euro, the relations between people who do not know each other are not necessarily good. To create a good relationship in euro you often have to seek out your customer, talk to him and then contact him again; in Sardex my customers call me (E. 34).

The "demolition of walls" evoked by this entrepreneur can be interpreted as overcoming distrust of *alter* behaviour by stabilising behavioural expectations. The way in which entrepreneurs relate to one another shortens social distances and transforms economic transactions in Sardex into a form of social bond that is stronger than the traditionally weak ties usually found in the economic sphere. Entrepreneurs feel the Sardex network has a recognised ethical code and this is associated with a desire to sanction members who do not respect the rules. The operations of the Sardex device ensure that entrepreneur members have a high degree of confidence that *alter* will not choose the free-riding option but will choose to cooperate.

The social mechanisms which foster trust in Sardex, the low cost of Sardex credit and the brokerage activity carried out by Sardex Ltd are the three elements that foster a willingness to cooperate among members and consequently generate high levels of economic transactions. The 26% average increase in turnover of Sardex network member companies, net of the euro substitution effect, together the more rapid circulation of the Sardex compared to the euro (Littera et al. 2014), confirm that the system of relations based on cooperation fostered by the Sardex device effectively promotes the economic development of member companies,[12] see Fig. 4.7.

[12]For a discussion of the risks and benefits associated with high levels of cooperation in the market see Sub-sect. 5.1.3 Competition, cooperation and innovation.

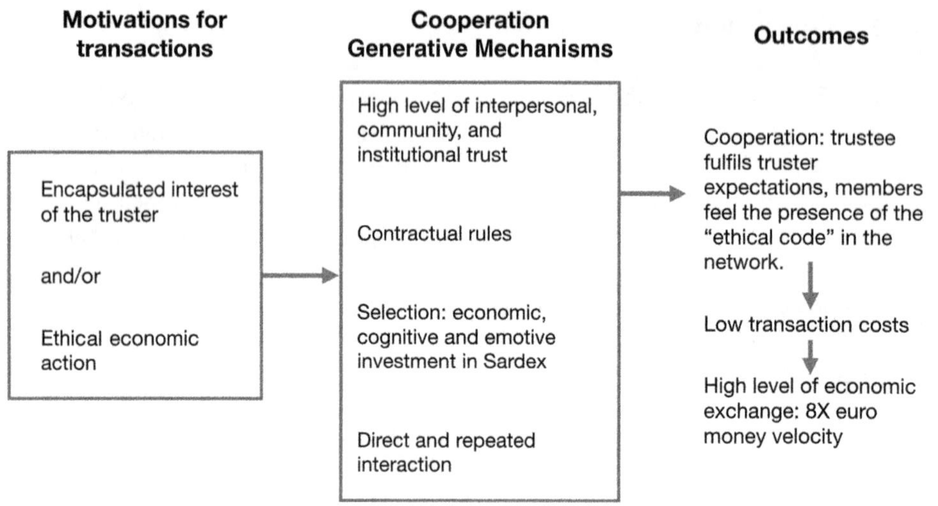

Fig. 4.7 Sardex cooperation generative mechanisms. (Source: own figure)

4.3 Solidarity

Solidarity is a much-used concept, both in the common sense meaning of the term, and in the scientific language, where it finds numerous semantic declensions. In sociology the term solidarity refers to the nature of the social bond. Describing the form of this bond allows us to study the constraints of reciprocity, and of adhering to behavioural norms, that are traditionally associated with the concept of social solidarity, and to understand how these constraints are created. Researching forms of solidarity involves many sociological research topics, ranging from philosophical questions regarding the nature of society and its origin (Simmel 1910), to studies on concrete interactional forms that generate solidarity constraints. The numerous interpretations of the form and functioning of solidarity cannot be included here, but some interpretations of the bond between individuals and society, potentially useful for interpreting the bonds between individuals and the collectivity found in Sardex, will be discussed.

The classical theory underpinning the modern state is based on contractualism; it explains the transfer of individual sovereignty to a political power as a rational act in the collective and individual interest (Hobbes 2010 [1651]). This theory maintains that delegating power management ensures individuals have the best possible conditions of freedom. Political power, through the imposition of laws and norms, would be the basis of the social bond that guides social behaviour towards solidarity. The conceptual distinction between individual advantages and the collective advantages of the social order made it possible to consider the form of the social bond, in its solidaristic sense, as a secondary effect of individual utility. The utilitarian approach *(Homo economicus)* explains the form of the social bond, with its normative and solidaristic constraints, as an aggregate effect of rational individual choices that consider the social and political order as more advantageous than total individual freedom. The utilitarian approach to explaining individual action has had a huge impact on economic theory, to the point that it has become the anthropological basis traditionally used to explain how economies function.

In contrast to the utilitarian approach to explaining social order, there are conflict theories which see the social order as the result of struggles to dominate others, control resources and perpetuate privileges (Marx and Engels 2002 [1848]; Dahrendorf 1959). In this case solidarity can be imposed by those in power, or it can develop among those oppressed by the powerful as a function of their common condition of disadvantage.

Durkheim explains that the origin of social solidarity lies in the way society functions. In *The Division of Labour in Society* (1984 [1893]) he argues that the form of modern solidarity is an effect of the division of labour. The transition from an agrarian society to an industrial one requires a specialisation of work roles that make individuals more interdependent. In pre-modern societies, work in the fields allowed families a certain autonomy to support themselves and to produce the food required for their family. Industrial society, however, increases social interdependence because it requires a high degree of specialisation in order to function, which implies greater social coordination so all needs can be met. In traditional societies social solidarity is based on shared values and Durkheim describes it as "mechanical"; in modern societies, though, social solidarity is defined by Durkheim as "organic", because it is required to satisfy a primary need. Other approaches see the emergence of solidarity as a specific function performed by institutions that are distinct from the economy: for Parsons, family, politics and religion sustain the development of a civil society that guarantees inclusion and social solidarity (1971). The distinction between civil society, the economy and political institutions has sustained further explanations for the emergence of social solidarity as a sphere of social action distinct from others (Alexander 2006).

In the case of Sardex it is difficult, in principle, to distinguish economic action from other forms of social action that traditionally have been used to explain the emergence of social solidarity. The description of the social mechanisms that generate interpersonal trust among members of the Sardex network highlighted the fact that the entrepreneur members adopt reciprocal constraints, and forms of action oriented towards social norms, that cannot be explained only in terms of expected individual utility. The cooperative behaviours described, acquire forms of social reciprocity traditionally associated with social spheres of "civil society", not entrepreneurial activity.

The following four sub-sections will attempt to describe the social mechanisms that generate the forms of social action at work within the Sardex network which can be identified as solidaristic. The sub-sections Opportunities, Desires and Beliefs describe how the Sardex device modifies the context of the action in such a way as to bring forth the solidarity-based social behaviours described as a form of collective action in

Sub-sect. 4.3.4.[13] Collective action is associated with a form of solidaristic action because it is oriented towards the promotion and regulation of common goods. This framework is used to describe the mechanisms by which the collective interest becomes part of the individual interest and, in some cases, becomes a preponderant part of social action.

4.3.1 Opportunities

Opportunity Mechanisms

The concept of opportunity is fundamental for studying decision-making processes. Opportunities *"consist of the possible choices available once political, social, economic, and technical constraints have been taken into account"* (Petersen 2009, p. 115). Decision making is subjected to external constraints which limit the options available. These constraints guide individual choices: individual choices and behaviours emerge from the set of opportunities provided.

> To explain why a person in a given situation behaves in one way rather than in another, we can see his action as the result of two successive filtering processes. The first has the effect of limiting the set of abstractly possible actions to the feasible set, i.e., the set of actions that satisfy simultaneously a number of physical, technical, economic and politico-legal constraints. The second has the effect of singling out one member of the feasible set as the action which is to be carried out (Elster 1979, p. 86).

Constraints can be classified as physical, technological, socio-political and cognitive-psychological. A basic decision-making process is one where an isolated individual considers the choice options available. In this situation it may be possible to predict with relative certainty the outcomes of the choice; in a social context the outcomes of choices are very unlikely to be entirely predictable because social phenomena are complex and interdependent. Socially oriented actions necessarily take into consideration the behaviour of all the protagonists involved (Weber 1978 [1922]), even though these behaviours cannot be predicted with any certainty. Where outcomes are uncertain, opportunities and outcomes are evaluated on the basis of desired outcomes and expectations regarding *alter* behaviours (Beckert 2016). Game theory uses the term "strategic interaction" for this choice constraint (Gintis 2000; see also Goffman 1969). Opportunities are not static in strategic interaction situations, but vary according to the choices made by all the protagonists involved. The ability to predict the choices others will make, or to influence them, can be crucial for making the best choices: signalling mechanisms are often deployed for this.

---

[13] To explain the emergence of solidarity in Sardex, the following sub-sections adopt the action theory described by Hedström as DBO theory (Desires, Beliefs, Opportunities) (2005, p. 38 ff.).

The constraints associated with these opportunities can often be varied to optimise specific outcomes. Individuals and institutions can work to remove constraints and expand available opportunities (e.g., policies against inequality), or reduce them (e.g., policies restricting freedom of movement). Legislation that reduces opportunities is not necessarily a negative restriction of freedom. In Europe, for example, limiting the freedom to hold and carry arms is seen as a positive limitation, because it is believed that this will reduce the possibility of violent behaviour. This type of limitation is not viewed positively in itself, but rather for its effects on a chain of events. Subjects with violent motivations, who are willing to use arms, are less likely to access them if the circulation of arms is tightly controlled. This makes violent behaviour less likely, thereby reducing the damage that might be caused at the individual and aggregate level.

Previously expressed preferences are often modified when opportunities are expanded or restricted (Elster 1984). When a set of previously available possibilities is restricted (e.g., when the colour range for cars is reduced), it is reasonable to expect that the individuals making the choice, will opt for one of the available opportunities. Likewise, faced with an expansion of opportunities (e.g., when a car with a new type of automatic transmission enters the market), it is reasonable to expect that some individuals will modify their previous preferences and opt for the new possibility.

Opportunities in Sardex

The Sardex device creates new opportunities but also restricts some existing ones. The Sardex selection mechanism restricts the field of possible commercial partners to companies that are members of the Sardex network; trade promotion activities organised by Sardex for its members, on the other hand, facilitate the creation of trade networks that would probably never have arisen spontaneously.

Once participating companies have paid for goods and services in Sardex, or have obtained a Sardex line of credit, they need to find Sardex suppliers for the goods and services their company requires. In businesses such as catering, virtually the entire production chain, from producer to consumer, can be sourced using Sardex. In fact entrepreneurs who are Sardex members are often restaurant customers and spend their Sardex credit at restaurants. Sardinia produces significant quantities of food and wine, so it is easy to find suppliers of raw materials and semi-finished products who are Sardex members:

> I can source most of the production chain in Sardex. I am in the catering business and I can source wine, fresh pasta, cured meats, table cloths, crockery, equipment and most of my other needs from consortiums that are in Sardex (E. 33).

Owners of supermarkets that join Sardex usually have to change their habits significantly. Although many small Sardinian companies produce foodstuffs, large-scale food distributors often opt for suppliers from large companies located outside Sardinia. Large companies often look for suppliers of large quantities of products, with a wide range of goods, that small local producers cannot match. Large manufacturing companies can offer a wider variety of products than small local producers, simplifying supply management. Supermarket owners that enter the Sardex network rapidly accumulate large sums in Sardex and this gives them an incentive to find local suppliers of goods who can be paid in Sardex:

> When we signed the contract with Sardex, we obtained an € 8,500.00 line of credit. We didn't use it immediately because we had so many customers that we had a budget surplus. Then I blacked out my Sardex profile for three months, so as to have time to contact suppliers who could be paid in Sardex, and I created my product assortment. My suppliers of bread, cured meats, biscuits, pickles, dairy produce, fruit and vegetables are all paid in Sardex. They all produce locally. Now we still have a surplus but our budget is almost balanced. I still need to find some suppliers (E. 32).

The Sardex network is restricted and this constrains member entrepreneurs to seek out member suppliers who can be paid in Sardex. The Sardex network also provides opportunities for meeting other member entrepreneurs and facilitates the creation of new investment opportunities:

> The difference is, for example, that I have now renovated my office with 50,000 Sardex instead of € 50,000. That may not seem much to you! I borrowed 50,000 Sardex with no interest and I can pay back the money when it suits me. I repaid 30,000 Sardex in one year with instalments of 2,500 Sardex per month, but without any stress. I have to work and make money, but it is less stressful than doing it with the bank. When you have deadlines with the bank you are always worried, but I have fewer worries with Sardex. For example, I have two Sardex accounts, one for the ordinary loan and then a line of credit for the renovation work. If I am unable to repay the instalment at the end of the month, I can use the overdraft of the ordinary account. Of course, when you have a commitment you must respect it, both in euros and in Sardex. I bought everything in Sardex: the lawn, the seats, the dummy, the plants, the paint, the gravel, the blinds, the signage, etc. The most important thing is that, using Sardex, I met some professionals who I would never have met otherwise. I spent 100,000 Sardex to build my house and I met professionals I would never have met otherwise (E. 13).

Sardex can only be used in Sardinia and it cannot be used to pay mortgages, taxes or utility bills; raw materials can only sometimes be paid for using Sardex. Because of these limits, entrepreneurs who belong to the Sardex network tend to use Sardex to buy goods and services required for their business or for personal services:

> When you join Sardex you start moving all the fixed expenses of your business from euro to Sardex, so as to free up the euros for paying for all the things that can't be paid for with Sardex, for example, the building mortgage and the lease for the equipment. I try to pay in Sardex for any other services I use (E. 21).

Sardex cannot be used for many substantial business expenses: this means it is spent more "easily". Sardex cannot be saved to pay off euro debts or to meet future euro payments; this restriction means Sardex funds are of limited use for the future, so they tend to be spent rather than hoarded:

> The banking and monetary system have ruined us because no-one wants to spend, people are afraid. As soon as I have some Sardex I spend them; why should I keep them? I have heaps of things to do, and I spend them immediately. But I keep my euros because I am always worried that I might need them (E. 2).

For many businesses, Sardex revenue is considered a sort of "drawer" which can be drawn from for expenditures that cannot not be afforded in euros. The "Sardex drawer" creates new opportunities for spending and investing which otherwise would not be feasible:

> Unlike Sardex, in euros you always have to put off buying things because you don't have enough money. This is not the case with Sardex. The advantage is that Sardex customers are all new. The euro customers are still there. I call these new customers the "Sardex drawer" and they are quite separate from our regular customers … We have considered it practically as the "Sardex drawer", as if we had a bank account in Sardex and we spend from that account. We set aside Sardex to renovate the entire shop and we also went on holiday last summer–we would not have been able to do this without Sardex. We now use Sardex to do the shopping and repair the car, there is a bit of everything … I have been able to do things that I kept postponing. My initial line of credit in Sardex was € 3,000. Then, as my takings increased, my credit was also increased (E. 10).

Some entrepreneurs maintain that the restrictions regarding the use and circulation of Sardex money directly impact relationships between Sardex members because Sardex and euros are used differently:

> The relationship between Sardex and society is strong because we return to being the society that we have lost. In normal sales you just buy something; with Sardex you buy the same thing, but you also return to having a collaborative spirit. The difference comes from the fact that we belong to a network, as though we were a family. The first question you ask when you go to buy in Sardex is, "who are you", and only after that, "how much does it cost?". This happens because Sardex goes into a separate account which you can't use for paying your taxes or utility bills. Sardex is a money-box, which gives you a surplus that you can use to improve your business. Money in your euro account has to be spent on paying bills and utilities. I use Sardex to make investments that will improve my business: for instance, when I have 10,000 Sardex I will update my computers (E. 7).

Sardex is perceived as a "lighter" currency that is easier to spend: entrepreneurs know they will never be able to spend their Sardex on utility bills or taxes whereas the same amount in euros might be needed in the future to deal with these mandatory business expenses. The fewer opportunities for spending Sardex make them easier to spend because entrepreneurs, when deciding whether or not they should spend their Sardex, do not have to factor in future expenses which can only be paid in euros.

The evidence that takings in Sardex are extra to takings in euros, not just a substitution, encourages entrepreneurs to make new investments that had not been planned with euro income:

> With Sardex I can create extra services, for instance an automatic distributor. I wouldn't have done it in euro because I would have felt like I was subtracting resources from the business. But Sardex has a different weight. I don't mean to say that we don't value Sardex, I'd say that Sardex gives us something extra that we didn't have before. Our euro quota has remained unchanged but now we have Sardex as well. Our sales figures have increased by 9% so we have more money to spend and more resources to invest in the business (E. 32).

Sardex investments can come from credits received on the market, or from specific lines of investment provided by Sardex Ltd for specific projects for member companies:

> Sardex is a channel that at no extra cost allows you to pay for expenses that you wouldn't otherwise commit to, because with the euro you always give priority to other things such as suppliers, electricity and salaries. We have used Sardex to make small investments to improve our business … We plan to replace our electrical wiring. This will cost 100,000 euros and we have asked Sardex to support us. Even if we only have 50% of the investment in Sardex, we will manage; if we don't, we won't have enough euros to do the work (E. 31).
>
> Thanks to Sardex, I have been able to realise my dream of new rooms for my dental surgery, built using innovative technologies that keep energy consumption to a minimum. I was able to do this thanks to my earnings and the trust that was given to me with a handshake (E. 21).
>
> For me [Sardex] was a lever that allowed my company to be "beautiful". Now [my premises] have better lighting than when I was without Sardex and afraid to invest to improve the image of my company. I couldn't have done it in euros. To have an "elastic" euro budget the bank asks for your DNA. Sardex gives you credit to enable you to consume and invest more dynamically at no cost (E. 26).

For companies that do not require special credit lines or credit accumulation in Sardex, the decision to make further investments in Sardex may derive from a different perception of the Sardex cash flow. The highly cooperative attitude of Sardex members means the currency circulates far more rapidly than the euro; entrepreneurs feel it is easier to collect Sardex payments than euro payments—these are factors which guide some entrepreneurs towards investment choices they would avoid in euros:

> We have to renovate and paint the [restaurant] dining room and replace the furniture. The brokers have already given me a lot of contacts and I have obtained quotes. I will do all the work in Sardex because I have a good cash flow in Sardex, and the work will be done by companies that are also my customers. Giving them this work is also a way to have customers (E. 16).

Entrepreneurs can choose whether they use Sardex or euros for their investments: this puts them in the position of being able to compare the services offered by the banking system with those offered by Sardex:

> The less you use banks the better. Banks look after their interests, not yours. They charge for every service they offer, so in recent years we have used them as little as possible. You need freedom to live and make your business successful. The banking world totally discourages you because their figures are all wrong, they don't describe the world the way it really is. We are now independent so we can decide if we are going to use the banks or not (E. 22).

Prices and services offered by Sardex Ltd are considered far more advantageous than those offered by the mainstream banking sector. The services offered by Sardex Ltd, however, remain complementary to those of the banking system because Sardex circulation is limited and Sardex does not cover all the uses of the euro. The credit offered by Sardex Ltd for investments to improve businesses is seen as particularly advantageous compared to the credit available from banks.

The Sardex network's mode of operating also offers promotional opportunities that would not otherwise be accessible to small businesses due to the high costs of implementing them. Both the online platform of the Sardex network and the members' Facebook page allow members to publish promotional advertisements for their businesses, free of charge. Published posts which rapidly reach the many members who check these pages daily, have proved to be very effective, free marketing tools:

> Sardex allows you to make great promotions for free and then, in the twinkling of an eye, every business knows that on Wednesday and Thursday, I will be offering a 40% discount on paint. It's free publicity. I work a lot with promotions. I have a marketing consultant from Frosinone who is our teacher for the profession. If I see that the agenda on Wednesday is a bit empty, I put a promotion on Thursday, Friday and Saturday and fill the agenda. For Sardex customers I put promotions on the Sardex portal, for other customers I put promotions on WhatsApp and Facebook groups (E. 18).

For some entrepreneurs the free marketing tools provided by Sardex have become a significant part of their business activity. With these tools, appropriate *ad hoc* marketing strategies can be developed for products using Sardex technological devices and social mechanisms:

> I joined Sardex so my clients could pay in Sardex if they wished, and also to enlarge my business network. Then, as our business expanded and we got to know the Sardex network better, we started using Sardex to organise events and promote evening entertainment, for example, cultural aperitifs, organising tours, company partnerships. For example, at Christmas we suggested preparing and selling Christmas baskets containing a book and wine from a Sardex producer. I asked my Sardex broker what she thought of this idea, she thought it was a good idea and gave me a list of wine makers who were Sardex members. I chose one that I already knew, who lived nearby, and we promoted these Christmas baskets inside and outside the Sardex network. Customers could choose which book and which wine to put in the basket and the initiative was a success, especially the first year because it was something new. Now other businesses are following suit (E. 19).

The possibilities offered by the Sardex device can be used occasionally or strategically, as described by entrepreneur n°19. In this case the entrepreneur used resources provided by the broker area, other network members and the Sardex website, to create a specific product and service that would have been difficult to achieve with moderate costs and a similar sales success outside the Sardex network.

The "Sardex drawer" can also have effects on personal and family consumption choices. When entrepreneurs or employees receive part of their salaries in Sardex, they tend to orient their Sardex spending habits differently from their euro spending. The limited circulation and use of Sardex guides the use of Sardex in a similar way to the uses that entrepreneurs make for business expenses: Sardex is spent more readily for consumption or purchases that in euro would have been postponed:

> I am a fan of Sardex because over the years it has saved many companies from closing, helping them to remain on the market. I receive part of my salary in Sardex and this has allowed me to maintain consumption levels for my family which I would not have been able to do otherwise. Sardex has made it possible for my business to be more dynamic; I have made investments that I would not have been able to make in euro and I am more relaxed (E. 26).

The opportunities offered by the Sardex device have also had cognitive effects: those involved with Sardex have modified their perception of money and their system of preferences. This will be analysed in the following sub-section.

Conclusions

The regulations and technical-operational characteristics developed by Sardex Ltd have created the Sardex device, which limits some of the opportunities provided by ordinary money but also creates new ones. The limitations: Sardex currency can only circulate within the region of Sardinia, it can only be used by businesses that belong to the Sardex network and there are only limited opportunities for capitalising Sardex.[14] The opportunities created: access to a brokerage service, the online platform and the Sardex Facebook group, opportunities for socialisation among members.

The limitations imposed by the Sardex device, together with the intensified bonding among members, have resulted in Sardex money being used in a different way to the euro. Sardex cannot be used to pay utility bills, taxes, mortgages or raw materials which means entrepreneurs spend their Sardex more "lightly" than they spend their euros. The restrictions imposed on the circulation of the Sardex currency encourage entrepreneur members to invest in their businesses and to maintain higher levels of personal consumption. Investment is also supported by the low cost of obtaining credit compared to the cost of bank loans in euros. Entrepreneurs perceive the liquidity created by sales in Sardex as an "additional drawer" of resources that can be spent, whereas euros are kept in reserve to pay expenses outside the Sardex network. Sardex money can come from

[14]On the economic effects of these limitations see Sect. 5.1 Sardex as an instrument of economic policy.

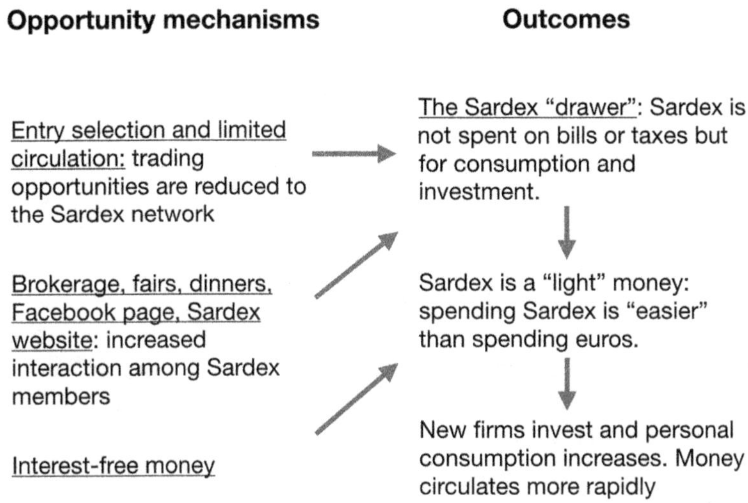

Fig. 4.8 Sardex opportunity mechanisms. (Source: own figure)

sales and also from special credit lines that Sardex Ltd offers companies with specific investment projects. This credit covers up to 50% of investment costs and allows entrepreneurs to carry out development projects that would not be feasible within the euro currency alone.

The Sardex device offers companies new opportunities for spending and investment: see Fig. 4.8. Restrictions on the use and circulation of Sardex currency are combined with increased exchange opportunities, facilitated by easier access to credit and a high level of cooperation among members.

4.3.2 Desires

Desire Mechanisms

There is no doubt that social actors have their own desires which can differ considerably. According to common perception and the scientific conceptualisation of social action, observed behaviours can usually be traced back to individual intentions formed on the basis of desires. The theory of rational choice considers this causal link between desires and behaviours to be the basic theoretical model for explaining social phenomena. If desires can be detected, and they determine the intentions of behaviour, then it may seem legitimate to use them as a causal factor in the processes that explain a certain observed behaviour. In reality, however, the way in which desires are formed and influence observable behaviours in everyday life is not so linear, and the causal link among them is not always clearly oriented from desire to behaviours. As was observed in Sub-sect. 4.3.1

Opportunities, desires are often formed on the basis of the available choice options and tend to have a situational character and to change over time when the options available vary ("sour grapes"). The idea of an "unstable" desire does not offer an adequate base for explaining what it generates of the observed social behaviours (Dennet 1987).

A different conceptualisation of desires uses them as trends or patterns of behaviour. In this case the desires observed express a statistical regularity to which the role of *explanans* of the behaviours observed cannot be assigned (Freese 2009, p. 97). In this conceptualisation the desires themselves can become the *explanandum* that needs to be explained by causes external to the desires and to the individual who expresses them. For example, the variation of customs, related to clothing, in different contexts, can be explained on the basis of desires endogenous to the individual or, in the second conceptualisation, the "causes" of the desires can be traced back, for example, to changes in climate external to the volition of the individual. In general terms, however, desires can be considered a valid *explanans* of the behaviours observed when the link between *explanans* and *explanandum* is sufficiently clear, and reasonably allows the exclusion of other factors, prior or external to the desires, that may have influenced the choices made. In this perspective, desires are not stable, objective elements within the individuals observed, but are situational in nature for the protagonists acting upon them, and their heuristic collocation, between *explanans* and *explanandum*, depends on the observer's perspective. Like beliefs, desires can themselves be considered a *black box* that requires its own explanation. Despite the conditional limitation of the explanatory validity of the concept of desires, desires can be used for specific research projects that limit and define their explanatory validity or describe how the *black box* operates.

Rational choice theory postulates that desires detected from choices made can be attributed to a greater expected utility of that choice with respect to the other options available (Fishburn 1970). The concept of utility, however much it may seem appropriate for describing the distance between the different options guiding the choice, only represents an abstract distance detected *ex-post* the choice was made from the options available. In general terms, the choice between different options can be correctly interpreted as an individual desire that rests on a greater expected utility. The concept of utility is abstract to the point of not providing any information regarding the elements considered which led to the particular decision being taken. Utility can describe a distance between options, but it does not provide information about the elements characterising this distance and cannot, therefore, be used by itself as *explanans* of the phenomena observed (Hedström 2005). In this perspective, a different collocation of behaviours on the utility curve is insufficient for explaining the observed behaviour, because the utility measured only represents a gap between options. Measuring the distance does not provide significant information about the factors that determine this gap in subjects' perceptions. The factors that really influence the choice may have heterogeneous characteristics that cannot be placed linearly on the continuous utility curve.

The case of studies on risk aversion are a clear example of how expressed desires are hard to generalise to other contexts of choice. In economic research, studies on risk aversion are increasingly used to try to identify stable personality traits that could act as predictors of subjects' behaviour in different contexts (Arrow 1971; Rabin 2013). Choosing a more-or-less risky option in a given situation could lead to the hypothesis that the choice is based on—and can be explained by—relatively stable personality traits, which guide choices in a more-or-less risky manner. If the preference for risk were the consequence of a stable orientation of the subject (variously interpretable in psychological, cognitive or physiological terms) then it would be reasonable to expect that in different contexts, interpretable as risky, subjects would opt for choices with similar levels of risk.

Empirical research shows that the hypothesis of risk aversion levels remaining stable in varying contexts is not confirmed (Berg et al. 2005; Freese and Montgomery 2007). Desires are therefore detectable as a result of contextual choices whose stability is hard to generalise, and often need to be explained in terms of elements that are not internal psychological traits. The sociological approach to the study of desires *"should consider as part of its project understanding how social dynamics can make preference variation more or less consequential for ultimate outcomes"* (Freese 2009, p. 103). The use of desires to explain social dynamics should, therefore, consider the contextual elements that influence the formation of desires, the ways in which desires guide subject behaviour and which aggregate effects are observed as a function of the desires detected.

A collective orientation in favour of the same desire can have aggregate effects similar to those described for selection mechanisms: the alternative options are disadvantaged in subsequent rounds, or by the subsequent involvement of other actors, and convictions can be formed regarding the quality of the choice that anticipate a rational cost/benefit evaluation. For example, trends in the fashion system follow expansive mechanisms of this type, to the point where the conformation of individual desires to collectively established desires is no longer considered to bring particular benefits to the identification of the subject's social identity. Desires in fashion that are then imitated and become "popular" often start from "subversive" choices made by public figures; these choices are imitated by "followers" and then appropriated by the big brands. In this case too, subjects express their own desires by choosing clothing with specific characteristics, but these desires can only be explained by following the action chain that links them to other protagonists, institutions and specific material characteristics.

Cases of panic in financial markets that are commonly referred to as "irrational" can also be considered an aggregate effect of beliefs and desires. S*elf-fulfilling prophecies* are fuelled by the desires of a few actors: these desires are then imitated, but are not based on particular inner motivations or cost-benefit calculations between the different options (Merton 1948). Social dynamics follow a logic of their own that cannot be explained as a function of a subjective stability of desires, but rather as a function of opportunities that arise within a network of actors. In these situations, desires acquire strong signalling values for interpreting the real intentions of *alter*.

Desires and beliefs are very interdependent in situations such as these. There are numerous forms of inter-connection between desires and beliefs that often operate at a sub-conscious level, however, the most common patterns can be summarised in three models:

> (1) Adaptive preferences, causal connections from beliefs to desires that lead actors to desire only what they believe they can get ("sour grapes"); (2) counter-adaptive preferences, causal connections from beliefs to desires that lead actors to desire only what they believe they cannot get ("the grass is always greener on the other side of the fence"); and (3) wishful thinking, causal connections from desires to beliefs that lead actors to believe only what they desire to be the case … Cognitive-dissonance theory also suggests important links between an actor's past actions and his/her current beliefs and/or desires. To reduce cognitive dissonance, "is" can become "ought" by beliefs and desires adjusting to the actions (Hedström 2005, p. 40; see Elster 1979 also).

Finally, subjects can use desires strategically to signal belonging and consequently attempt to guide the *alter* perception of their own social identity in a way they consider advantageous.

Desires in Sardex

The analysis of desires in Sardex focuses on the influence that the Sardex device has on the protagonists involved, especially the entrepreneur members of the Sardex network. In line with the results of scientific research on the subject, it is reasonable to expect that modifying the opportunity context of the protagonists involved, thanks to the mix of limitations and new opportunities thrown up by the way the Sardex currency operates, might, with repeated use, modify the desires of the protagonists involved.

The first significant change in entrepreneurs' desires concerns their general perception of the Sardex currency. Initially entrepreneurs approached the Sardex project with a mixture of curiosity and distrust; some of them thought the Sardex currency was worth less than the euro:

> At the start I was almost ashamed to pay in Sardex, I felt like I wasn't paying my supplier, because it seemed like a less valuable currency (E. 26).

This scepticism passed once entrepreneurs experienced the positive effects the Sardex currency had for their businesses; in some cases this diffidence was transformed into strong support for the Sardex project.

The motivations that drive entrepreneurs to join the Sardex network are primarily economic and can be traced back to their desire to expand their businesses by increasing customer numbers, profits and turnover:

> I joined Sardex when I opened my business in 2011 because you save by being part of the Sardex network: you meet new clients and then, if you get used to doing your shopping in Sardex, instead of in euros, the savings are immediate. I joined to have new clients and so I could spend Sardex and leave my euros in the cash-register (E. 27).

Most of those interviewed declared they had experienced difficulties in accessing traditional credit; they viewed Sardex as a resource because it offered low-cost credit:

> My main problem was my lack of liquidity–with adequate support I could have worked well … Unfortunately banks don't want me. Because of this credit crunch if you miss one repayment on a bank loan the bank revokes everything … If your shoulders are strong you can take this blow. My shoulders are not strong and so I suffered in this situation (E. 2).
>
> I went to the bank to ask for a line of credit and they told me I was too young, you have a company but you are "just boys" so you are not credible, maybe you have a fight and then you dissolve your company. Then Sardex arrived, you develop a project, they totally approve it, you have to give them some merit. They financed my project. Repayment was expected a year later but we will repay everything after 11 months, because we prefer it that way, it is our personal choice, to repay our debts as soon as possible, even if there is no advantage for us. Entrepreneurship is not done on debts. We pay all our suppliers and, if something remains we take it for ourselves, otherwise we don't take anything. We have seen how Italy has been reduced after years of debts. Debts bring more debts, it is a vortex (E. 13).

Difficulty in accessing bank credit was not generalised, however. Some entrepreneurs deliberately chose not to apply for bank credit because of the high costs, or because they doubted the transparency and fairness of the banking system or because they considered bank credit economically disadvantageous.

For 31 of the entrepreneurs interviewed, a variety of economic reasons were the decisive factor for them deciding to become members of the Sardex network. For two entrepreneurs economic and ethical reasons were equally important factors. The ethical motivations centred on the belief that the Sardex project could provide collective benefits that would exceed the economic benefits obtained by the member companies. Ethical reasons were the decisive factor for joining Sardex for four entrepreneurs:

> Today there are 4,500 businesses [in the Sardex network] and probably those who become members now have different reasons than we did at the start, when there were only four of us. This depends on the fact that you join up if you are animated by the values of the network. I personally did not become a member for economic reasons. Economic interest was probably the least important reason for joining (E. 9).
>
> I decided to join because I think it is an instrument that gives something extra to businesses. There is a social aspect as well as the economic aspect. In the sense that relationships between businesses and people are valued more highly. It is a project that has extra value because it gathers us all together within the local economy. I joined to find new customers, but also because you can be sure that what you do remains within the local economy and you contribute to it with your work. (E. 30).
>
> A friend told me the story of Sardex and it fascinated me. The reasons that led us to join were merely ethical ones. At the beginning there was great enthusiasm for the idea of solidarity among companies. We do not have a primary supplier within the network (there are no companies that can supply me with paper, ink or electricity). It could have been a way of expanding our customer network, but we were struck by people's enthusiasm when they told us about Sardex and all the ethics and values that surround Sardex products (E. 37).

Table 4.2 Motivations for joining and using Sardex. (Source: own presentation)

	Business	Ethical	Both
Joining	31	4	2
Using	17	3	17

In the course of the interviews it was possible to distinguish the motivations that had inspired the entrepreneurs to join the network from their current motivations for remaining within the network and continuing to use Sardex currency. About half the entrepreneurs interviewed admitted that the ethical goals of the Sardex project were very relevant to their continued support for Sardex. 14 entrepreneurs joined the Sardex network mainly for economic motives, but they continue to support it also for ethical reasons. This difference can be interpreted as a demonstration of how using the Sardex device has guided the desires of member entrepreneurs. Economic motivations have maintained their relevance, confirmed by the positive economic effects of Sardex, but members perceive ethical motivations as having become more relevant in their decision to continue to use Sardex currency (Table 4.2).

For two of the entrepreneurs interviewed, using the Sardex device completely changed their reason for remaining in Sardex. They had joined Sardex for almost exclusively ethical reasons but then began to appreciate the positive economic returns for their companies. Both these entrepreneurs were very well educated and their companies were doing well economically:

> I joined because I met the founders and their ideas seemed really original, something that could be supported without running any serious risks. Now I use it because it's good for business, the other factors remain, but now I use it because it is good for business: to increase the number of customers and turnover, also because it offers me reliable interlocutors (E. 34).

For some entrepreneurs using Sardex currency has made them aware of the uses and effects of money, and they now see the Sardex as a possible alternative to the euro:

> The reason I joined the Sardex network was to increase the number of my customers, now that I am using Sardex, it has become a way of replacing the euro for me. Regardless of the Sardex, I like bartering, I use it in my business (E. 33).

This shift in desire orientations can be interpreted as the result of a pattern of *adaptive preferences* linked to the context of Sardex-modified opportunities, together with a pattern of *reduced cognitive dissonance* with respect to the cognitive, emotional and economic investment linked to the initial selection mechanism for joining the Sardex network.

The second order of desires where it is possible to observe a change linked to the use of the Sardex currency regards the ways this currency is used. At first members were uncertain how to use it and did not follow any strategies in their Sardex spending. Many entrepreneurs are paid part of their salary in Sardex and use this money for personal and family expenses. In this way they experiment different ways of using the Sardex, trying different suppliers and they familiarise themselves with this currency. They soon realised that the Sardex, sustained by the confidence-building mechanisms described above, is easy to spend and can be used for economic transactions in a way that very efficiently meets the requirements of their companies.

> At first I used [Sardex] for personal expenses (groceries restaurant, etc.), because that is the easiest thing to do. Then, the more you use it and the more you realise its potential, and I started using it for larger company expenses (E. 35).

Using Sardex to make important investments for a company means finding reliable companies for the supply of goods and services. Thanks to the high probability that member companies of the Sardex network will remain cooperative throughout all phases of investment implementation, the risks involved in entrusting an important investment to a single supplier are reduced if the supplier is part of the Sardex network.

For three entrepreneurs, using Sardex currency has resulted in a shift in their motivation for so doing that widens the spectrum of choice. Sardex can be used to create additional business to that in euros, or it can be used to create business that replaces the euro; now three entrepreneurs have started using Sardex as an instrument to expand their business in euros. The market tools provided by the Sardex device allow the development of strategies that can also expand economic activities in euros:

> At the beginning I joined the network to find new customers among Sardex members. Then I realised that I could use Sardex credit and the Sardex network to promote my company outside Sardex as well, thanks to communication services among members (radio, newspapers, webmaster, etc.), and to revamp my shop (E. 26).

When entrepreneurs use Sardex currency for their own personal expenses or for those of their family this can affect consumption styles and habits. The most significant testimony comes from a retailer who notes how he is able to identify if a buyer is in Sardex, or not, from his consumption style when shopping. Customers only express their intention to pay in Sardex when they are about to pay and are not obliged to notify the seller beforehand. The common trend of consumption during the years of economic crisis was for customers to go and buy only one item from his shop, with much hesitating because of the uncertain economic situation.

> My impression was positive after the very first transactions because I realised that people buying with Sardex did so with greater serenity. Times are difficult, but Sardex customers will buy two or three items, rather than just one. This is because Sardex gives you greater buying power: having Sardex is like having an extra bank account with money you have to spend within the network, and this gives you the serenity to go shopping–even for the more instinctive types of shopping that in recent times people tend to reject (E. 35).

The different opportunities for spending Sardex compared to euros has modified members' spending preferences, favouring a greater ease of spending and consumption:

> The banking and monetary system are ruining us because people don't want to spend, they are afraid too. As soon as I have some Sardex, though, I spend them, why should I keep them? I have a hundred things to do and I spend them immediately. I keep my euros, though, because I am always afraid that I might need them (E. 2).

Other entrepreneurs also report how the consumption habits of Sardex customers are different from those of euro customers. Sardex customers tend to buy more than euro customers and even family consumption habits change:

> What I like about Sardex is that when a member comes shopping, his entire family comes along as well. I don't know why this is, but they all come (E. 18).

The greater ease of spending in Sardex compared to the euro, noticed by entrepreneurs as larger sums spent for single-item purchases in Sardex than in euros, is also confirmed by the average increase in the business of Sardex network members. As reported previously their customers have increased by 23% and their turnover has increased by 26%. In the light of members' comments the 3% difference between the increase in customers and the increased turnover can be interpreted as a greater average value of purchases in Sardex than in euros. A Sardex customer tends to spend more than a euro customer.

The tendency for entrepreneurs to spend more, and more readily, in Sardex than they do in euros also emerges from an examination of company investments:

> I use the liquidity generated by Sardex to make purchases I wouldn't otherwise make. For example, if I need to install a burglar alarm, it is not a priority, because I normally use money for more urgent things. Sardex allows us (for the way in which we use it) to make important, sometimes essential, purchases, which in that moment we would have avoided making with euros. If you can spend money you don't have [Sardex line of credit] obviously you use it because you know you can compensate with sales. To give an example, we have installed a LED lighting system in our offices. Without Sardex I would have changed two light bulbs, I certainly wouldn't have replaced the entire lighting system. But with Sardex I thought I would re-do the company's entire lighting system to improve it. With Sardex we have changed all the office furniture too. We have also bought a mechanised sweeper with Sardex. We found a tool that could be useful for us in a Sardex company. We also converted all worker safety expenses into Sardex. Some maintenance work on the building was done in Sardex too (E. 32).

In times of economic crisis, investments that are not absolutely essential to ordinary company business, are frequently postponed until the economic situation improves. The Sardex device guides entrepreneurs more towards consumption and investment and less towards saving than the euro does.

Conclusions

The modified opportunities for using the Sardex currency, as compared to the euro, enable the Sardex device to guide the desires of its entrepreneur members. The most significant effects regard how the Sardex currency is perceived and the uses to which it can be put. Once entrepreneurs have used Sardex for a while, they start to appreciate it and increase the range of activities where they use it: from personal consumption to company expenses and investment. A greater understanding of how the Sardex device operates, and its economic and social effects, has generated a shift in the motivations for using Sardex currency: thanks to their use of Sardex, the motives of fourteen entrepreneurs have gone from being purely economic to having an ethical component. Ethical motivations identify beneficial economic effects for the community as deriving from using the Sardex currency. For a small number of entrepreneurs a shift in the opposite direction has also been observed: entrepreneurs who entered the network for purely ethical motives, began to appreciate the economic benefits of the network once they had used it for a while and to consider these economic benefits a valid reason for using the Sardex currency on a par with ethical reasons.

Finally, the Sardex device affects individual consumption and investment desires. There is significant evidence that using Sardex currency generates greater "ease of spending" among customers and sustains the propensity to invest. In times of economic crisis, the aggregate effects of this influence on desires can be interpreted as an anti-cyclical action. The change in preferences fostered by the use of the Sardex device can be interpreted as a decision-making orientation in specific contexts. Given the situational nature of the desires, the influence of Sardex can explain the change within the socio-economic context of reference, a context that potentially is not far removed from other, weaker economic areas within developed economies, see Fig. 4.9.

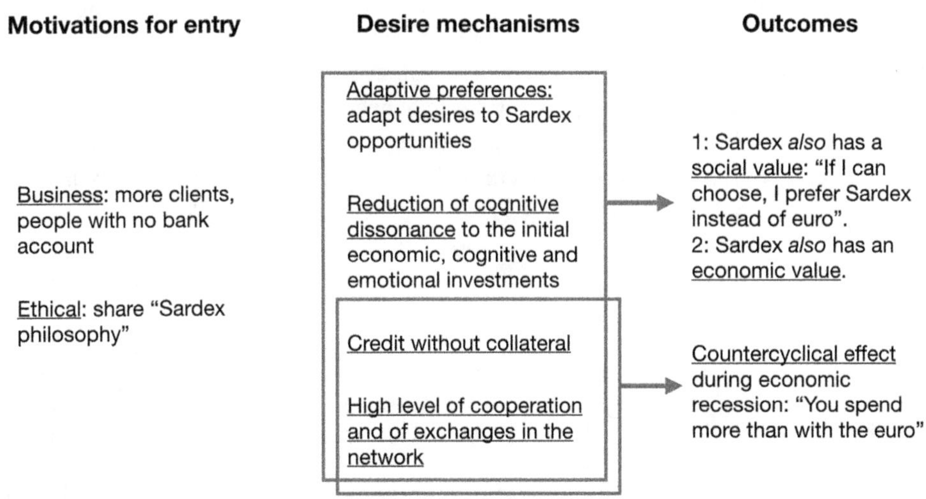

Fig. 4.9 Sardex desire mechanisms. (Source: own figure)

4.3.3 Beliefs

Belief Mechanisms

The definition of desires is not in itself a sufficient element for predicting social behaviours, especially if the guidelines are generic and have not been considered in relation to a specific context. For example, the desire to use a non-polluting means of transport, by itself, is unlikely to be able to predict or explain the real decisions that individuals will make in the different contexts in which they find themselves choosing from different means of transport. The possible choices these individuals will make need more precise assessment: the different opportunities offered in the various contexts need to be known, as does the belief system adopted regarding the functioning and effects of the different transport opportunities in relation to the general desire expressed. Opportunities are only perceived as such in relation to beliefs that link the functioning of some of the characteristics of the situation to a general guideline attributable to the desire system (Elster 1983). In this perspective, the requirement that the belief system be classified as objectively "true" or "false" takes second place: beliefs are useful for explaining social action because they provide information on the causal links between the social phenomena used by the actors. An example: although a circumscribed economic shock does not have the potential to impact global economic dynamics, financial investors' beliefs about the reactions of other financial investors to the shock have the potential to create panic situations in financial markets, which then really do influence global economic dynamics (Felin and Foss 2009). Destructive beliefs about the economic effects of a limited economic shock need not be "objectively" proven to motivate uncontrolled sales behaviour by investors. The beliefs about the expected effects of an observed phenomenon may be enough to explain the behaviours, regardless of the expected validity of the forecast.[15] The widespread effects of the social mechanism of self-fulfilling prophecies on financial markets make the effects of beliefs real. Regardless of the expected validity of the causal mechanisms of the observed social phenomena used by the individuals involved, the aggregate effects of behaviour based on beliefs are real, and tend to confirm the correctness of the belief system and to stabilise the consequent social behaviours (Merton 1948).

From the sociological point of view, the precise definition of the beliefs at stake does not offer a definitive *explanans* that can reliably explain social phenomena. Beliefs, in fact, are such only within a specific context and their very genesis can be considered

[15]The possibility of predicting explanations of social phenomena is very limited and the validity of doing so is debated. For an introduction to the topic see Clarke et al. 2016, part. 1.

a phenomenon that requires a proper sociological explanation.[16] For example, the individual beliefs of German citizens regarding the stability of the value of their currency during the historical period of hyper-inflation are easily explained sociologically by the previous frequent devaluations of their currency. Repeated observation is, in fact, one of the social mechanisms associated with forming beliefs (Rydgren 2009a).

Sometimes however, observation alone does not provide enough information to explain the causal links among observed social phenomena or, in any case, does not provide enough information to guide social action. Educational choices, for example, are a topic of much debate, even among specialists: the causal links between the way in which reference adults behave towards children and the behaviours that these children will display years later, when they are adults, cannot be defined unambiguously. Faced with situations in which the causal link between the observed phenomena and the events they have generated, or the events they will generate in the future, is not clear, it is considered reasonable to introduce an ethic of intention (Weber 2004, p. 32 ff.) or an external epistemic authority (Zagzebski 2015) to guide the action. Pedagogues and psychologists, for example, provide comprehensible behaviour models that educators can draw inspiration from: external epistemic authority often helps resolve the problem of choice under uncertain conditions and allows actions to be guided.

If repeated observation, or epistemic authority, allow the development of beliefs that appear to be plausible, with regard to the causal links that generate the social phenomena observed or the effects that these will produce, it is very likely these beliefs will be readily reutilised in different contexts. Using beliefs in contexts different from those in which they were generated is referred to as the analogy mechanism (Chwe 2001). For example, the repeated observation that University X graduates obtain more prestigious and better paid jobs than their counterparts at University Y, in the same city, can lead, through generalisation, to a belief that University X trains university students better than University Y does. If information to this effect is repeated frequently, this observation can easily turn into a widespread belief, to the point where students prefer to attend University X. Students have limited information for effectively assessing the quality of the teaching they will receive in the future, and tend to adopt an inductive style of reasoning to guide their choice making. Inductive logic does not offer certainties that the expected effects will be realised, but it is often considered a valid strategy for guiding

[16]"*The mechanisms through which beliefs are formed tend to be 'causal' (as distinct from intentional) from the focal individual's point of view, and typically operate 'behind the back' of the individual. Dissonance reduction ... is an important example of a process in which the actions of some bring about dissonance and subsequent changes in the beliefs of others. Although the process is an unintended outcome of other individuals' actions, actions nevertheless are what make them tick, and therefore analyses of social interactions between intentional actors are the core concern. This was certainly an important reason why Weber explicitly defined sociology as a science that concerns itself with understanding and explaining the causes and consequences of social action*" (Hedström 2005, p. 43).

choices in conditions of uncertainty (Holland et al. 1986). Repeated observation and inductive logic constitute a mechanism of beliefs formation.

Following the diffusion of beliefs thus formed, through the dissemination of information regarding the "quality" of the two universities, it is reasonable to expect, all other conditions being equal, that the labour market will prefer University X graduates to University Y graduates. In this case the belief-formation mechanism uses deductive logic, not inductive logic. The reasoning used by employers in this case is as follows: if University X graduates are highly skilled then also individual N who studied at University X is skilled. The reasoning is based on a categorisation of individuals on the basis of some known characteristics (e.g., the university they attended) and assigning these individuals some unknown characteristics as well (e.g., good working skills), in the belief that all the individuals belonging to that group will share similar characteristics.

Arguments based on inductive logic and those based on deductive logic can lead to erroneous beliefs when explaining social phenomena: University X might offer Student N a low quality education, just as Graduate N might not possess the skills the employer assumes he has. Both types of logic are however commonly used to form beliefs and they are also useful for guiding social action: *"tentative guides for perception and behaviour. When they are relied on heavily, there are bound to be inferential errors and misguided actions"* (Nisbett and Ross 1980, pp. 8–9, cit. in Rydgren 2009b, p. 77). The effects of these beliefs, however, are real and objective: in this case it is reasonable to expect that University X will attract many students and its graduates will probably be preferred by employers, at least until the current beliefs are replaced by others (Pierce 1957).

Beliefs, therefore, have a situational value linked to the specific context in which they are formed and to the effects they can produce. Repeated observation and inference, information dissemination, analogy, recourse to epistemic authority and categorisation are common social mechanisms for producing beliefs and spreading their effects.

Beliefs in Sardex

In line with the theoretical approach used, the role of beliefs in Sardex is analysed in relation to the effects of the Sardex device on the belief system of the individuals that use it. As was observed in the section dedicated to trust-generating mechanisms, Sardex members, in the process of using Sardex currency, begin to perceive relations with other member entrepreneurs differently from relations with entrepreneurs who use only euros. A high level of reliability is attributed to other entrepreneurs in the Sardex network, simply because they are members. This different way of relating to members is perceived from the first transactions in Sardex:

> The first exchanges in Sardex were positive because negotiations started differently. Relations with companies in Sardex have well identified values: trust, a desire for reciprocity, and to help the network grow, improve negotiations and relations. This seems to me a common quality among Sardex members, especially those who have been a part of the network from the beginning (E. 9).

Members observe that economic relations are conducted differently in Sardex, and this leads them to characterise other members as trustworthy, desirous of reciprocity in their transactions and of fostering the Sardex project. These beliefs, formed by observing the behaviour of others, are then used to categorise other network members. In fact, armed only with the knowledge that an interlocutor is a member of the Sardex network, without any specific feedback, entrepreneurs attribute to that member a reliable character, a desire for reciprocity and a desire to promote the Sardex network. Beliefs are used in this case to categorise other entrepreneurs and to deduce some characteristics, without having to collect specific data. The reliability of other entrepreneurs is deduced simply from their belonging to the Sardex network, thanks to the mechanism of belief forming through categorisation.

These beliefs relating to the functioning of the Sardex network are quickly confirmed by subsequent interactions, where, thanks to high levels of cooperation, defections from expected cooperative behaviour are very rare occurrences.

> When a member meets another entrepreneur member the relationship is different because they have both chosen to belong to the same group and they have both placed their bet on the network and this generates a strong sense of belonging. Over time we all experience the two sides of the same coin: when I give credit and let the others go away with a smile (the average receipt is higher), I have also had the experience of being in debt to others in the network. I had the opportunity to make an investment that otherwise I could not have done or to improve the wellbeing of the workforce which, with the crisis, I would never have been able to do (F. 1).

These experiences show members a different way of conducting economic relations. Over and above the different social relationships, the economic system activated by the Sardex currency is also founded on providing credit, using criteria that differ from the ordinary ones. Entrepreneurs perceive the provision of credit in Sardex as being "easier" than credit in euros. This is due to the low cost of the annual membership fee, compared to the costs involved with bank interest rates and also to the selection criteria for joining the network, which assesses an entrepreneur's potential to conclude transactions within the network, rather than traditional collateral to guarantee credit. For many entrepreneurs these different selection criteria mean they do not need bank credit because they can access Sardex credit to develop their business. Different ways of relating to economic transactions, and different ways for entrepreneurs to access credit in order to develop their business projects, are readily summarised by these entrepreneurs as a different approach to doing business:

> With their first purchase or their first sale, members realise there is a different way of doing business, they can touch it and see it on their account statement. Then they meet up with other entrepreneurs who made the same choice and it becomes their daily life … it gives a sense of belonging and of security … I wasn't a fool (F. 1).

Many small Sardinian companies have suffered a decline in their business following the economic crisis and the competitive pressure of the large retail chains. Personnel laid off, profit margins reduced, and closure of economic activities have been common experiences for Sardinian entrepreneurs since the 2008 economic crisis. Many entrepreneurs consider the different way of doing business in Sardex as a sign that a different economic system might be possible:

> I joined Sardex to get around the growing crisis and I must say I was right. This allowed me to save myself and attract new customers to counteract the loss of those who use the internet or who only care about price and not service. It is not these people's fault, because the system doesn't leave them much money and prices are all aligned in a downward direction. Workers and entrepreneurs are doing without the profit margins required for the company to exist. Twenty years ago, a company with my turnover, managed to feed 4/5 people without any problems. Today I can barely manage with just my son. The gross operating margin has decreased and consequently the net operating margin has also decreased. The State doesn't believe this is my real net operating margin, and I am told it is impossible and that I am cheating. A tragedy. This is everyone's condition: it is Europe that is in this situation. In a while Germany will also fall into this situation because poverty is born of poverty. If we don't get it into our heads to make our small businesses grow again and give value to our work, we won't get out of this situation. With Sardex our work is valued (E. 15).

The positive characteristics of how the economy functions using the Sardex currency are then generalised by members, through an inferential process, as a potential possibility for the functioning of the economic system in general. In this generalising process, in addition to the ways members relate to each other and the easy access to credit, the geographical limitation of circulation of the Sardex currency also comes into play:

> Sardex gives a sense of belonging that is missing today. Members recognise that the Sardex project gives them a chance of keeping their money here. This is the basic mission that members recognise in the Sardex project, then soon this mission is transformed into relations between people who trust each other. This is a condition never experienced in any other type of economic operation. For work I have visited over a thousand companies, but a situation of this kind is absolutely unique in history, an incredible demolition of barriers. Sardex is an element of commonality that encourages you to share experiences. The positive experiences you make in the network reinforce this image (E. 34).

The conviction that easy access to credit and trusting relations among members are positive effects, combines with the limited circulation of the Sardex currency, which makes entrepreneurs feel that it is a less abstract mediator of their economic transactions than the euro. The money spent in euros may well pass through banks, companies or other financial intermediaries that can move it to other countries or use it for a variety of other purposes. Money spent in Sardex, because of its technical characteristics, remains in Sardinia and is only used by Sardinian companies that are Sardex network members. It is commonly believed that the presence of money in a place has the capacity to increase wealth and collective wellbeing there. This belief has been borrowed, using an analogy mechanism, and adopted by entrepreneurs to hypothesise the future effects of using the Sardex currency. The explanation of the effects of the money used by the entrepreneurs rests, in this case, on the belief that its local circulation can favour local business development. The data on business growth of the member companies confirm the entrepreneurs' interpretation of the positive economic effects of the Sardex device.

> Using Sardex I learned to better appreciate its goals and objectives because I see that it is working. Its turnover among local operators is increasing especially among professionals and artisans because they don't have the problem of buying raw materials. This has the effect of increasing monetary circulation and purchasing power because there are companies, professionals and artisans that are increasing their turnover. The positive effect on my activity and on the local economy have made me judge Sardex more favourably (E. 14).
>
> Sardex is a very positive experience, both for our company and for the region, because it keeps the Sardinian economy turning over (E. 25).
>
> With Sardex I keep the product in our region. It is easy to buy online, on the internet, but with Sardex we keep the product in our region, and we don't need to look for it elsewhere. If I can, I do my shopping locally, not elsewhere. It is also a way to support the Sardinian economy and the smaller economies (E. 27).
>
> I strongly believe in Sardex, it is a very, very important instrument, everyone should believe in it more, because it gives you job opportunities and allows you to contribute to the local economy (E. 30).
>
> It is useful for our region because it gives you a chance to work "at home", to belong to a regional network in which you have the opportunity to provide and obtain work in the area you live in (E. 33).

Entrepreneurs interpret the beneficial effects of using the Sardex device not only through the increased availability of credit for companies, but also for its capacity to develop particular types of networks among small businesses:

> Sardex helps develop small economies. Businesses active in small centres are put online along with larger economic areas and they are given the same publicity in the network (E. 34).

In the euro market, large companies have far more effective marketing tools at their disposal than smaller companies, but in the Sardex network the same marketing tools are available to all companies, both large and small. Many micro-businesses make strategic use of the marketing resources offered by the Sardex device and successfully increase their sales. The size of the company using these tools does not seem to influence their effective use. This feature of the online Sardex platform is appreciated by small businesses: they understand that it gives them the chance to compete more effectively with larger companies. In this sense they interpret the effects of the Sardex device as a redistribution of resources for competitiveness between small and large businesses:

> In my opinion Sardex is the alternative to the large retailers who do not appreciate our products, because we don't have the large quantities of goods they require. With Sardex, small local businesses can make themselves known. Leaving aside the currency, the Sardex network is an opportunity to make contact [with potential customers] (E. 17).

The difficulties, for small-scale producers who want to sell their products to large retailers, are not usually due to the poor quality of their produce, but rather that the quantity is limited and fluctuates over time. For small-scale producers, especially those in the food and wine sector, who are unable to access the sales channels used by large retailers, using the Sardex device is seen as a valid alternative for making their business known, and for attracting new customers. Thanks to this interpretation of the expected effects of the Sardex device, entrepreneurs attribute this device with redistributive capacities within the economic system, increasing the competitiveness of small-scale producers at the expense of larger-scale producers and large-scale retail chains.

In addition to beliefs regarding the overall functioning of the local economic system, the Sardex device also affects the way in which entrepreneurs interpret individual choices in the economic field. As was observed for the effects of the Sardex device on desires, members tend to spend the Sardex currency more readily than they spend euros. These behaviours, thanks to the mechanism of repeated observation and inference, change beliefs about the expected spending behaviour of Sardex customers compared to euro customers:

> Another interesting aspect concerns the amount spent in Sardex. For example, we prepare gift coupons for a haircut and styling. Customers spend a bit more in Sardex. Just think … a customer bought products that cost 270 Sardex, she was worried about emptying my window display! I told her not to worry because we had a good supply in stock (E. 18).
>
> Sardex customers usually spend a little more because they let themselves be tempted. Maybe they take a cellulose product with nicer graphics compared to the euro customer who may try to keep the price low (E. 23).
>
> Sardex provides a bit of oxygen in moments of crisis. I am aware that the people who come and buy from me in Sardex feel easier when they are buying trousers, or a shirt or jacket, in recent years it has been hard to buy these items (E. 35).

The propensity to spend more is partly legitimised by the greater ease of accessing credit and partly by the belief that any Sardex spent will quickly return in the form of more sales:

> When I buy something in Sardex I don't worry much about the price because you don't feel like you are spending. Even though, rationally, you know you are spending, you also know you can recuperate the Sardex by selling (E. 31).
>
> Sardex has no risks: you don't pay interest, you don't pay arrears, you are permanently overdrawn, and nothing happens, on the contrary, you are encouraged to spend [Sardex] even if you don't have any. So, we have done a very useful thing [joining Sardex]: we lend the money but then, in one way or another, people come back. And, if we lend money, we introduce money, work, labour, products. In my opinion it is a very good monetary philosophy. I manage quite a few business activities and I have realised that if you give people a chance to spend, they will do so (E. 28).

The conviction that it will be easy to earn the spent Sardex again, reduces the uncertainty which is felt when there is a spending decision to make. For some entrepreneurs, this easy "return" of spent Sardex is also clearly identifiable in direct reciprocity relationships established between entrepreneurs:

> You often spend without realising. For example, we have become good friends with an optician in the city who is a Sardex member. He often comes here to eat, and I bought glasses from him that were worth a thousand euros. In euros I wouldn't have been able to afford them, because it is difficult to spend a thousand euros on glasses, for a person like me, who has started a new business and is full of payment deadlines. With Sardex though, if you have money available you spend it. Earning money in Sardex is as tiring as it is in euros, but I see it as something "witty" and "inspiring": I do the shopping in Sardex for the restaurant and for myself. The shopping for the restaurant you do in a different way because you know that the people you buy from will come and spend Sardex at your [business] (E. 23).

Although earning money in Sardex is as "tiring" as it is in euros, spending in Sardex is seen as "wittier" and "more inspiring" than normal euro spending. The rapid circulation and limited use of the Sardex facilitates a different attitude that makes spending in Sardex "easier" than spending euros.

Some entrepreneurs believe that using the Sardex not only changes Sardex spending but it also allows a general increase in the standard of living:

> I have acquired customers thanks to word of mouth from Sardex clients and others who entered Sardex later. For example, I have a car dealership in Nuoro which joined Sardex later. I hired a rental car from them for fiscal convenience: the engine was 3,000 cc and I would never have chosen that car, if I had not been paying in Sardex. I pay for hire cars in Sardex, the dealership pays the consulting service that my company provides for them. We made a trade agreement by exchanging advice and car rental, paying both in Sardex: it is a step forward for both parties with both sides paying what they owe. As I provide advice in Sardex they accept 100% of the rental in Sardex. In the end I get myself a large-cylinder car that otherwise I would never have been able to afford. It is advantageous because everyone's living standard improves. I acquire a currency that I have to spend, that I cannot accumulate, because it makes no sense to accumulate it. My standard of living grows automatically. I worry less when I have to go to a restaurant or hotel (E. 34).

Expenses considered financially unattainable in euros are considered sustainable if they are paid for with Sardex. This different perception of the use of money can also change family behaviour with respect to money:

> Around Christmas time one of our employees said he was able to give gifts "much more willingly" to his wife who had to up-date her wardrobe and went shopping in the network. In euros you have more scruples about spending because you know that you might get unexpected expenses to deal with, for example a higher-than-normal electricity bill. Instead in Sardex you spend them because you will have to spend them anyway, you can't use them for the electricity bill, you have them, you spend them, and you spend a bit more too. You inject liquidity into the network at a time when we are in deflation because no one is spending (E. 23).
>
> In the periods when I know I cannot spend euros, I have the opportunity to spend in Sardex. Euros are always needed for specific things, like taxes. If I need to buy something and I can't spend in euros, then I use Sardex. For example, a few days ago it was my daughter's birthday, we went to the restaurant opposite, with all the family, to celebrate and I paid in Sardex. In euro I wouldn't have done it because I would have thought about it a thousand times before. Nowadays, we have to think a lot before spending euros (E. 29).

Money that cannot be used to pay taxes or utility bills creates less anxiety when it is spent on celebrating a birthday. A birthday party, which would be too expensive to pay for in euros, is not so expensive that it cannot be paid in Sardex, even though the nominal value is exactly the same, thanks to the fixed parity of the two currencies established by contract.

Members believe that their living standards have improved and that the Sardex device has provided positive economic effects for them: this leads them to believe that the Sardex device can provide both individual and collective benefits. The two categories of benefit do not exclude one another but have synergistic effects instead. Entrepreneurs do not believe that the Sardex device provides tools to achieve these benefits separately or inversely proportionally, but instead they believe that within the Sardex network, the pursuit of individual utility will also produce collective benefits. Individual and collective benefits coexist in the operation of the network increasing personal living standards and sustaining the local economy go hand in hand:

> Members are promoting their own interests and helping others at the same time. Obviously, everyone buys where they prefer to but, by buying within the network, I am helping the network to operate well. This increases the number of my customers, and also my spending capacity (E. 12).

This different interpretation of the functioning of the monetary system and of its effects tends to be extended to other areas of the economic system as well.

The importance of the quality of relations for the functioning of the economic system is particularly emphasised by the way the Sardex device operates. The relationships among entrepreneurs within the network change qualitatively, compared to relationships in the euro system. For some entrepreneurs this difference can contribute to a different connotation of the economic system in general:

> Sardex has helped me to understand the meaning of money. We grow up thinking that we need money: we don't need money, we need to satisfy our basic needs, eat, sleep and have relationships. If we shift our focus to money, we associate our well-being with having money, but this is misleading. We always think we have too little money to feel good, but our well-being is tied to our satisfaction in what we do, and in satisfying our basic needs. Sardex has helped me to rediscover that there are more important things than money, we must not be slaves to money, we should work more at our relationships. The network obliges you to work at relationships. When a customer of mine comes to the cash register to pay I ask him what he does in the network and I see if I can advise him on how to use the network (E. 2).

Some entrepreneurs refer to experiences and functioning modes from the past to interpret the different way the economic system operates in Sardex. Strong social relations within the economic system were common in Italy until the country was industrialised in the 1950s and 1960s and remained a common way of relating in small towns for many years after:

> The first time was positive because it was possible to pay for the shopping with Sardex. The first payment was exciting, I was paying without taking any money out of the till. It reminded me of the barter system that operated after the war: I'll give you some potatoes and you'll give me some beetroot (E. 10).

Barter is a common form of exchange in rural economies where production is intended for family consumption. The evolution of financial capitalism in recent decades has made this form of exchange obsolete in the eyes of most economic operators. The ease of using money for transactions and their immediacy on a global scale, thanks to the financial markets, have been considered an important conquest, a motor for modernising the economy that has made other forms of exchange obsolete. Despite the redoubtable innovative capacity of the financial markets, though, ever since the economic crises of 2001 and 2008, brought about by speculative financial bubbles, the economic effects of the financial markets are viewed with suspicion by some:

> I thought the tremendous economic crisis underway could only be countered by exchanging [goods] with barter. We should return to nature, give new meaning to human work. We are machines who work for the state and international finance. We don't even know who we are working for, we can't stop, we have undefined goals to reach. For opticians the main enemies are Luxottica and the state. With Sardex, though, we return to a system of barter. If you have four apples, you can come to me and in exchange I can give you a pair of glasses. In this way, work has a value again. I make a pair of glasses for someone who grows apples or who paints a room. This is really the way the economy works, but it has been upset by uncontrollable financial systems. With the euro it would perhaps be possible if we weren't governed by people linked to the world of finance. The point is bad money management. Even today there is the tendency to further separate those with money from those without … There is this sense of community in Sardex because we have set up a system that can save the economic system of our small companies. With Sardex we have the chance to not depend entirely on the barbaric system of the global economy (E. 15).

Despite the perception of uncontrollable global financial flux, the Sardex currency makes barter and money seem manageable on a local scale, an element that helps with the economic exchanges of daily life. A few entrepreneurs used the mechanism of analogy with Sardex operations to extend the idea of barter to economic exchanges with no Sardex mediation:

> I have extended the idea of Sardex to pure barter. A wine producer came to me for dinner and I suggested he pay the rent of the room in wine and we agreed on this. Now, every time he comes to Cagliari he sleeps here, and he pays me in wine. It is cheap for him and good for me, as I would have had an empty room and I would have bought his wine for the restaurant anyway (E. 2).

The general perception of entrepreneurs is that the Sardex "circulates" but the euro "doesn't move" or "doesn't exist". In the years of economic recession and low interest rates, the interest rates on money invested in banks were close to zero but companies requiring credit for investments or current expenses often continued to pay high rates of interest. In this context, entrepreneurs preferred their experience with the Sardex currency with some of them going so far as to imagine the effects of applying the Sardex operating system to the euro:

> With Sardex I immediately felt at home from the very first transactions because I met people who respected my work. People who respected the dignity of my work without putting the price as the number one problem. This happens because the Sardex has no financial value, you can't accumulate Sardex, in fact, if you hold your Sardex, they burn. With Sardex we have finally invented a money that circulates. The absurdity of the euro is that its financial value is non-existent, but for a 0,25% interest rate [difference] we are capable of changing our bank or changing our investment or squabbling with our financial advisor, it is an aberration! When, really, they are kidding us because even the euro no longer has financial value. Today is the first time that money costs 10/11%, whilst collecting it doesn't cost anything for banks. The way Sardex circulates in just one day gives many families enough to live on. If we were a bit more intelligent, we could do it with the euro. When I can, I choose Sardex (E. 15).

The complex belief system that has developed around the Sardex device has inspired entrepreneurs to the point where some of them believe that Sardex could be an instrument for changing the current economic system:

> In Sardex we are a kind of brotherhood, a trade union, a private club, we all feel like one family and, in the end, this makes us frighteningly loyal in our purchases and it also means we create friendships. We all share the hope of being able to change something in this economic system which penalises those who work, and which has increased the distance between those who have enough money and those who do not. Sardex is a payment system that gives you the chance to make a living. It shortens distances. People with lots of Sardex to spend have more problems than those who don't! (E. 15)

Conclusions

The Sardex device is able to influence the beliefs of members through the following mechanisms: repeated observation and inference, information dissemination, analogy and categorisation. The beliefs concern the form of social relations in the economy: a high level of trust in relations is observed from the first transactions and the high level of reliability is soon generalised through inference and categorisation to all members of the Sardex network. The positive economic effects observed by entrepreneurs encourage them to assume, through the analogy mechanism, the operational model of the Sardex currency as an operational model for currencies in general. The entrepreneurs believe that Sardex has a positive influence on their living standards and that it supports the economy of small local businesses at the same time. Faced with the economic crisis, which then became a banking credit crisis, and faced with the competitive pressure of large companies, entrepreneurs see Sardex as an economic instrument that redistributes development opportunities from large to small businesses, as well as supporting local development. Increasing individual wellbeing by increasing the business of one's own company and increasing collective wellbeing by supporting the local economy are not seen as alternative options by Sardex entrepreneurs but rather as synergies: maintaining a high level of transactions in the network benefits individual businesses, but it also benefits the local economic system. The limited circulation of the Sardex currency is central to this mechanism because it legitimises the idea that money "stays here". Moreover, this limited use, which precludes payment of taxes, mortgages or utility bills, makes it easier to spend Sardex because, given the high level of transactions, entrepreneurs believe that Sardex will be re-cashed more readily than euros. When translated into consumption habits, these beliefs result in spending choices that provide a higher living standard: people buy more when they pay in Sardex or they allow themselves little luxuries that would be considered unaffordable in euros, even though goods and services have the same nominal value in euros and Sardex.

The Sardex operating model is also seen as a model for operating the euro currency; some entrepreneurs even see it as a tool capable of modifying how the ordinary economy functions. The widespread perception that the regulations guiding economic operations are stable and autonomous ("the markets"), or that they are the task of distant, independent authorities, has been countered by the Sardex currency experience, which has brought regulation of the economy back to a level closer to everyday life. The presence of the Sardex currency, which only exists in Sardinia, and which operates in the form of mutual credit between entrepreneurs, modifies members' perceptions of how the economic system operates. Entrepreneurs now feel it is concretely possible for them to influence how the regional economy operates and how interpersonal business relations are organised, see Fig. 4.10.

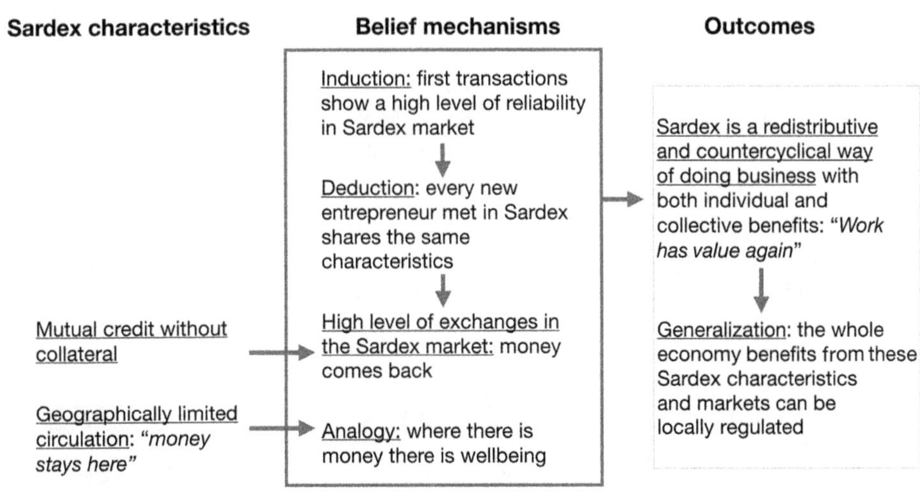

Fig. 4.10 Sardex belief mechanisms. (Source: own figure)

4.3.4 Collective Action

Collective Action Mechanisms

Collective action can be defined as a wide range of social dynamics that see individuals cooperating for a common goal. Unlike other forms of cooperation, collective action is oriented towards producing, regulating or requesting a collective good.[17] A collective good differs from other goods because it can only be produced or managed collectively, individuals cannot produce or manage it. Common goals can only be attained through coordination, in many possible forms, of several people. Social movement scholars traditionally associate the concept of collective action with extraordinary events (McAdam 1999 [1982]; della Porta and Diani 2006), such as revolutions or protests, but a broader interpretation also associates this concept with aspects of the ordinary functioning of society. Voluntary participation in the activities of political parties or social volunteering, for example, are not extraordinary events but they can be interpreted as a form of collective action, oriented towards producing collective goods. From an analytical point of view, even a musician playing in an orchestra or the act of signing a petition can be analysed as problems of organising collective action because both activities aim to produce a collective good that cannot be obtained individually (Baldassarri 2009, pp. 391–392). The analytical problem of explaining the social mechanisms that allow individual actions to be coordinated in view of a collective good, through collective action, involves explaining social behaviour which is partly indifferent to the objectives and forms of coordination of collective action that are being analysed. A revolutionary uprising or signing a petition can both be treated as problems of coordinating collective action, in view of a collective good, that require sociological explanation, although the explanations provided will necessarily be different. Finally, Ostrom (1990) extended the problem of collective action to the management of common-pool resources: assets, for the most part natural resources, whose use by one person necessarily reduces availability for others.

The explanation of the social phenomenon of collective action has been the subject of contention among different social science disciplines; within the disciplines there are different theoretical approaches as well. Rational choice theorists argue that collective action, like cooperation, can be explained as a function of individual interest: the decision to avoid free-rider behaviour is explained by the positive personal effects on an individual's reputation or personal identity (Elster 1989). The sociological tradition, however, has long preferred an interpretation of collective action based on the idea of "social norm" to which individuals feel attached and which guides their actions

[17]The definition of collective action is linked to different interpretations, often connected to specific research areas that use a particular concept. The following discussion refers mainly to the definition adopted in *The Oxford Handbook of Analytical Sociology* (Baldassarri 2009).

(Durkheim 1982 [1895]). The psychological approach tends to explain the predisposition of individuals towards collective action as an effect of their own psychological traits (Stroebe and Frey 1982). These different approaches are not easy to compare because they start from different theoretical assumptions about the causal links that explain social action: it is possible to obtain empirical confirmation using different approaches, but it is not possible to definitively confirm or exclude one or the other explanatory hypothesis. It is interesting to note how, in recent years, the experimental approaches used to study collective action are changing the scenario of traditional explanations of the phenomenon. The experimental context provides evidence of how collective action can be carried out, by individual interest, but also by people's attitude to *"reciprocity, cooperation, and punishment of defectors, as well as recognising the distinctive role of communication, face-to-face interaction, and personal relationships in fostering and maintaining cooperation"* (Baldassarri 2009, p. 392). Experimental research has shown that a substantial part of the population chooses to avoid free-riding even when they have no prior experience or incentive to do so. Even in the non-repeated version of the Public Good Games, where the rational strategy, from a utilitarian point of view, would be to not contribute to the collective good, individuals still contributed between 40 and 60% of their resources (Ostrom 2000, p. 140). Furthermore, the possibility of direct communication, the presence of incentives and the possibility of sanctions affect the amount contributed to the common good (ibid.). So neither the utilitarian model nor the presence of social norms fully explain, jointly or alone, the emergence of social action which requires *"the study of the contextual and institutional aspects that favour the emergence and maintenance of social norms [which become] central to the collective-action research agenda"* (Baldassarri 2009, p. 401; Ostrom 1990, 2000).

This experimental evidence does not resolve the dispute as to the ultimate nature of the collective action phenomena, but it does tend to shift the focus of research interest towards the contextual and institutional conditions which favour its emergence. In this context, the use of formal models for studying the individual utility trade-off between cooperative and free-rider behaviours does not lose heuristic validity (Olson 1965; Hardin 1982), but it can acquire new information by studying the contextual and institutional elements from which collective action emerges. For example the class *in sé* becomes a class *per sé* only when it enters a phase of self-representation shared with members of the class it is part of (Marx 1963 [1852]). The explanatory mechanism of collective action that Marx adopted is based on a mutual recognition that the working classes were exploited. In this perspective it could be said that without class awareness there is no possibility of collective action. But what factors encourage the emergence of a common sense of belonging to a social group with common goals? Scholars of social movements have focused attention on various factors: a functioning political system

(Marwell and Oliver 1993), the distribution of inequalities (Calhoun 2015), the role played by elites in mobilising the masses (Bearman 1993), the role of culture (McAdam et al. 1996), the role of technical devices (Marres 2016); the role of social networks (Gould 1993; 1995; Kim and Bearman 1997).

The contextual factors that favour the emergence of collective action, therefore, cannot be considered interstitial elements that deviate utilitarian action towards adherence to social norms, but they are the behaviours, defined as utilitarian or cooperative, that need to be analytically explained as a situational effect of social interaction and the elements that influence it.

> In this perspective, there is no need to assume norms or ideology (or some other metaphysical entity) as the driving force of people's commitment; the specific interest that becomes relevant to the individual and shared among group members is elicited through interaction and the experience of group affiliation (Baldassarri 2009, p. 402).

Past experiences and interaction contexts create the conditions for specific interests or objectives to emerge and to elicit a form of collective action to achieve them. The distribution of roles in the situation and the context of opportunities guide the action and can influence the system of beliefs and desires. Collective action can therefore be interpreted as the effect of this situational device that guides individual and collective action and makes the collective interest part of each actor's individual interest (Ibid., p. 412).

Collective Action in Sardex

Use of the Sardex device by entrepreneurs, creates reciprocal constraint towards both the member network and Sardex Ltd: this pushes members to become promoters of the Sardex project themselves (see Sub-sect. 4.1.3). Thanks to social mechanisms of belief formation, Sardex users develop specific beliefs regarding the role of Sardex currency in the economic system, comparing its operation and impact with that of the euro (see Sub-sect. 4.3.3). The Sardex currency is often used in contexts where traditional credit has disillusioned entrepreneurs:

> The banks have always given us a slap in the face. But now I say thank you, because I no longer trust the banks. I did well, because now what is mine, is mine, and nobody can touch my things. With the banks you never know where you are going to end up … We asked for a billion lire to build this shed. After a year they told us they weren't going to give us the money. Slowly, slowly, over time we managed to do it, by ourselves. With time we managed to do it. (E. 32).
>
> We don't use traditional credit. We didn't ask for it, we needed it in some periods, but I don't consider the banks to be trustworthy. Not because they might fail but because nowadays banks' intentions are not to help customers prosper, but to damage them. We have a traditional bank account, but I see that there is no interest in increasing a customer's wealth, but only to make sure the figures are correct and that everything is precise, and the right procedures adhered to. Today the situation does not allow companies to be in top form, I don't see the banks providing any assistance to companies, quite the opposite. Sardex, though, sustains companies by offering them credit lines (E. 31).

The banking system is (no longer) seen as supporting local economic development, but as a closed system, more interested in its own development than in sustaining business projects. The limited circulation of the Sardex currency affects perceptions regarding currency circulation and the economic effects thereof. Entrepreneurs interpret this limited circulation as the currency's explicit support for developing local businesses whose value is recognised:

> Sardex provides benefits for our territory because the money stays here, with salaries and taxes. The greater the number of Sardinian companies working, the greater the benefits for Sardinia (E. 19).
>
> From the socio-economical perspective it is very important that only Sardinian companies are members of the Sardex network and that we keep our money within the region. Without being aware of it, we make important economic choices when we do the shopping, from banal purchases to important acquisitions. Choosing to buy locally sourced products means helping your neighbours and ensuring money circulates in your area. When you buy something at the supermarket you are ensuring that money leaves the area, buying non-local goods means you impoverish your area. Post-war Italy was rebuilt thanks to money sent by Italians who had gone to work abroad. Their remittances made the Italian post-war economic boom possible. When money is subtracted from one community and transferred to another, the first community becomes poorer. When you buy from Amazon, you are mostly buying from shops that are far away and you are reducing the amount of money circulating in the area. With Sardex, though, you give that money the opportunity of circulating only in Sardinia. I used my Sardex to buy sheep wool as a thermal insulator for my new dental clinic. The seller will never be able to use that money to go and buy on Amazon, but he will go and buy other goods or services in Sardex. This money will circulate within Sardinia and will enrich the Sardinian social fabric. In 2015 there were 51 million Sardex in circulation: a significant figure for a poor region like Sardinia, where there are the poorest regions of Italy like Sulcis, where there is no industry, where politicians are determined to stop using coal, where they are spending huge amounts trying to prop up the chemicals industry, where they continue to waste money, where there is no future (E. 21).

Entrepreneurs still consider Sardex as primarily a tool for increasing their company's business but, once they use the Sardex currency, almost half the entrepreneurs interviewed, begin to associate it with ethical goals linked to the collective benefits they recognise as deriving from the Sardex project. Entrepreneurs use the Sardex currency to improve their business prospects, but also because they believe the Sardex benefits the collective more than the euro. Although it could well be true that increased circulation and use of the euro would result in collective economic benefits, entrepreneurs tend to associate the use of the euro with exclusively individual benefits (becoming wealthier), or onerous obligations such as paying bank interest and taxes.[18] The benefits attributed to

[18]In peripheral EU countries, the most recent tendency among the so-called "anti-system" political movements, when interpreting the effects of the euro currency, is to associate it with an instrument used by the central more powerful countries or by supranational financial institutions for controlling or even exploiting weaker countries.

the Sardex currency go beyond mere individual gain; they include the collective benefit which extends to the geographical boundaries defining the area where the currency can circulate. The Sardex, unlike the euro, is used because it is widely perceived to have collective goals.

Using the Sardex currency stimulates a new sense of belonging that unites traditionally separate aspects: regional identity, and the sense of belonging this generates, are heightened by the functioning of the Sardex economic system. The Sardex can only be used by companies with headquarters in the region, and this generates a feeling of belonging and identity among network members that is totally absent from traditional economic instruments. The euro has negative connotations because it does not remain within the region but sustains investment elsewhere:

> It is not a problem when some money moves, but it is a problem when it all moves. The banks here do not invest but just collect savings and only invest a part of these in the local territory. This does not help local businesses, but if I leave the money locally that does help local businesses (E. 34).

It must be remembered that the development of global trade and financial markets has damaged peripheral economies like Sardinia's: this negative experience has influenced perceptions of the workings of the financial system. Compared to the wealthy regions of Northern Italy, Sardinia is chronically under-developed and traditional economic policies, advocating opening up to external competition, do not seem to have borne fruit. The Sardex offers a new way of belonging with which entrepreneurs can identify and which links using Sardex to the socio-economic well-being of their region:

> Friendships can develop in commercial relationships outside Sardex as well, but it is the concept of Sardex that goes beyond making money. Sardex will always circulate in Sardinia and the profits will remain here for ever. Without financial resources the local economy will not develop. Those who think of their children are pleased their region benefits from the network. Those who join the network and understand it realise its value for our region (E. 2).

The Sardex device creates opportunities because business activity is not seen as being entirely guided by entrepreneurs' individual interests but is also perceived as being guided by the collective interest. The currency's *modus operandi* allows entrepreneurs to address ethical issues, traditionally confined to non-economic, philanthropic issues through their normal business activity:

> In Sardex it's different, I don't know why, but an atmosphere of trust and collaboration is created. It is as if there were a common mission which does not exist in any other type of commercial activity. This common mission is developing our region through the participation of its residents: I know that what I spend here in Sardinia will remain in Sardinia (E. 34).

Doing business in Sardex becomes a way for entrepreneurs to contribute to a collective interest related to the socio-economic development of their region.

The idea that the Sardex currency contributes to local development is deeply rooted in almost half the respondents. Some have identified with this ideal to the point of imagining possible developments of this virtuous link between currency and local development: For example, many entrepreneurs would like to be able to pay their local taxes in Sardex.

> It would be useful if the opportunities for spending Sardex were expanded, for example if the State could accept Sardex for tax payments or if they could be used for buying on a national network outside the region. How useful Sardex is today depends on the type of business and its market. Companies which buy and sell in Sardinia benefit greatly but companies that have to buy outside the region, but sell here, may experience difficulties because they may have to limit their sales in Sardex, because it is hard to spend them as they cannot be used to pay their suppliers of raw materials (E. 24).

The synergic link between currency circulation and local development is seen as an effective policy instrument that should also be supported by municipal administrations. One of the responsibilities of these administrations is to create the conditions for socio-economic development and, in the entrepreneurs' eyes, the Sardex project seems an innovative and very effective way of reaching these goals:

> If the Region or the Municipal Government allowed us to pay our taxes in Sardex, it would be a great help, and it would advantage local businesses. If we could at least pay our local taxes in Sardex, then employees would be encouraged to use Sardex also (E. 23).

Paying local taxes in Sardex would also increase opportunities for spending Sardex and, according to the entrepreneurs, this would make it easier for employees to accept part of their salaries being paid in Sardex.

For entrepreneurs with raw material suppliers in Sardinia (mostly the food and wine sector), using the Sardex currency also signifies changing the traditional production chain. As the Sect. 4.3.2 Desires highlighted, using the Sardex device in these cases offers the opportunity and the requirement to use small local producers as suppliers. This selection of a production chain which favours small local businesses at the expense of larger companies is perceived as a further effect of the Sardex currency which helps support the regional economy. In these cases, it is not just the limited circulation of the Sardex currency that supports the regional economy, but also the limitation of network membership to companies based in Sardinia, most of which conduct nearly all their business within the region.

> Reasoning in euros is mostly a reasoning of convenience, while the reasoning in Sardex is a project which grows together with the community. In our sector there are small food-producing companies with quality products which promote their territory. By choosing to buy the products of these companies, we complete the production chain, from the producer to the customer, describing that land, that product, that company, promoting them together with our region (E. 22).

Entrepreneurial activity and collective action are forms of social action that are traditionally kept separate. With the birth of the euro and the end of national currencies, the separation of currency regulation from political control is generally perceived to have increased: political regulation has, for the most part, maintained national boundaries but monetary policy has been delegated to the Central European Bank. The central bank, commercial banks and entrepreneurs are usually considered the central elements of an economic system which tries to avoid political constraints and objectives in order to operate effectively. The collective benefits expected as a consequence of market efficiency are not a form of politically controlled social regulation, but are considered to be secondary effects of entrepreneurs pursuing individual profit. Some entrepreneurs involved in Sardex currency operations, however, consider that using the Sardex currency to pursue their individual profits brings collective benefits to their region. In other words, it can be argued that entrepreneurs associate company business conducted in Sardex as an economic activity with "values" that traditionally are extraneous to company's economic activities:

> This happens because in Sardex there is a return to barter, economists describe [Sardex] as a clearing house, but it is nothing more than barter with values that some people choose to call compensatory credit. I give you ten chickens for a piece of gold (E. 7).
>
> The product my restaurant offers works really well with Sardex because it is a new way of understanding the world and managing money. It is an ethically correct world. Just look - Sardex invests in marketing and the workforce, not in multinationals. They are not speculative investments that only benefit a few people, Sardex by its nature benefits everyone (E. 20).

This conviction that using the Sardex currency brings collective benefits can result in entrepreneurs enthusiastically supporting the Sardex project. Some entrepreneurs become promoters of the Sardex currency among their contacts even when they will obtain no direct economic advantage. When an entrepreneur joins the membership network other members often expect that he/she will provide economic opportunities for trading their goods and services. If the new company membership of the Sardex network is not expected to create opportunities for trade (i.e. because its belong to a different economic sector), the promotional activity engaged in by members toward the new entry is more similar to a form of proselytism or propaganda, close to the activism of political party volunteers:

> I talk in my shop with Sardex customers, I explain how it works and, when they tell me they would like to join, I call the brokers and tell them to visit them. For example, there is a really nice toy shop, I talked to [the owner] for a year to persuade him to join and now he is really happy. Now he complains that he would have liked to join the network earlier. I always advise trying it for a year, if you realise that it doesn't work for you, then don't renew your membership. But they have all remained, even the creche. Our creche and kindergarten are both in Sardex (E. 18).

Entrepreneur No.18 has become a real promoter of the Sardex network in his neighbourhood. Neither his family or his business use the kindergarten or the toy shop, but he encouraged them both, together with other companies, to join the network. Entrepreneur No.18 is not motivated by personal gain (the membership of these companies has not provided him with any noticeable economic returns) but by personal conviction. This entrepreneur believes that developing the Sardex network is intrinsically positive, benefitting both himself and the entire collectivity, even when there is no direct economic gain. In the eyes of entrepreneurs such as these, the regional economic system becomes a real collective good to which they believe they should dedicate time and energy:

> I use the broker service for finding companies and for proposing companies for network membership. This happens naturally, no money is exchanged for this – it is all done because we believe in the project and we want it to grow (E. 22).
>
> I became a promoter of Sardex myself. If there is a chance to talk about it with someone, I always ask why they are not members. I spoke for a whole year with the restaurant next door to get him to join and we finally managed to overcome his doubts (E. 30).

For almost half of those interviewed, the economic system activated by the Sardex currency acquires characteristics that make it possible to consider it a collective asset. Within the network there are also occasions, though far more sporadic, in which using the Sardex device generates the development of pro-social behaviours that go beyond the boundaries of the economic system. These occasions are sporadic in comparison with the ordinariness of members perceiving the collective value of the Sardex network: they represent episodes which only some entrepreneurs know about. These episodes are often related to natural disasters where members found the Sardex network proved to be a valid tool for solidarity:

> A few years ago, there was a flood in Olbia and entrepreneurs spontaneously suggested donating [Sardex] credits to help the flood victims and we collected the credits. There was a similar dynamic for the earthquake in the Marches where donations were received from other networks as well. That time we were better organised, and we suggested that members buy a Christmas basket filled with products of companies that suffered damage in the earthquake (F. 2).
>
> We organised an oral-hygiene evening for our Sardex patients where all the proceeds of the evening were destined to people affected by the earthquake. We did it for our Sardex customers because it was a rapid way of conveying information and also because Sardex was already organising a fund raising. We had an evening where the surgery had no bookings and with Sardex it was possible to immediately spread the word. If we had put the notice on Facebook for our normal patients, probably none of them would have read it, but instead we spoke to the brokers and then we posted the information on the Sardex Facebook page which members follow (E. 21).

A special case concerns how the presence of the Sardex currency made it possible to develop local voluntary work in a small village in Sardinia:

> I am a member of the Festivities for Patron Saints Committee in our village and I got the committee to join the Sardex network. We accept Sardex sponsorship and we buy equipment for shows in Sardex. For example, Sardex credits are used to buy the children's show from agencies that organise children's entertainment in Sardex. If I go and ask a company for one hundred euros sponsorship, they don't give it to me but, if I ask for one hundred Sardex, they do give it to me. I don't know why, but this is what happens. But it is also the same for me: if I have to make a donation of one hundred Sardex, I do it. We counted the committee's funds yesterday and we noticed that we had acquired 27 Sardex sponsors which corresponds to € 2,700.00. We also collected € 25,000.00, but we wouldn't have been given those 2,700 Sardex in euro. So, a thousand Sardex will be used to pay for the children's entertainment, other Sardex will buy sausages for the rolls, other provisions, the gas for the cook tops, etc. (E. 18).

This case confirms the greater "ease" of spending Sardex which also applies to donations for voluntary activities.

The manager of a medium-sized company considers the Sardex currency operating system to be an ethical model for the functioning of economic relations. His plan is to pay part of his employee's salaries in Sardex, but he would like to do this in such a way as to not create economic difficulties for their families. For this entrepreneur his employee's use of Sardex should follow the principles of mutual aid that are the basis of Sardex credit:

> We have now understood its potential and we are planning to build a photovoltaic system that is worth more than € 500,000.00 and we will pay 50% of the cost in Sardex credit. Also for a new building for our company, worth € 200.000, we were allowed to pay € 95,000.00 of this sum in Sardex. The reasons for solidarity are still important today, moral and ethical values are still important [with reference to the moment of the entry of the company in the network, when they were the only reasons for entry, A/N]. The economic component has now expanded enormously, economic interest in the network has also greatly increased. Now that the network is expanding to embrace customers, I have the opportunity to pay part of my employees' salaries in Sardex. We, the owners, started paying ourselves small sums in Sardex and then we suggested to our dependants that they too, could be paid small amounts in Sardex. The idea is that together we would assess how much of their monthly expenses could be sustained in Sardex without creating difficulties for their families. This line of reasoning mirrors the network's solidarity: the network was not set up to create difficulties for companies so, it must not create difficulties for company employees who decide to be paid also in Sardex. I don't think we will go over 10% of their salaries to be paid in Sardex. I want the vision the company has of Sardex to be coherent with our employes' vision of Sardex, I want us to share the same spirit (E. 37).

Conclusions

The Sardex device is able to develop new forms of collective action among entrepreneur members which work towards the region's socio-economic development. The change in beliefs regarding how the economic system functions gives rise to an unusual interpretation of the link between economic activity and collective well-being. The traditional economic interpretation considers any collective benefits of the economic system to be secondary effects that depend on entrepreneurs pursuing their individual profits, but entrepreneurs who are Sardex members begin to associate the economic operations and their own entrepreneurial activity with the positive effects that they bring to collective wellbeing. Entrepreneurs associate their Sardex transactions with positive, collective socio-economic effects, but do not view business transactions in euro in the same light. Entrepreneurs' primary goal of improving their companies' business is associated with the belief that business done in Sardex also leads to collective benefits. The Sardex only circulates in Sardinia and this encourages members in their conviction that its circulation helps sustain the local economy. With this in mind, half of those interviewed, declared that they use the Sardex currency, not just to improve their company's business, but also to contribute to the socio-economic development of their region. At a time when the regulation of currency circulation is commonly perceived as something that no-one can change, the Sardex currency reactivates, in the eyes of entrepreneurs, the link between currency and the possibility of intervening in economic dynamics. Entrepreneurs consider the circulation of the Sardex currency to be an effective instrument for economic development that creates collective benefits.

The traditional distinctions between individual utility and collective well-being are redefined by the use of the Sardex currency, so that business transactions within the Sardex network are an instrument for increasing company business, but are also a form of collective action for promoting a common good, identified as the region's socio-economic development. This form of collective action is normally put into practice by using the network to carry out economic transactions that include business motivations, but also the collective purposes described, while some entrepreneurs actively promote network expansion with their acquaintances without having any direct economic return (see Fig. 4.11). The Sardex network is also used occasionally for philanthropic activities and as a tool to support voluntary work.

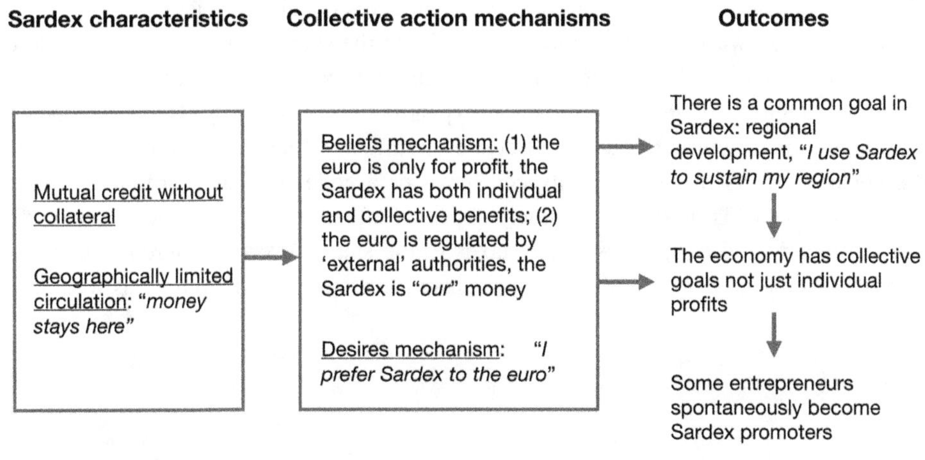

Fig. 4.11 Sardex collective action mechanisms. (Source: own figure)

4.3.5 Conclusions: Solidarity in Sardex

Recent approaches to the study of the genesis of collective action have shown that it is difficult to provide a stable, unambiguous explanation with reference to a single generative mechanism. Behaviour oriented towards solidarity norms emerges in experimental contexts, even when no utility is expected and, in parallel, the joint presence of norms and incentives is not the only factor sustaining solidaristic behaviours. Other factors which can play a very important role in promoting solidarity include the context of opportunities, opportunities for direct interaction, and the belief system regarding causal links among social phenomena.

In the Sardex case, a system of social relations based on a high level of cooperation, together with the limited circulation and use of the currency, seem to be the elements which determine the emergence of solidarity-based behaviours, identifiable in the forms of collective action described in the previous sections. The context of opportunity directs preferences towards companies based in Sardinia. This limitation of the Sardex currency is interpreted by entrepreneurs as a solidaristic choice that offers a competitive advantage to Sardinian companies at the expense of larger companies with headquarters outside Sardinia. In fact, for almost half the interviewees, the use of the Sardex currency is motivated by ethical reasons (the network benefits the entire community) as well as expectations of economic utility. The Sardex can only circulate in Sardinia and this makes it possible for members to adopt an idea of this currency as being less abstract, and more embedded in the region, than the euro. The Sardex costs less than the euro and, in the eyes of the entrepreneurs, this confirms that the Sardex is a tool for sustaining local development. Access to "ordinary money" is very expensive or impossible for many entrepreneurs, while access to the Sardex currency is seen to be inexpensive and Sardex Ltd also provides entrepreneurs with free marketing opportunities and other opportunities for increasing customer numbers.[19]

The participating entrepreneurs thus find themselves readily associating the use of the Sardex currency with collective purposes involving the socio-economic development of the region. Using Sardex thus becomes a way of contributing to the community, identified within regional boundaries, as well as expanding one's company. The Sardex device as a whole allows entrepreneurs to associate the effects of their economic activity with the positive effects that this activity can have for a collective (the Sardinians). When "ordinary money" is used the commonly expected effects relate to business benefits for one's company and obligations to pay taxes to the state. Diversely, entrepreneurs consider that using the Sardex currency has positive effects on the community as well as on

[19]For the effects on innovation see Sub-sect. 5.1.3 Competition, cooperation and innovation.

their own businesses. This step allows the establishment of a collective that focuses on a common goal that can be summarised as the socio-economic development of the region. Within this type of social-action orientation there are also many members who spontaneously became real promoters of Sardex network membership among their acquaintances. The identification of a collective value in the Sardex network pushes some members to recommend membership to some of their social circle even when there is no chance of them benefitting from economic transactions because the companies involved belong to different production chains.

In the Sardex network there are forms of group solidarity, where members help each other, as well as more general forms of solidarity that guide social action in favour of a collective defined by the region of Sardinia. In the case of solidarity among members, the reasons for the action can be attributed to an expected individual utility resulting from the repeated interactions among members and the existing reputational system, but in the event that the action is oriented towards regional solidarity, the possibilities for direct individual benefits are very low and spread out over time. This form of social action is more comparable to a value-oriented form of action than the more common instrumental action with which economic activity is traditionally interpreted.[20]

Among the members of Sardex, further forms of solidarity, of a more occasional nature, can also be detected. The Sardex network has, in fact, been used for fundraising following natural disasters in other Italian regions. The "ease" of spending, used to characterise the Sardex currency, has also supported fundraising for local volunteering initiatives, funds that would probably not have been donated in euros.

In conclusion, it can be noted that the solidarity observable in the Sardex network is not the effect of particular individual characteristics or of functional requirements of the social system, as traditional interpretations of this form of social bonding postulate, but rather, it is the effect of contextual factors - in particular the functioning characteristics of the currency - that guide social interaction so that, at the aggregate level, social phenomena that can be defined as "solidarity" can be observed.

[20]The presence of hybrid forms of social action harks back to one of the classic debates in the social sciences. Among the various assumptions that led to disciplinary differentiation in the social sciences, the concept of economic action played an important role in developing different research methods and explanatory models for understanding social phenomena. Neoclassical economists explain individual social action as being constantly guided towards maximising individual utility, while for the sociologists *"actions oriented towards finding a means of subsistence are not necessarily characterised by a rational allocation of scarce resources"* (Trigilia 2002, p. 18). To explain economic action, one needs to consider *"actions oriented towards different non-utilitarian goals (ibid.), as human beings are "driven by conflicting, antithetical impulses which we "understand" as a whole"* (Weber 1922; cit. Trigilia 2002, p. 20).

4.4 The Generative Mechanisms of the Social and Economic Effects of Sardex

Sardex device functioning is a complex bond which combines the characteristics of the Sardex currency with the regulation of the operations carried out by Sardex Ltd and with activated social mechanisms. The combination and interaction of these elements create specific social effects that have been summarised as effects on trust, cooperation and solidarity. The conceptual map "Sardex generative mechanisms" (Fig. 4.12) summarises the elements considered, dividing them into three categories: the characteristics of the Sardex complementary currency, the adjustments Sardex Ltd makes to the membership network, and the social effects. Within these three categories, the collocation of the social mechanisms described in the previous sections can also be identified. The arrows indicate the explanatory relationships that link the characteristics of the currency and its adjustment by Sardex Ltd to the observed social effects.

The social mechanisms are present individually in the three categories of elements described and they explain how the action is carried out by one of the elements considered in the following direction. In general terms, the explanatory relations between the elements considered (see arrows in Fig. 4.12) can be interpreted as "possibility conditions" within which the action takes place. However, an analysis of the social mechanisms allows greater analytical precision in describing which characteristics of the elements considered are significant and which effects they produce in the situation in

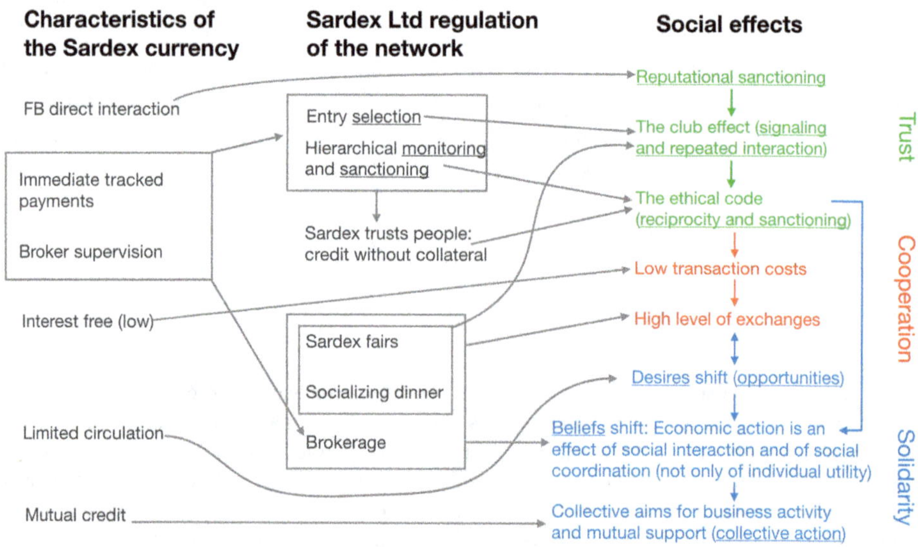

Fig. 4.12 Sardex generative mechanisms (the underlined words indicate social mechanisms). (Source: own figure)

relation to the other elements. In this perspective, the explanatory relationship between the elements described can be considered as an explanation of the observed social phenomena because it allows to identify the characteristics of the single elements that generate these observed social phenomena.

It is extremely important for creating trust that all transactions in Sardex are traced and monitored by the Sardex broker team. These monitoring activities make it possible to select those applying for membership of the Sardex network and to monitor the progress of each individual member company's transactions. Selection and hierarchical monitoring are fundamental for activating signalling and reciprocity mechanisms. Selective entry to the Sardex network makes it possible to recognise a common sense of belonging, through signalling, considered an indicator that the interlocutor is extremely reliable. Joining the Sardex network requires a high level of cognitive investment because entrepreneurs have to change their habits and seek out new suppliers; joining the network is also an economic investment because an annual membership fee has to be paid to Sardex Ltd. Sardex Ltd selects members on the basis of their expected ability to exchange goods and services within the Sardex network. Every company applying to become a member of the Sardex network has to compile a "buying list" and a "selling list" which list everything the company has bought or sold in the last year. The lists are then assessed by the Sardex brokers who verify whether the company will be able to trade with other network members, and whether there is a risk of creating a surplus or scarcity of certain goods or services within the network. This selection process is only possible because the Sardex IT platform tracks all transactions carried out in the network and observes them in aggregate form.

The nature of Sardex money is that of mutual credit between entrepreneurs. The operation of the currency can in fact be linked to that of a multilateral barter system and the role of Sardex Ltd to that of an exchange clearing house. The mutual credit characteristic of the Sardex currency means the Sardex Ltd manager has no need to buy money from the central bank to provide credit, unlike the traditional banks. Sardex Ltd provides credit to entrepreneurs on the basis of a process of creating money that is independent of the creation of money by the central bank. In fact, the credit granted to entrepreneurs is based on an estimate of their ability to carry out economic transactions within the network. The "buying" and "selling" lists, are evaluated to ensure they are complementary to supply and demand in the network. This complementarity of company business with the supply and demand for goods within the Sardex network is the best guarantee that the credit granted to a company will be repaid through the sale of goods and services to other members.

Sardex Ltd, therefore, unlike ordinary banks, can provide credit to its members without requesting collateral to guarantee the credit. Sardex members have the perception that Sardex lends them money on the strength of a handshake; this is far removed from the experience that most entrepreneurs have with banks. Many Sardex entrepreneurs who have no access to bank credit can relatively easily access Sardex credit. These entrepreneurs perceive Sardex credit as an important investment of confidence in them and their businesses; this trust generates a strong desire to reciprocate which takes the form of fostering the optimal functioning of the Sardex network.

Signalling and repeated interaction among members in turn creates a strong bond of reciprocity in transactions. Members can report any misconduct of other members directly to Sardex Ltd or bring it to other members' attention on the Sardex Facebook page. This makes members feel "protected" against fraud and misconduct within the Sardex network. When transacting in the euro market, though, entrepreneurs usually request more guarantees, especially when it is the first transaction with a company. The potential for horizontal monitoring within the Sardex network means that members consider other Sardex entrepreneurs reliable from the first time they meet them. The correct behaviour that members experience in relations within the network is described by the members themselves as an "code of ethics" which regulates behaviour within the Sardex network. The presence of a code of ethics in transactions, combined with the low cost of providing Sardex credit, makes economic transactions within the network extremely easy compared to similar transactions in euro currency. Compared to the high costs of bank credit, the only cost associated with Sardex credit is the annual membership fee which not only provides access to credit but also allows members to use all the services provided by Sardex Ltd, available on the on-line platform or, in the case of the Sardex brokers, via telephone.

The constant brokering activity of the Sardex brokers fosters transactions among members: brokers carry out the functions of a buying and selling office for members, free of charge. Entrepreneurs have recounted that even on the day they joined the Sardex network, their area broker called them to suggest possible transactions or other members called spontaneously. Entrepreneurs are very surprised when they discover that, in the Sardex network, customers often call the company, a marked difference from the euro market where acquiring a new customer requires considerable time and company resources. Organising social dinners or small trade fairs further foster face-to-face encounters among Sardex entrepreneurs, as well as providing an opportunity for economic transactions. The presence of an ethical code of conduct, the low cost of Sardex credit and the brokering activity, all foster a high level of cooperation among member entrepreneurs and, as a consequence, a large number of economic transactions.

Another important feature of the Sardex currency is that it only circulates in Sardinia and within the Sardex membership network. These limits modify the traditional use of money, precluding some opportunities but also creating new ones. The Sardex currency does not generate positive or negative interest rates, but positive credits only last for a year, before they disappear, and unpaid debts must be repaid in euro after a year. This means it makes little sense to accumulate Sardex money, the best strategy is to spend Sardex money quickly and stay at the highest debt level allowed by your account. The high level of cooperation among members and the convenience of spending Sardex money quickly have changed company spending patterns and the personal consumption of entrepreneurs and their families. Entrepreneurs spend their Sardex more readily and with less concern than their euros: they know they can only use euros, not Sardex, to pay taxes, utility bills or supplies of materials procured outside Sardinia. Limited use and ease of spending of the Sardex put entrepreneurs in a position to spend their Sardex to invest in their company, investments that would be frequently put off if they were paid for in euros, and for personal consumption that would not be considered sustainable in euros. When entrepreneurs pay in Sardex they usually spend more and they allow themselves little luxuries they would otherwise avoid.

Changes to their consumption patterns, and to the way business is conducted, cause entrepreneurs to perceive Sardex market operations differently to those conducted in the euro market. Transactions are smoother, other members behave correctly and the Sardex spent return rapidly to the till: these factors are a decisive improvement for entrepreneurs compared to operations carried out in the euro market. The entrepreneurs are able to observe operations in two different markets (the euro market and the Sardex market) and this allows them to assess the effects of the two different *modus operandi*. Many entrepreneurs prefer operations in the Sardex network. Although the transactions conducted in Sardex necessarily remain a minor, complementary part of company business, the Sardex network is increasingly preferred by entrepreneurs because they believe that: (i) the economic system works better because the Sardex is “easy” to spend; (ii) the limited circulation of the Sardex leads to collective benefits for Sardinia–Sardex cannot be spent or invested outside Sardinia so every Sardex spent will necessarily continue to circulate among Sardex companies. The limited circulation of the Sardex is interpreted by member entrepreneurs as a choice that has had the effect of fostering the Sardinian region’s socio-economic development.

The effect that entrepreneurs expect from using Sardex, combine an economic utility for their company and collective benefits for Sardinian region. Half the entrepreneurs interviewed were of the opinion that individual and collective interests are combined when Sardex is used. These entrepreneurs continue to use Sardex because they believe it benefits their company economically, as well as providing the collective benefit of fostering regional socio-economic development. In fact these two factors—the beliefs matured regarding the positive effects of limiting Sardex circulation to the region and the economic benefits Sardex provides for their company—foster the use of the Sardex in function of a collective good that can be identified in the socio-economic development of their own region.

A particular feature of this form of solidarity is linked to its origin within the economic system. Traditionally the functioning of the economic system was thought to be based on the idea that entrepreneurs only seek ever greater profits for their businesses. The Sardex experience, though, has shown that entrepreneurs, in addition to seeking economic benefits for their companies, are starting to perceive and pursue a collective benefit within their own business activity.

References

Akerlof, G. A. (1970). The market for 'Lemons': Quality uncertainty and the market mechanism. *Quarterly Journal of Economics, 84,* 488–500.

Alexander, J. C. (2006). *The civil sphere*. New York, NY: Oxford University Press.

Arendt, H. (1973). *The origins of totalitarianism*. Orlando, FL: Harcourt.

Arrow, K. J. (1971). The theory of risk aversion. In Y. J. S. Helsinki (Ed.), *Aspects of the theory of risk bearing* (pp. 90–109). Chicago: Markham Publishing Company. Reprinted in Essays in the Theory of Risk Bearing.

Arrow, K. J. (1974). *The limits of organization*. New York, NY: Norton.

Axelrod, R. (1984). An evolutionary approach to norms. *American Political Science Review, 80,* 1095–1111.

Bacharach, M., & Gambetta, D. (2001). Trust in signs. In Karen S. Cook (Ed.), *Trust in society* (pp. 148–184). New York, NY: Russel Sage.

Baldassarri, D. (2009). Collective action. In P. Bearman & P. Hedström (Eds.), *Oxford Handbook of Analytical Sociology*. Oxford: Oxford University Press.

Baldassarri, D. (2015). Cooperative networks: Altruism, group solidarity, reciprocity, and sanctioning in Uganda producer organizations. *American Journal of Sociology, 121*(2), 355–395.

Baldassarri, D., & Grossman, G. (2011). Centralized sanctioning and legitimate authority promote cooperation in humans. *Proceedings of the National Academy of Sciences, 108*(27), 11023–11027.

Baldassarri, D., & Grossman, G. (2013). The effect of group attachment and social position on prosocial behavior: Evidence from Lab-in-the-Field experiments. *PLoS ONE, 8*(3), e58750.

Banca d'Italia. (2018). *Economie regionali. L'economia delle regioni italiane nel 2017.*

Bearman, P. (1993). *Relations into Rhetorics: Local Elite Social Structure in Norfolk, England: 1540–1640*. New Brunswick, NJ: Rutgers University Press.

Beckert, J. (2005). *Trust and the performative construction of markets*. Cologne: Max Planck Institute for the Study of Societies. MPIfG Discussion Paper 05/8.

Beckert, J. (2009). The social order of markets. *Theory and Society, 38*(3), 245–269.

Beckert, J. (2016). *Imagined futures*. Cambridge, MA: Harvard University Press.

Berg, J., Dickhaut, J., & McCabe, K. A. (1995). Trust, reciprocity, and social history. *Games and Economic Behavior, 10,* 290–307.

Berg, J., Dickhaut, J., & McCabe, K. A. (2005). Risk Preference Instability Across Institutions: A Dilemma. In *Proceedings of the National Academy of Sciences*, 102: 4209–14.

Bohnet, I., & Frey, B. S. (1999a). The sound of silence in prisoner's dilemma and dictator games. *Journal of Economic Behavior & Organization, 38,* 43–57.

Bohnet, I., & Frey, B. S. (1999b). Social distance and other-regarding behavior in dictator games: Comment. *American Economic Review, 89,* 335–40.

Bowles, S., & Gintis, H. (2011). *A cooperative species: Human reciprocity and its evolution*. Princeton, NJ: Princeton University Press.

Burt, R., & Knez, M. (1995). Kinds of third-party effects on trust. *Rationality and Society, 7*(3), 255–92.

Buskens, V., & Raub, W. (2002). Embedded trust: Control and learning. In S. R. Thye & E. Lawler (Eds.), *Advances in group processes, 13,* 167–202. Oxford: Elsevier Science.

Calhoun, C. (2015). *Democratizing inequalities: Dilemmas of the new public participation*. New York, NY: New York University Press.

Camerer, C., & Fehr, E. (2004). Measuring social norms and preferences using experimental games: A guide for social scientists. In J. Henrich, R. Boyd, S. Bowles, C. Camerer, E. Fehr, & H. Gintis (Eds.), *Foundations of human sociality: Economic experiments and ethnographic evidence from fifteen small-scale societies* (pp. 55–96). New York, NY: Oxford University Press.

Chwe, M. S. (2001). *Rational ritual: Culture, coordination, and common knowledge*. Princeton, NJ: Princeton University Press.

Clarke, A. E., Friese, C., & Washburn, R. (2016). *Situational analysis in practice: Mapping research with grounded theory*. London: Routledge.

Coleman, J. S. (1989). Rationality and society. *Rationality and Society, 1,* 5–9.

Coleman, J. S. (1990). *Foundations of social theory*. Cambridge: Belknap Press.

Cook, K. (Ed.). (2001). *Trust in society*. New York, NY: Russell Sage Foundation.

Cook, K., & Gerbasi, A. (2009). Trust: Explanations of social action and implications for social structure. In P. Bearman & P. Hedström (Eds.), *The Oxford Handbook of Analytical Sociology*. Oxford: Oxford University Press.

Cook, K. S., Hardin, R., & Levi, M. (2005). *Cooperation without trust*. New York, NY: Russell Sage.

Dahrendorf, R. (1959). *Class and class conflict in industrial society*. Stanford, CA: Stanford University Press.

Dasgupta, P. (1988). Trust as a commodity. In Diego Gambetta (Ed.), *Trust. Making and breaking cooperative relations* (pp. 49–72). New York: Blackwell.

Della Porta, D., & Diani, M. (2006). *Social movements: An introduction*. Malden, MA: Blackwell.

Dennett, D. C. (1987). *The intentional stance*. Cambridge, MA: MIT Press.

Dini, P. & Kioupkiolis, A. (2014). *Community currencies as laboratories of institutional learning: emergence of governance through the mediation of social value*. In: Inaugural WINIR Conference, London, UK. http://eprints.lse.ac.uk/59307/. Accessed: 1 March 2020.

Dirks, K. T., & Ferrin, D. L. (2001). The role of trust in organizational settings. *Organization Science, 12,* 450–67.

Durkheim, É. (1982). *The rules of sociological method*. London: Palgrave. (First Publication 1895).

Durkheim, É. (1984). *The division of labor in society*. New York, NY: Free Press. (First Publication 1893).

Elias, N. (2000). *The civilizing process: Sociogenetic and psychogenetic investigations*. Malden, MA: Wiley-Blackwell. (First Publication 1939)

Elster, J. (1979). *Ulysses and the Sirens*. Cambridge: Cambridge University Press.

Elster, J. (1983). *Explaining technical change: A case study in the philosophy of science*. Cambridge: Cambridge University Press.

Elster, J. (1984). *Sour grapes*. Cambridge: Cambridge University Press.

Elster, J. (1989). *The cement of society*. Cambridge: Cambridge University Press.

Erikson, E., & Parent, J. M. (2007). Central authority and order. *Sociological Theory, 25,* 245–267.

Fehr, E., & Gachter, S. (2000). Fairness and retaliation: The economics of reciprocity. *Journal of Economic Perspectives, 14,* 159–81.

Fehr, E., & Gachter, S. (2002). Altruistic punishment in humans. *Nature, 415,* 137–40.

Fehr, E., & Gintis, H. (2007). Human motivation and social cooperation: Experimental and analytical foundations. *Annual Review of Sociology, 33,* 43–64.

Fehr, E., & Schmidt, K. M. (1999). A theory of fairness, competition, and cooperation. *Quarterly Journal of Economics, 114,* 817–68.

Fehr, E., Gachter, S., & Kirchsteiger, G. (1997). Reciprocity as a contract enforcement device: Experimental evidence. *Econometrica, 64,* 833–60.

Felin, T., & Foss, N. J. (2009). Social reality, the boundaries of self-fulfilling prophecy, and economics. *Organization Science, 20*(3), 654–668.

Fishburn, P. C. (1970). *Utility theory for decision making*. Huntington: Robert E. Krieger.

Freese, J. (2009). Preferences. In P. Bearman & P. Hedström (Eds.), *The Oxford Handbook of Analytical Sociology*. Oxford: Oxford University Press.

Freese, J., & Montgomery, J. D. (2007). The devil made her do it? Evaluating risk preference as an explanation of sex differences in religiousness. In S. J. Correll (Ed.), *Advances in group processes: The social psychology of gender* (pp. 187–230). Oxford: Elsevier.

Fukuyama, F. (1995). *Trust: The social virtues and the creation of prosperity*. New York, NY: Simon & Schuster.
Gambetta, D. (1988). *Trust: Making and breaking cooperative relations*. Oxford: Blackwell.
Gibbons, R. (2001). Trust in social structures: Hobbes and coase meet repeated games. In K. Cook (Ed.), *Trust in society* (pp. 332–353). New York, NY: Russell Sage Foundation.
Gintis, H. (2000). *Game theory evolving*. Princeton, NJ: Princeton University Press.
Goette, L., Huffman, D., Meier, S., & Sutter, M. (2010). *Group membership, competition, and altruistic versus antisocial punishment: Evidence from randomly assigned army groups*. Bonn: Institute for the Study of Labor. *IZA discussion paper* no. 5189.
Goffman, E. (1969). *Strategic Interaction*. Philadelphia, PA: University of Pennsylvania Press.
Gould, R. (1993). Collective action and network structure. *American Sociological Review, 58*, 182–96.
Gould, R. (1995). *Insurgent Identities: Class, Community, and Protest in Paris from 1948 to the Commune*. Chicago, IL: University of Chicago Press.
Gouldner, A. W. (1960). The norm of reciprocity: A preliminary statement. *American Sociological Review, 25*, 161–178.
Granovetter, M. (1985). Economic action and social structure: The problem of embeddedness. *American Journal of Sociology, 91*(3), 481–510.
Greig, F., & Bohnet, I. (2008). Is there reciprocity in a reciprocal-exchange economy? Evidence of gendered norms from a slum in Nairobi, Kenya. *Economic Inquiry, 46*(1), 77–83.
Hardin, R. (1982), *Collective action*. Baltimore, MD: Johns Hopkins University Press.
Hardin, R. (2004). *Trust and trustworthiness*. New York, NY: Russell Sage Foundation.
Hedström, P. (2005). *Dissecting the social: On the principles of analytical sociology*. Cambridge, MA: Cambridge University Press.
Hirschman, A. O. (1970). *Exit, voice, and loyalty: Responses to decline in firms, organizations, and states*. Cambridge, MA: Harvard University Press.
Hobbes, T. (2010). *Leviathan: Or the Matter, forme, and power of a common-wealth ecclesiasticall and civill*, Ed. by Ian Shapiro. New Haven, CT: Yale University Press. (First Publication 1651).
Holland, J. H., Holyoak, K., Nisbett, E., & Thagard, P. (1986). *Induction: Processes of inference, learning, and discovery*. Cambridge, MA: MIT Press.
Ingham, G. (2004). *The nature of money*. Cambridge: Polity.
Iosifidis, G., Charette, Y., Littera, G., Tassiulas, L., & Christakis, N. (2018). Cyclic motifs in the Sardex monetary network. *Nature Human Behaviour, 2*(11), 822.
Keynes, J. M. (2007). *The general theory of employment, interest and money*. London: Palgrave Macmillan. (First Publication 1936).
Kim, H., & Bearman, P. S. (1997). The structure and dynamics of movement participation. *American Sociological Review, 62*, 70–93.
Kimmel, M. J., Pruitt, D. G., Magenau, J. M., Konar-Goldband, E., & Carnevale, P. J. (1980). Effects of trust, aspiration, and gender on negotiation tactics. *Journal of Personality and Social Psychology, 38*(1), 9.
Kosugi, M., & Yamagishi, T. (1998). General trust and judgments of trustworthiness. *Japanese Journal of Psychology, 69*, 349–57.
Kreps, D. M., Milgrom, P., Roberts, J., & Wilson, R. (1982). Rational cooperation in the finitely repeated prisoners-dilemma. *Journal of Economic Theory, 27*, 245–252.
Littera, G., Sartori, L., Dini, P. & Antoniadis, P. (2014). *From an idea to a scalable working model: Merging economic benefits with social values in Sardex*. In Inaugural WINIR Conference, Greenwich. Available at: http://eprints.lse.ac.uk/59406/. Accessed: 1 March 2020.
Luhmann, N. (1979). *Trust and power: Two works by Niklas Luhmann*. New York, NY: John Wiley & Sons.

Luhmann, N. (1988). Familiarity, confidence, trust: Problems and alternatives. In D. Gambetta (Ed.), *Trust* (pp. 94–107). Oxford: Blackwell.

Macaulay, S. (1963). Non-Contractual relations in business: A preliminary study. *American Sociological Review, 28,* 55–67.

Malhotra, D., & Murnighan, J. K. (2002). The effects of contracts on interpersonal trust. *Administrative Science Quarterly, 47,* 534–59.

Manzo, G. (Ed.). (2014). *Analytical sociology: Actions and networks*. Chichester: John Wiley & Sons.

Marres, N. (2016). *Material participation: Technology, the environment and everyday publics*. London: Palgrave Macmillan.

Marwell, G., & Ames, R. E. (1979). Experiments on the provision of public goods, I: Resources, interest, group size, and the free-rider problem. *American Journal of Sociology, 84,* 1335–60.

Marwell, G., & Oliver, P. E. (1993). *The critical mass in collective action: A microsocial theory*. Cambridge: Cambridge University Press.

Marx, K. (1963). *The Eighteenth Brumaire of Louis Bonaparte*. New York, NY: International. (First Publication 1852).

Marx, K., & Engels, F. (2002). *The communist manifesto*. London: Penguin. (First Publication 1848).

Maurer, A. (2016). Social mechanisms as special cases of explanatory sociology: Notes toward systemizing and expanding mechanism-based explanation within sociology. *Analyse & Kritik, 38*(1), 31–52.

McAdam, D. (1999). *Political process and the development of black insurgency: 1930–1970*. Chicago, IL: University of Chicago Press. (First Publication 1982).

McAdam, D., McCarthy, J., & Zald, M. N. (1996). *Comparative perspectives on social movements: Political opportunities, mobilizing structures and cultural framing*. Cambridge: Cambridge University Press.

McAllister, D. J. (1995). Affect- and cognition-based trust as foundations for interpersonal cooperation in organizations. *Academy of Management Journal, 38*(1), 24–59.

Merton, R. K. (1948). The self-fulfilling prophecy. *The Antioch Review, 8*(2), 193–210.

Molm, L. D., Takahashi, N., & Peterson, G. (2000). Risk and trust in social exchange: An experimental test of a classical proposition. *American Journal of Sociology, 105,* 1396–1427.

Nisbett, R., & Ross, L. (1980). *Human inference: Strategies and shortcomings of social judgment*. Englewood Cliffs: Prentice-Hall.

Offe, C. (1999). How can we trust our fellow citizens? In M. E. Warren (Ed.), *Democracy and trust* (pp. 42–87). Cambridge: Cambridge University Press.

O'Gorman, R., Henrich, J., & Van Vugt, M. (2009). Constraining free riding in public goods games: Designated solitary punishers can sustain human cooperation. *Proceedings of the Royal Society B: Biological Sciences, 276,* 323–329.

Olson, M. (1965). *The logic of collective action: Public goods and the theory of groups*. Cambridge, MA: Harvard University Press.

Ostrom, E. (1990). *Governing the commons: The evolution of institutions for collective action*. Cambridge, MA: Cambridge University Press.

Ostrom, E. (2000). Collective action and the evolution of social norms. *Journal of Economic Perspectives, 14*(3), 137–58.

Ostrom, E., Walker, J., & Gardner, R. (1992). Covenants with and without a sword: Self-Governance is possible. *American Political Science Review, 86,* 404–17.

Parsons, T. (1971). *The system of modern societies*. Englewood Cliffs: Prentice Hall.

Peirce, C. S. (1957). The fixation of belief. In C. S. Pierce, *Essays in the philosophy of science*. New York, NY: Bobbs-Merrill.

Petersen, T. (2009). Opportunities. In P. Hedström & P. S. Bearman (Eds.), *The Oxford handbook of analytical sociology*. Oxford: Oxford University Press.

Pizzorno, A. (1983). Sulla razionalità della scelta democratica. *Stato e Mercato, 7,* 3–46.

Poteete, A. R., Janssen, M. A., & Ostrom, E. (2010). *Working together: Collective action, the commons, and multiple methods in practice*. Princeton, NJ: Princeton University Press.

Rabin, M. (2013). Risk aversion and expected-utility theory: A calibration theorem. In L. C. MacLean & W. T. Ziemba (Eds.), *Handbook of the fundamentals of financial decision making: Part I* (pp. 241–252). Hackensack: World Scientific Publishing.

Rotter, J. B. (1980). Interpersonal trust, trustworthiness and gullibility. *American Psychologist, 35,* 1–7.

Rydgren, J. (2009a). Shared beliefs about the past: A cognitive sociology of intersubjective memory. In P. Hedström & B. Wittrock (Eds.), *The frontiers of sociology*. Amsterdam: Brill.

Rydgren, J. (2009b). Beliefs. In P. Hedström & P. S. Bearman (Eds.), *The Oxford handbook of analytical sociology*. Oxford: Oxford University Press.

Sally, D. (1995). Conversation and cooperation in social dilemmas. *Rationality and Society, 7,* 58–92.

Sartori, L., & Dini, P. (2016). From complementary currency to institution: A micro-macro study of the Sardex mutual credit system. *Stato e Mercato, 36*(2), 273–304.

Scholz, J. T., & Gray, W. B. (1997). Can government facilitate cooperation? An informational model of OSHA enforcement. *American Journal of Political Science, 41,* 693–717.

Simmel, G. (1910). How is society possible? *American Journal of Sociology, 16*(3), 372–391.

Simmel, G. (1990). *The philosophy of money*. London: Routledge. (First Publication 1907).

Simmel, G. (2010). Englischsprachige Veröffentlichungen 1893–1910. In Simmel, G. *Gesamtausgabe*, vol. 18, edited by Otthe in Rammstedt and David P. Frisby. Berlin: Suhrkamp.

Spence, M. (1973). Job market signaling. *Quarterly Journal of Economics, 87,* 355–374.

Stroebe, W., & Frey, B. S. (1982). Self-interest and collective action: The economics and psychology of public goods. *British Journal of Social Psychology, 21*(2), 121–137.

Sztompka, P. (1999). *Trust: A Sociological Theory*. Cambridge: Cambridge University Press.

Tönnies, F. (1887). *Gemeinschaft und Gesellschaft*. Leipzig: Verlag di Fues.

Trigilia, C. (2002). *Sociologia economica* (Vol. 2). Bologna: II Mulino.

Van den Assem, M. J., Van Dolder, D., & Thaler, R. H. (2012). Split or steal? Cooperative behavior when the stakes are large. *Management Science, 58*(1), 2–20.

Walras, L. (2013) [1877]. *Elements of pure economics*. London: Routledge

Weber, M. (1946). *From Max Weber: Essays in sociology*. Oxford: Oxford University Press.

Weber, M. (1978). *Economy and society*. Berkeley, CA: University of California Press. (First Publication 1922).

Weber, M. (2004). *The vocation lectures*. Indianapolis, IN: Hackett Publishing.

Weber, M. (2013). *The protestant ethic and the spirit of capitalism*. London: Routledge. (First Publication 1905).

Williamson, O. (1975). *Markets and Hierarchies*. New York, NY: Free Press.

Yamagishi, T. (2011). *Trust: The evolutionary game of mind and society*. Tokyo: Springer.

Zagzebski, L. T. (2015). *Epistemic authority: A theory of trust, authority, and autonomy in belief*. New York, NY: Oxford University Press.

Zak, P. J., & Knack, S. (2001). Trust and growth. *Economic Journal, 111,* 295–321.

Zucker, L. G. (1986). Production of trust: Institutional sources of economic structure, 1840–1920. *Research in Organizational Behavior, 8,* 53–111.

5 Conclusions

The previous chapter drew attention to the rich variety of social mechanisms activated by a specific currency. Far from being a universal neutral equivalent, the Sardex complementary currency activates heterogeneous social configurations and creates a hybrid economic activity that cannot be explained in terms of traditional utilitarianism. The objective of this final chapter is to outline a preliminary synthesis of the social functioning of money which will be described from a perspective of increasing abstraction. The first section considers the effects and the potential of Sardex as an instrument of economic policy; the second section presents sociological categories within which to conceptualise the social functioning of money and provides a preliminary comparison between modern money, Sardex and crypto-currencies; the third section proposes a theoretical reading of the nature of money as a mediator of the relationship between the individual and society and its performative capacities. In conclusion, some implications of the research are introduced for the elaboration of a monetary policy in a sociological perspective and some suggestions for further research are given.

5.1 Sardex as an Economic Policy Tool

5.1.1 The Economic Effects of Sardex

Sub-sect. 4.2 *Cooperation in Sardex* laid out the principle economic effects that joining the Sardex network had on member companies. Among the economic data collected, the most significant results from an economic point of view, were the increases in revenue and number of customers, which grew by 26% and 23% respectively, net of the substitution effect between the euro and Sardex. Sardex device operations account for

G. Bazzani, *When Money Changes Society*, Wirtschaft + Gesellschaft,
https://doi.org/10.1007/978-3-658-28533-3_5

this increase: they activate social mechanisms that generate a high level of trust between members and a willingness to cooperate that facilitates market transactions.

Trust creation can be traced back to the presence of the following social mechanisms: horizontal and hierarchical monitoring and sanctioning, signalling, repeated interaction reciprocity with other members and reciprocity norm towards Sardex Ltd (see Sub-sect. 4.1 *Trust*). The high level of cooperation among members can be explained as an effect of the high level of trust in the network, combined with the low cost of Sardex credit and the brokerage activity carried out by Sardex Ltd (see Sub-sect. 4.2 *Cooperation*). In summary, it can be argued that entrepreneurs who are members of the Sardex network willingly engage in economic transactions with other entrepreneur members because they consider them very reliable, while the Sardex broker team and the online tools available to members foster the matching of supply and demand (ibid.).

5.1.2 Transaction Costs and Brokerage

Transaction costs have been a central theme in the development of economic analysis and its relationship with sociology (Trigilia 1989). In particular, the current of economic research known as neo-institutionalism has made transaction costs a key element to understanding the way in which a company expands (Williamson 1975; Alchian and Demsetz 1972; Moe 1984). Transaction costs are important in the study of economy because economic transactions always have a more or less high degree of uncertainty with respect to the transaction outcome: this uncertainty is mainly due to the information gap between the actors and to the risks of opportunistic behaviours. The information uncertainty refers to the seller having more information than the buyer about the quality of the goods being sold, as well as possible future situations not known at the time of the transaction. This uncertainty may encourage the seller to behave opportunistically—for instance, by providing inadequate or false information. The buyer too, can behave opportunistically, for example, by not respecting the payment amount or time initially agreed upon (Beckert 2009). The presence of this uncertainty requires the entrepreneur to properly evaluate the terms of the exchange and the costs to be applied, based on the estimated defection risks. In the case of exchanges for large sums, the transaction costs take the form of formal contracts in which attempts are made to regulate most future situations that could occur. The time and the cost of creating these contracts are costs that are added to the costs of producing the goods in determining the final prices.[1]

---

[1]In traditional neo-institutional analysis, transaction costs are decisive in a company's decision to internalise the production of specific goods or to buy them on the market (Williamson 1975). The higher the transaction costs, the greater the incentive for the company to produce these goods itself, while low transaction costs encourage the firm to obtain supplies from the market.

The Sardex device improves *alter* reliability by guaranteeing less uncertainty about his or her future behaviour. Similarly, the entrepreneur who uses Sardex is unlikely to implement opportunistic behaviour, and he or she is very likely to encounter high levels of cooperation. These characteristics allow transactions to be carried out with low-level guarantees even when the two parties transacting are not known to each other. Even when the products being sold are inadequately described, and the guarantees on payment times are ineffective, it is likely the transaction will be successfully concluded, thanks to the social mechanisms activated by Sardex.

A final element considered by Williamson for defining transaction costs is more elusive and is defined in terms of "transactional atmosphere" (1975, p. 38). Transactional atmosphere refers to the socio-cultural context within which a transaction takes place which may, or may not, favour the transaction (Trigilia 1989, p. 135). Socio-cultural factors influence transaction costs independently of others: the propensity for a high level of interpersonal trust and cooperation can be influenced by cultural characteristics that transcend the interactional context of the transaction. For example, changing historical and political contexts can influence entrepreneurs' propensity to cooperate.[2]

The influence of the socio-cultural context on transaction costs in the Sardex experience is complex to interpret. The cultural tradition of Sardinia is described as tending to closure and not very open to innovation (Pinna 1971). The historical presence of a language that is different from Italian, the geographical condition of being an island and strong local traditions are some of the reasons used to explain this trend. This tradition is also seen as one of the factors that has contributed to the chronically low economic development of the region (Bottazzi 1999; Sartori and Dini 2016, p. 286). It could be hypothesised that this cultural tradition provides valid cultural support for a currency that circulates exclusively within the region: if this were so, support for the Sardex project would have exogenous causes (cultural characteristics of historical origin). If this hypothesis were correct, interpretations of Sardex operations would be comparable to those of the functioning of "community markets" in support of industrial districts where

[2]For example the fragmentation of textile and automobile production in Japan cannot be explained by a theory of transaction costs that does not take into account the cultural context which fosters strong individual motivations for cooperation (Dore 1983). The functioning of Italian industrial districts can also be explained thanks to the cultural support for cooperation among entrepreneurs, and between entrepreneurs and workers, as well as community forms of production organisation (Trigilia 1986). In this context, small, highly specialised companies, coordinated by the final seller of the finished product, each realise a part of the productive chain. The agreements among companies for realising these different productive phases are often based on frequently used, informal agreements. If they had to be described in formal contracts, it would create transaction costs that would be unsustainable for the industrial district. Those who defect or adopt opportunistic behaviours, in the industrial district, as in Sardex, are rapidly identified and isolated (Becattini 1989). These high levels of cooperation makes the transaction costs within the industrial district very low and this makes high productivity levels possible even where the production chain is very fragmented.

the local identity and cultural heritage facilitate the functioning of the market (Dei Ottati 1995). Indeed, a common cognitive and sense-of-belonging dimension would facilitate economic relations on a local scale (Trigilia 2001; Becattini 2004). Although these causes cannot easily be excluded from the analysis of the Sardex experience, their influence does not seem to be decisive for the observed social effects. In fact, the expansion of the Sardex device into other Italian regions, and the presence of similar, successful projects in other European regions, including some with less intense cultural traditions than the Sardinian ones, suggests that the cultural causes linked to Sardinia's historical legacy are not decisive in explaining the success of the Sardex project and its influence on transaction costs. On the contrary, in the Sardex experience, it can be argued that a strong sense of belonging to the local community is fostered by Sardex currency operations and is not a precondition for Sardex operations. Although a strong sense of belonging to regional cultural characteristics is part of the local tradition, the *modus operandi* of the Sardex currency makes it possible to perceive a link between economic activity and local development.[3] A secondary consequence of this *modus operandi* is that entrepreneurs identify more strongly with their own region once they start using the Sardex currency.[4] Furthermore, in the same Sardinian context, the strong social ties observed in Sardex are not extended by member entrepreneurs to economic relations with non-Sardex members.

In the Sardex experience, the influence of the socio-cultural context in determining transaction costs can be linked to the trend of the economic cycle. With the 2008 economic crisis, company business progressively deteriorated, and Sardinia's GDP fell by 9.1%. The liquidity crisis and reduced consumption fuelled each other by inducing negative economic expectations with entrepreneurs making fewer investments as a consequence. This economic recession made company bankruptcies a common phenomenon, as well as causing chronic delays in payments between companies. The entrepreneurs interviewed related how they would spend a large part of their working day trying to collect credit they were owed by other companies, instead of dealing with the development and management of their own business. This engendered very negative expectations about interlocutor reliability and sometimes entrepreneurs preferred not to sell their products unless payment was immediate or there were certain guarantees for future payment. So when there is an economic recession, the socio-cultural context puts a firm brake on market transactions. In contrast to this socio-cultural context, the role of

[3]See Sub-sect. 4.3.2 *Desires* and 4.3.3 *Beliefs*.

[4]Although industrial districts and the Sardex network are both characterised by a strong sense of community membership, the relation between this sense of community membership and economic operations do not seem to follow the same pathways: in the industrial district, membership is a precondition of good economic operations, but in the Sardex experience this sense of community membership seems to be more an effect of how the economy operates. In fact as Sub-sects. 4.1.1 *Selection* and 4.1.2 *Signalling* demonstrate, the type of relationship experienced with other entrepreneurs changes inside the Sardex network, with the development of strong social ties.

the Sardex device, in periods of economic recession, is one of significantly facilitating transactions and contrasting the negative expectations surrounding economic transactions. Payments in Sardex are immediate and certain and any opportunistic behaviour is quickly sanctioned by hierarchical or horizontal sanctioning mechanisms.[5]

In addition to the forms of hierarchical and market production coordination aimed at reducing transaction costs, Ouchi introduces the "clan" model as a form of organisation (1980, p. 131). Clan organisation reduces uncertainty about the behaviour of its members thanks to a high fiduciary investment, with shared rules and values. The practice in Japanese industries of employing workers for life is an example of the attempt to have workers involved in the values and norms of the company they work for. Clans can also emerge in the productive organisation in relationships between different companies, to the point of creating a "market assisted by clans" (Barney and Ouchi 1986). In this case, "*it is certainly possible that the motivations and behaviours of the actors are modified by solidaristic mechanisms*" (Trigilia 1989, p. 149).

When describing the system of strong social relations within the industrial district, Dei Ottati (1995), prefers to use the term "community" instead of "clan" because:

> *It seemed better suited for underlining both the fact that the coordination of the subjects' actions takes place here through mutual adaptation, rather than by command, as if there were a hierarchy, and the fact that intersubjective relationships are jointly based on cooperation and competition, rather than on competition alone, as happens in the market in its pure form (ibid.: 26).*

The Sardex device directs the functioning of the Sardex market towards a community model. Sardex influences market transactions by sustaining very high levels of regulatory control in their everyday operations. The low levels of opportunistic behaviour can be interpreted as an alignment of behaviour in economic transactions with stricter rules of behaviour than ordinary ones. Thanks to the social mechanisms described, entrepreneurs do not adopt opportunistic behaviour but adapt their behaviour to rules that do not find the same cogency in the euro market. In the Sardex market, entrepreneurs adherence to predictable rules of behaviour reduces uncertainty about *alter* behaviour, reduces the perceived risk in market exchanges and therefore lowers transaction costs, which has the secondary effect of encouraging a high level of economic transactions.[6]

---

[5]See Sub-sect. 4.1.4 *Monitoring and Sanctioning*.

[6]A high level of interpersonal trust that sustains transactions is a characteristic shared by economic district operations and those of the Sardex complementary currency. Although their social relations operate in a similar way, their organisational forms and the nature of their trust are different. Industrial district operations are based on the possibility of dividing the productive process among different companies united by uncertainties regarding technological development or by the need for production flexibility (Becattini 1989; Scott 1998). The network of companies in Sardex is not based on the division of production among small, specialised companies with a few, large final sellers like it is in the industrial district. The Sardex member companies carry out economic transactions with one another, and are complementary so as to complete the production chain

The most important economic effects therefore concern the reduction of transaction costs which favours exchanges, and also the direct brokerage activity which further supports the match between demand and supply. In fact, although low transaction costs are already an incentive to trade in Sardex, these low costs do not necessarily mean that they produce large amounts of trade. On the contrary, as described in Sect. 4.2 Cooperation, the broker that calls an entrepreneur to ask for quotes on behalf of other companies changes the flow of the entrepreneur's daily activity: being put in contact with new customers who will be expected to pay immediately is seen as an extraordinary opportunity not to be missed.

Even the small fairs and socialisation opportunities promoted by Sardex Ltd are important for the opportunities they provide for making transactions. The opportunities for Sardex entrepreneurs to get to know each other on these occasions is an element that greatly facilitates the start of economic transactions. In summary, the brokerage activities implemented by the Sardex device facilitate the match between supply and demand and create, for the member companies, that part of demand for goods and services that for many companies has been cancelled by the economic crisis.

5.1.3 Competition, Cooperation and Innovation

The increase in demand generated by the functioning of the Sardex currency has well-defined geographical and economic limits: the additional demand comes exclusively from Sardinian companies. This increased demand with its exclusively local base can be criticised from the point of view of economic theory as a limit to the expansion of global competition. In fact, member companies with a credit in Sardex to spend, are "obliged" to spend their credits with other member companies that are based exclusively in Sardex. Competition between companies to acquire customers in Sardex is limited to members, whose membership is in turn limited to Sardinian companies. Even assuming a potential expansion of the Sardex network to all companies in the region, due to the current system of currency operation, non-Sardinian companies would still not have access to the network and could not compete with other companies. From a theoretical point of view, considering the positive effects of competition on prices and innovation, Sardex's complementary currency could be accused of not favouring a reduction in prices and of limiting the stimulus for Sardinian companies to innovate that would have come from competing with more competitive non-Sardinian companies. Exchanges in Sardex take place only between companies in the region for which it is possible to assume that it

both horizontally and vertically, but any form of coordination of production, in the current state of development of the Sardex project, unlike the industrial district, is occasional and comparable with production coordination already present in the euro market.

may happen that products of local companies, that would be less competitive on the euro market, may be preferred to products of external companies, simply because the external companies do not have access to the Sardex market. These dynamics would be negative both for final consumers, because they would lose part of the innovative potential of market competition, and also for Sardinian companies because, if protected for a long time from external competition, in the medium term they could find themselves in a condition of ever-decreasing competitiveness with respect to external competitor companies, because they were able to sell their products with less need for innovation.

This interpretation of the potential negative aggregate economic effects of the Sardex currency, however, does not take into account two dynamics that act in the opposite way to the negative effects described. The Sardex is a complementary currency that does not aspire to becoming an alternative currency to the euro. Sardex is a special money (Zelizer 1995), created and developed to perform specific functions, different from the traditional universal currency of modern states (see Sect. 5.3 *Performative money: between individual and society*). Entrepreneurs know that in order to maintain their business balance sheet in good order, transactions conducted in Sardex should not exceed 20% of the company's overall business. However, each sector of activity has its own specificities: companies that use expensive raw materials that are not produced in Sardinia have to carefully evaluate how to grow their Sardex business in order to avoid having large numbers of Sardex credits from the sale of their products but insufficient euro liquidity for buying raw materials or paying utilities and taxes, etc. Companies whose production processes require significant quantities of energy also have to be vigilant because there are no energy-producing companies in Sardinia so energy consumption has to be paid in euros. Artisans, professionals and companies in the food and wine industry, find it is considerably easier to expand their business in Sardex without risking imbalances in their balance sheets because they can readily find all or most of their suppliers within the Sardex market. Therefore, for the member companies, the Sardex market is still a complementary and marginal market compared to the euro market. The limited Sardex market has the effect of making it necessary for companies to maintain a large part of their business in euros. This means that Sardex companies, in order to survive economic competition, also need to remain competitive in the euro market as well as the Sardex market. A company that largely or exclusively relies on the Sardex market would be forced to close after a short time because it would not have the resources to pay taxes, bills, wages and any raw materials not produced in Sardinia. The Sardex currency is in fact used for specific purposes within the company (see Sub-sect. 4.3.1 *Opportunities*). The companies that use Sardex are therefore companies that remain competitive on the euro market and the Sardex network offers very limited protection from the competition of the euro market.

From the price point of view the negative effects of the Sardex currency also seem limited. Sardex members are contractually obliged to charge the same price in euros as in Sardex. Although the Sardex market is more limited than the euro market, and therefore could theoretically accept higher prices because there is less competition, this is unlikely to happen. As the Sub-sect. 4.1.4 *Monitoring and sanctioning* highlighted, price differences between the euro and Sardex are not tolerated by members and are promptly sanctioned. It is therefore reasonable to expect that the influence of the limited competition within the Sardex market will not have significant effects on prices, and that these will remain aligned with prices on the euro market.

Although Sardex entrepreneurs have to remain competitive on the euro market and therefore are forced by the competition to innovate at least on a par with other competitors, it could be assumed that the Sardex market is not particularly dynamic from the point of view of innovation. However, the complementarity of the currency makes it possible to argue that once companies have made innovations that make them competitive on the euro market, they have every interest in extending these innovations to the Sardex market to acquire greater market shares in Sardex. The Sardex market, however, is unable to create long innovation networks that can generate technological or professional transfer (Ramella and Trigilia 2010). These aspects remain a prerogative of euro market operations, thanks to the long-distance transactions that the currency allows. Among the processes that generate economic innovation, though, the complementary currency Sardex can impact positively on the capacity to cooperate with customers and sub-suppliers (Soskice 1993). A high level of trust and a willingness to cooperate with customers and suppliers makes it possible to exchange information and build networks that can generate product and process innovation, albeit outside the production specialisation model of the industrial district. From this point of view, as was explained in Sects. 4.1 *Trust* and 4.2 *Cooperation*, the complementary currency Sardex generates the conditions for developing strong social ties among members and this creates an optimal context for the exchange of information.

Unlike the industrial district, the companies in the Sardex network are not developing significant innovations for coordinating and subdividing production activity among companies. The research carried out showed few examples where the Sardex network of companies, characterised by their high level of trust, develops joint business projects. Some entrepreneurs strategically use the member network to produce and sell specific products (see Sect. 4.2 *Cooperation*), but their number is limited. The most significant case concerns a company in the tourism sector that is developing with the aim of providing an on-line presence for small businesses in the tourism sector that are Sardex members: the company hopes this development will counteract the strong competition of large companies in the tourism sector that are constantly increasing their market share at the expense of smaller local ones. The strategic use of the Sardex business network—characterised by a high level of trust and ability to cooperate—for the development of innovative business projects could be a new frontier for the mature phase of the Sardex network, with significant positive effects for the local economy. Currently, the positive economic effects of the Sardex device can be found on the demand side, but the network's mode of operation makes it possible to hypothesise that the potential already present could also be used in a more systematic way to foster economic innovation.

5.1.4 Sardex Between Local Development and Convergence Policies

Sardex member companies are obliged to carry out economic transactions with other members of the Sardex network. Membership of this network is limited to companies based in Sardinia. This has an aggregate effect of fostering transactions between local companies and supporting the local economy. The products of local companies have an advantage in the attribution of value and preferences by other members, compared to the products of non-regional companies. From the point of view of a general theory of economic equilibrium, which lets the market select the best and most innovative companies, the effect of the Sardex currency might be negative. The Sardex market restricts the possibilities of exchange and competition, favouring companies based in Sardinia. These companies, therefore, have a competitive advantage over the others which does not derive from market selection mechanisms but from characteristics that are exogenous to the functioning of the market: the geographical location of the company.[7] This restriction on market functioning can be viewed negatively for its potential long-term distortion of prices and the competitiveness of the economic system.

Political intervention to orientate market equilibrium, however, is often used in economic policies. European Union convergence programmes for less developed regions are an example of these policies. Economic convergence policies use funds obtained from ordinary taxation to foster economic competitiveness in weaker regions. These redistributive policies do modify market equilibrium, but are considered legitimate in order to avoid the short-to-medium term negative economic and social effects that competition from more competitive companies and regions can have on economically weak regions. These policies are not interpreted as protection from international competition, but as instruments that reinforce the contextual factors supporting the local economy (Crouch et al. 2004). Traditional policies for supporting weak economic regions involve education, vocational training and support services for local businesses. In fact, economic theory stipulates that policies should not intervene in market equilibrium, but only in contextual factors that facilitate transactions and company competitiveness.

The Sardex project can be considered as a local monetary policy and as market regulation for the development of economically depressed regions, without the negative political effects of traditional convergence programmes.[8] Traditional EU programme use direct money transfers financed by national fiscal policies or the more recent debt-risk sharing with the ECB's quantitative easing programs (Valiante 2017). Traditional support programmes for economically weak regions of the EU are currently facing

[7]See Sub-sect. 4.1.1 *Selection*.

[8]Unlike weak economies, the economic effects might not be particularly significant for strong economies, able to compete autonomously in external markets, which require currencies that can be transferred easily.

growing political opposition from richer EU countries: this opposition can be linked to an increase in political populism and nationalism (Streeck 2015). A non-complementary but alternative local currency could be accused of strengthening a sense of local identity as well as reinforcing cultural processes of political fragmentation and economic closure. A complementary currency like Sardex, although it reinforces the bond of belonging to one's own region, seems to avoid the risks of economic closure because it is complementary to the ordinary currency. From this perspective, the political projects of alternative currencies and complementary currencies differ. An alternative local currency could be accused of promoting economic and political fragmentation whereas a complementary currency like Sardex, does not involve a departure from monetary and political unions belonging to higher orders of governance. In fact, Sardex seeks to encourage local transactions but it ensures that the exchanges in complementary currency remain a marginal part of the business of member companies, which for the most part remains in euros. Considering the growing political opposition of wealthy regions to convergence programs based on tax redistribution, Sardex can be considered an instrument of economic policy for local development that will generate less resistance in wealthy regions than traditional convergence policies. The Sardex project allows an economically depressed region like Sardinia to strengthen its economy on its own, without the use of financial resources deriving from the taxation of wealthier regions, which in the long term entails the risk of being considered a burden with the consequent increase of nationalism in the wealthy regions.

The Sardex project also avoids the risk of financing a shadow economy and tax evasion[9]: all market transactions are tracked by the online platform and entrepreneurs cannot avoid paying taxes on their economic transactions. Total market transparency for Sardex Ltd would also allow the implementation of very specific economic policies. For example, if the complementary currency were regulated with purposes more closely aligned to economic policy, in certain economic circumstances (economic bubble or recession for specific economic sectors) currency operations could easily expand or restrict credit for specific economic sectors. Total market transparency would allow very specific economic policy interventions, and the effects of these interventions could be accurately assessed by observing all market operations before and after policy implementation. Total market transparency may appear to the monetary regulatory authority to be a sort of "big brother" of social life,[10] but it would be an economic policy instrument that would allow an easy but effective regulation of monetary policy for the political purpose of redistributing competitive opportunities in the market.

[9]This risk is well known for other virtual currencies such as Bitcoin (Cheah and Fry 2015).

[10]Fiscal authorities currently are allowed to access the bank accounts of all citizens. This is a situation close to Sardex market transparency. The debate involves a discussion on the nature of money as a commodity (which belongs to the person who owns it) or as a political project (collectively regulated) and also affronts the question of the quality of the democratic controls exercised by citizens on public institutions.

5.2 The Social Functioning of Money

The research has demonstrated that a currency's functional characteristics can influence social relations in terms of trust, cooperation and solidarity. One of the most interesting aspects of the effects of money that emerged from the research, concerns the transition from a utilitarian perception of entrepreneurs' economic behaviour to a more realistic understanding of economic action as a collective good that manifests itself together with the pursuit of company business, thanks to the role played by money (see Sub-sect. 4.3.3 *Beliefs*). The social mechanisms described, show that entrepreneurs are often rational actors who maximise their utility, however the form this utility takes can vary, and includes a complex and collective perspective that cannot be reduced to individual profit alone. The concept of "personal utility" does not seem sufficient to describe the forms of interaction that develop between Sardex entrepreneurs: there are in fact forms of reciprocity (see Sub-sect. 4.1.3 *Reciprocity*) and action oriented towards collective goods (see Sub-sect. 4.3.4 *Collective action*), which require a more precise description of social interaction, and the social mechanisms this activates, than the traditional conceptualisations of utilitarian economic action can provide.

The research provides a preliminary account of the social mechanisms involved in money functioning which influence individual behaviour. These mechanisms are activated by the currency's technical characteristics, by how its circulation is regulated by Sardex Ltd and by the effects on social interaction these factors generate (see Sect. 4.4 *The generative mechanism of the economic and social effects of Sardex*).

The research provides evidence to suggest that the way money functions has a wide spectrum of social effects that are not considered in traditional definitions of money and monetary theory, by either the man in the street or by the experts who determine monetary policies. Traditional economic theory assigns four economic functions to money: it is a means of payment, a unit of account, a medium of exchange and a store of value. The section 3.1 Money and complementary currencies and section 3.2 The forerunners of Sardex describe how combining these four functions into one single currency was an achievement of the modern state. Currencies from earlier times, as well as the experience gained from the many CC currencies, show that the way modern money functions is not the only combination of possible characteristics and functions and that the present currency configuration has possible negative effects. The description of the economic and social mechanisms activated by Sardex CC operations make it possible to propose a tentative preliminary classification of the social functioning of money which will allow the recognisable or expected effects of implementing specific forms of money to be more faithfully described. The classification of the relevant aspects of the social functioning of money has been deduced from the analysis of Sardex's social mechanisms. The tables 5.1 and 5.2 summarise a possible typology of the economic and social functioning of money by comparing modern state currencies, Sardex and a crypto-currency.

Table 5.1 Typology of the economic functioning of different currencies. (Source Own presentation)

Currency	Economic functioning			
	Means of payment	Medium of exchange	Unit of account	Store of value
Tribal gifts	X			
Medieval currencies	X	X		partly
Wörgl	X	X		
Bancor			X	
Modern state currencies	X	X	X	X
Sardex	X	X		
Cryptocurrency (e.g., Bitcoin)	X	X	X	X

The proposed typology, which does not exhaust the possible social effects of money, was developed using the relevant social effects found in Sardex operations as a reference. These effects were compared with those of ordinary currency operations. In addition to the four functions of money described by economic science, the typology adopted here divides the social functioning of money into three different categories. Each represents a group of aspects that are distinct, but connected, when explaining how Sardex functions. The first category considers the technical and social characteristics of the currency—how it circulates, why was it developed, its legitimation criteria, the moral values it incorporates, the type of social embeddedness adopted—and then considers the social effects that these characteristics generate: extension of social networks, the types of trust encouraged or discouraged by the currency and whether the actors involved became more or less cooperative or competitive. The aggregate effect of these specific forms of social interaction, mediated by the role of money, can be described as the macro scale social effects of the functioning of money. In this perspective when, as in the case of the three currencies considered, the social effects of the functioning of money clearly direct the form of social interaction, it is possible to identify towards which form of social solidarity the social functioning of money orientates the community. The proposed typology, although it does not exhaust the possible social aspects to be considered when studying the social effects of money, offers a model to conceptualise some possible explanatory relationships between currency characteristics and social phenomena. The relationships between currency characteristics and social effects can be empirically tested; hypotheses regarding relations between money characteristics and social effects when there are different currencies operating, would allow specific research questions to be elaborated regarding the real social mechanisms activated in each case.

Table 5.2 Typology of the social functioning of different currencies. (Source Own presentation)

Currency	Social functioning								
	Currency characteristics					Social effects			Macro effects
	Means of circulation	Design objectives	Legitimation criteria	Moral values incorporated	Social Embeddedness	Extension of the social network	Trust orientation	Cooperation and competition	Forms of solidarity
State currency	Bank notes coins and online finance	Circulation of goods within the country and economic development	State universalism	Social contract; individual freedoms from community constraints	State administrations	State	Generalised trust in the state and its administration	Reinforces competition at the national and international level	Fiscal redistribution undertaken by the state
Sardex	Online network limited to members	Circulation of goods locally and regional development	Community self-development	Cooperation among members	1: Strong bonds among the founders 2: Social interaction mediated by network rules	Local	High levels of trust in the membership network and the Sardex Ltd hierarchy	Reinforces cooperation and reduces competitive pressure at the local level	Mutual credit among members
Cryptocurrency (e.g., Bitcoin)	Block-chain online	Subtract money from State control	Individual freedom	Self-made man	Anonymous actors with weak social ties	Global	Technology and interaction among equals	Removes community and State cooperation and regulation	None

5.3 Performative Money: Between Individual and Society

5.3.1 The Nature of Sardex Currency

Research shows that Sardex money is a very different type of money from the abstract type of money described by Simmel (1990 [1907]). The functioning and effects of Sardex are far removed from the idea of money as a universal equivalent that depersonalises social relations and separates exchanges and money from all cultural values. A century after Simmel's analysis of modern money, Sardex money seems to take on the characteristics of an indirect response to the effects of modern money and its more recent financialization. Financial money flows are increasingly characterised by free international circulation, often independent of national legislative constraints. Moreover, in recent decades there has been a progressive deregulation of financial transactions and instruments, as well as a gradual reduction in capital gains taxes in various national states (Epstein 2005; Palley 2013). Some nation states provide favourable financial regulatory conditions so as to attract new capital to their territory. However, the rapid shift of capital into one place also means its rapid outflow from somewhere else. From the point of view of a theory that postulates that markets regulate themselves, these financial flows can be legitimised by the idea of a more efficient allocation of resources: capital holders move their capital towards investments considered more profitable. Following the hypothesis of market self-regulation generated by competitive pressure, it could be hypothesised that, in the event of capital outflows and business closures, the workforce also moves towards more productive areas or the cost of labour decreases, making these areas again attractive to capital influx. As is known, however, while technology makes it relatively easy to move money, moving people from one country to another is not so easy, nor is the creation of new social capital and new companies following economic crises (Trigilia and Burroni 2009). For economically weak regions such as Sardinia, the outflow of capital and the emigration of the younger generations has had very negative economic and social effects which will be very difficult to recover from.[11]

Money, considered as an abstract form of universal equivalent has, as Simmel noted, freed people from pre-modern community bonds but, in its current financial form, it is also capable of producing very negative economic and social effects, without there being

[11]The negative economic and social effects described, do not take into account ethical considerations as to whether or not it is acceptable, from a normative point of view, that people having to emigrate are considered less important than the freedom of capital to move so as to maximise profits. In this sense it is possible to affirm: *"The neoliberal utopia of a borderless and peaceful globe requires that millions of ordinary people throughout the world have the flexibility to tolerate—perhaps as often as every five or ten years—a prolonged spell in which they must survive on half or less of what they previously earned. Polanyi believes that to expect that kind of flexibility is both morally wrong and deeply unrealistic. To him it is inevitable that people will mobilise to protect themselves from these economic shocks"* (Block 2001, p. XXXIV).

any obvious, simple short-term solutions. The easy international mobility of money is undoubtedly a stimulus to competition and productivity increase but, for the "losers" in this global competition, there remains only the possibility of emigration or the hope that (increasingly rare) local development policies will be implemented and supported by redistributive political choices between rich and poor regions.

The Sardex currency is an example of how money can be conceptualised in forms other than a universal equivalent, with obvious effects on economic regulation, redistribution[12] and social interaction. The Sardex can be described as a form of "community" currency[13] though it is not based on the presence of a community with strong pre-existing social ties, but rather, some of the characteristics of the community social bond emerge in the social interaction among members following the use of the Sardex CC (see Sub-sect. 4.1.5 *Conclusions: trust in Sardex*). Sardex currency cannot "leave" the member network: it can only circulate within the region and among entrepreneurs belonging to the Sardex network. In this sense, it is a form of "closed" currency that does not favour exchanges with the outside world, because not only can it not circulate there, but it cannot be converted into other currencies. The Sardex currency, however, due to its complementary nature, does not hinder trade with the outside world because entrepreneur members are "forced" to remain competitive on the euro market as well. Sardex, therefore, is a form of money that influences the form of the social bond between users, without necessarily translating into closure towards the outside. In fact, although Sardex members develop strong social bonds, that are unusual in ordinary economic relations, most of their business, of necessity, remains in euros, a currency that is readily transferred and converted.

The nature of the Sardex currency is such that it can be considered as a form of community money. Modern state currencies have their origin in political legitimacy and states holding the right to the exclusive use of force (Ingham 2004). The modern state has claimed the exclusive role of issuing money whose value is guaranteed by the state's ability to collect taxes from citizens and by that state's economy's capacity to produce wealth. Ordinary money is in fact issued by central banks, through a process of *fiat* money, whose mode of operation is regulated by political power in a more or less direct manner depending on the country. Sardex money, though, originates from mutual credit among entrepreneurs. Mutual credit is similar to a multilateral exchange system between entrepreneurs in which Sardex Ltd acts as a clearing house (see Sect. 3.4 *Sardex at work*). Sardex money is therefore similar to a form of credit whose collectability and convertibility in goods or services is not guaranteed by the state, but by the network of member companies. Companies agree to receive Sardex in payment for their products because

[12]Limiting the circulation and use of Sardex (see Sect. 4.1.3 *Opportunities*) provides local companies with a competitive advantage which can be interpreted as a redistributive element that offers greater value to products from an economically weak region like Sardinia, compared to products imported coming from more competitive regions.

[13]Thanks are owed to Jens Beckert for his useful suggestions regarding this aspect of the Sardex currency.

they are convinced they will be able to spend their credits with other companies for the purchase of goods or services of equal value. The value of money is therefore guaranteed only by the confidence that other entrepreneurs will accept Sardex as a means of payment. A complex system of social norms and operating rules maintains this high level of interpersonal trust as well as trust towards Sardex Ltd (see Sect. 4.1 *Trust*). It is also necessary to consider that taxes cannot be paid using Sardex: unlike the euro, its acceptability does not have the state as final guarantor. The entrepreneurs belonging to the network can therefore be considered as those who really "issue" the money by registering their credits in Sardex, and together with the functions performed by Sardex Ltd, they guarantee its value, its acceptability and that it can be converted into goods or services. The nature of the Sardex currency is therefore very different from that of modern currencies and their recent financialization. However, these differences do not make the Sardex an alternative currency but a complementary one: the objectives of its operation are different from those of the euro and the way in which it was designed does not allow it to perform some of the functions performed by ordinary money.

Sardex money has local development as its primary objective but, from the point of view of its nature and functioning, it is a form of credit that differs from microcredit. Neither microcredit nor Sardex credit have the traditional guarantees requested by the banks, and for this reason they provide credit access to a wider range of possible entrepreneurs. Microcredit, though, is paid to an entrepreneur without the ancillary services offered by the Sardex Ltd broker team. The specificity of the services offered by the Sardex brokers (see Sect. 4.2 *Cooperation in Sardex*) lies in their ability to match demand and supply within the Sardex network. Sardex members, in addition to receiving a credit that can be spent, as also happens with microcredit, also receive additional demand from other members for their products which they would not otherwise have had. So the Sardex network creates additional demand for goods for its members that ordinary forms of microcredit do not offer. The nature of Sardex money is also different from microcredit. Microcredit provides loans on the basis of ordinary money issued by central banks; Sardex money, on the other hand, originates in mutual credit among members.

Money that originates in mutual credit has fewer expansionary constraints than ordinary money: the money supply can be expanded without particular inflationary risks. In fact, what is decisive for maintaining the value of the Sardex currency is not the direct relationship between the money supply and the productive capacity of the economic system, but rather the ability of the companies to exchange goods and services among themselves (see Sub-sect. 4.1.1 *Selection*). Sardex credit will always be spendable provided the company that owns the credit is able to find suppliers of the goods required for their business in the network. Sardex money supply, therefore, can potentially expand independently of the trend of the economic cycle—the only restriction being that companies maintain a sufficient part of their business in euro so they can pay all their expenses not payable in Sardex (see Sub-sect. 4.3.1 *Opportunities*). Sardex money, as a credit loan, therefore, facilitates an increase in the amount of money circulating without generating the risk of inflation, because the correspondence of value between the goods on the market and their value in Sardex uses an external unit of account which is the euro. For this reason, having more Sardex available to spend within the system does not generate an increase in the prices of the goods to be purchased, whereas a strong monetary expansion of the ordinary currency will increase prices.

5.3.2 Aspects of Monetary Policy from a Sociological Perspective

The central bank's monetary policy manipulates the interest rate to encourage investment or savings and to control inflation. Empirical evidence shows that the response of the real economy to this manipulation varies according to the economic context (Fratzscher et al. 2016; Eser and Schwaab 2016). In the event of an economic downturn, investment may not take off again even with a zero or negative interest rate. This observation is at the heart of the Keynesian monetary policy which, in the event of an economic recession, suggests financing direct government investment with the public debt to restore the economic cycle of investments.[14] In fact, even when central banks have ample monetary liquidity during an economic recession, entrepreneurs often avoid investing and consumers avoid spending because they both lack confidence in the future of the economy (Keynes 2007 [1936]). In this situation, according to Keynesianism, the state should invest and create jobs to facilitate the circulation of money, thus encouraging expectations of a positive economic future. In this perspective, the Sardex device seems well placed to substitute the state in creating trust between economic actors, ensuring correct behaviour in the market and increasing demand for goods and services. The functioning of Sardex does not allow the capitalisation of money and financial investment but "forces" economic actors to quickly use their credit (see Sect. 3.5 *A Summary of How Sardex Works*). The credit granted by Sardex Ltd to members rapidly becomes an equivalent demand on the market: even in an economic recession, unlike ordinary currency (Cho and Rhee 2014; Kapetanios et al. 2012), the Sardex cannot become a financial investment. The ineffectiveness of traditional monetary policy in creating demand during the economic recession is avoided by the functioning of Sardex and in particular by the functions performed by the Sardex broker team.

A monetary policy inspired by the functioning of Sardex, with the goal of creating demand during a recession, needs to include the objectives of creating trust and cooperation among the actors. The reduction of interest rates may not be a sufficient incentive to shift the propensity to save towards investment or consumption: a good level of cooperation among the actors and positive expectations as to future demand are required for investments and consumption to pick up. Evidence from the Sardex experience suggests that expansive monetary policies function well; such policies could become a significant variable for developing monetary policies for ordinary currencies in periods of

[14]The previous conception of money was Marshall's which affirmed that: "*the quantity theory of money told them that prices would adjust to make sure that this could not happen. With a fixed quantity of money, prices would adjust to ensure that the demand for money equalled this fixed supply, and that all goods produced would actually be purchased*" (Vines and Wills 2018, p. 6).

recession. The social mechanisms that create trust and cooperation are not necessarily the same in Sardex operations as they are in ordinary currency operations, but despite these differences, the social effects on trust and cooperation could still be considered as a part of innovative monetary policies involving ordinary money.

The Sardex case suggests, by analogy, similar considerations for macroeconomic policy: a competitive economy requires a high level of competition and cooperation between economic actors (Beckert 2009). The expansion of competition into all economic sectors and in social life, advocated by recent macroeconomic policies, may not automatically lead to a more competitive economy. Structural reform programme of the common euro currency are commonly considered as ways of increasing competition in economic and social life between individuals, companies and countries (Eggertsson et al. 2014; Veltmeyer et al. 1997). Their results are ambivalent, both in macroeconomic results (Faini et al. 2015) and in social effects (Barro and Lee 2005; Stubbs and Kentikelenis 2018). Sardex's evidence suggests that in macroeconomic policies the levels of trust, cooperation and solidarity among economic actors, are also important objectives to consider for strengthening the economy. In the Sardex project, trust, cooperation and solidarity are not excluded from the economic field, as exogenous context, like education, values and norms are, but are considered as the effects of a specific form of economic interaction and, more precisely, of the Sardex currency *modus operandi*. In the context of the economy organised around the Sardex currency, forms of social action commonly belonging to different fields interact, influencing each other (see Sect. 4.3 *Solidarity*). While values and norms are commonly considered as contextual factors that influence economic action and behaviour (Zelizer 2010; Tabellini 2010), the Sardex experience shows how values and norms can be influenced by the form of economic interaction mediated by a specific mode of currency operation.

The theoretical framework of classical utilitarianism does not explain the behaviour of Sardex entrepreneurs: this behaviour would be better understood if complex hypotheses were used to explain economic action;

- There is evidence of direct and group reciprocity mechanisms in economic action;
- Personal utility and profit are not the only goals of economic action for entrepreneurs: collective and group utilities can coexist with personal utility or even exist without it[15];
- Neither the model of social interaction in the economic sphere, nor individual motivations for economic action, are exogenous to the economy: both can be influenced by how the currency operates. Depending on these operations the motivation for individual behaviour will move between individual and collective utility.

[15]This coexistence of individual and collective goals associated with Sardex operations, recalls the principles and functioning of Islamic finance (for an introduction to this topic, see Ricucci and Moiso 2017). The Islamic principles of prohibiting interest, sharing risk, prohibiting uncertainty clauses in contracts, equitable wealth distribution and prohibiting the use of money for prohibited activities have many affinities with the operating principles of the Sardex currency.

5.3.3 Performative Money

The empirical evidence regarding the social functioning of money suggests that money can have performative effects in the social sphere.[16] In this perspective, attention needs to be drawn to how beliefs about the functioning of social or economic systems can influence policy design. The effects of these policies then tend to be aligned with the theoretical assumptions that played a part in their design. The performative approach to the study of economics does not pay particular attention to the degree of "truth" that a given economic theory possesses, but it is interested in understanding how certain theoretical assumptions are able to model policies that steer social behaviour in the direction indicated by the economic theory adopted.[17] The Sardex experience offers interesting elements that can be used to evaluate the extent to which a theory of money that is supposed to explain how Sardex operates, in reality contributes to implementing the social phenomena that are expected from Sardex currency operations.[18]

Contemporary macroeconomic policy is based on the paradigm shift in monetary theory from Keynesianism to monetarism during the 1970s (Hall 1993); this "*led to policies that facilitated industry deregulation, as well as the privatisation of firms, tax cuts, market liberalisation, and the reform of the welfare state*" (Beckert 2016, p. 264).

---

[16]Performative effects are the social effects of policies developed in accordance with specific theoretical approaches (Callon 1998; Callon et al. 2007; Caliskan and Callon 2009; Muniesa 2014). Classic studies in this field include forms of market expansion (Aspers 2007; Hawkins 2012), financial markets (MacKenzie and Millo 2003; MacKenzie 2004; MacKenzie 2008) and more recently the first studies of the performative effects of the central banks' monetary policies have appeared (Braun 2015; 2016a, b).

[17]This observation is not intended to relativise all theories and deprive them of validity but rather wishes to draw attention to the secondary effects of the functioning models adopted that are often ignored, and also to consider how different explanatory models can contribute to creating social phenomena that are in line with the models utilised.

[18]Guseva and Rona-Tas provide a very clear description of the "performative" role of economic theories in developing new forms of money in Eastern Europe: "*Although limited in application, economic models are nevertheless very useful. First, as a* descriptive *device, they can shed light on the functional rules of a market if certain expectations are met about who the players are, what ways they are willing to cooperate and what the actors value … The analytic function of economic theories is not just to supply what Max Weber called an ideal type, a simplification and clarification of reality, and not only to reveal the necessary preconditions that markets require; it is also to provide cognitive coordination, a common language for participants to use in thinking about a market. Next, as a* prescriptive *tool, economic theories can help the coordination of action among market players. By prescribing what to do, they can narrow the universe of actions that people are likely to take, making markets more predictable … As an* ideological *instrument, economic theories establish the market's legitimacy … It is in this sense that economic theories protect these markets and contribute to their overall stability. Performativity of economics is laid bare here: for its theories to work, the market must be stable, and this very stability is advanced by those theories*" (Guseva and Rona-Tas 2014, p. 244–5).

The global financial crisis after 2008 can be considered as a side effect of international financial deregulation (Barrell and Davis 2008; Crotty 2009; Reinhart and Rogoff 2009). After the economic crisis, monetary policies have reconsidered the Keynesian approach and the new Dynamic Stochastic General Equilibrium (DSGE) has become the "reference model" for central banks (Vines and Wills 2018, p. 2; Blanchard 2008). This new model has partly alleviated the liquidity problems of the banks, but it has not provided a clear alternative to the previous macro-economic policy model. It seems to be a strategy for marking time during a period of financial turbulence (Streeck 2014), before restoring ordinary activity when the financial environment is more stable.

Monetary theory and the approach to monetary policy—e.g., the DSGE model—have significant effects on economic policy. In the theoretical monetarist approach, money is considered as a commodity, like other goods. As noted previously, the general theory of market functioning postulates that markets should tend towards equilibrium, that goods should circulate freely and that, in the long run, a competitive market will always provide the best aggregate utility. The efforts of companies to survive on the market will lead to the best possible results for consumers: prices will decrease and the best quality products will emerge through competition. Although there is no empirical evidence available that can confirm or deny with certainty these long-term effects (Atkinson and Stiglitz 1969; Rappaport 1996), the expectations associated with this theory of market functioning are assumed in the monetarist theoretical framework of reference and they produce economic forecasts and cause real effects when related economic policies are implemented (MacKenzie et al. 2007, p. 5; Çalışkan and Callon 2009)

In accordance with the expectations of general equilibrium theory as it applies to market functioning, regulatory policies should not intervene in market equilibrium, but only modify contextual factors so as to facilitate the competitiveness of companies and transactions. The long-term benefits to be expected from companies competing freely in the market would, in fact, be reduced by political intervention in the market equilibrium: the best companies would have difficulty in emerging if competition were altered by factors external to the functioning of the market itself. In the real markets of weak economies though, direct intervention to change the assignment of value in the markets in order to favour weaker sectors of the economy, or weaker economic areas (as in the Sardex experience), is a useful instrument of economic policy. This evidence, even though it is supported by empirical research results from the Sardex experience, can only be accepted within a theoretical framework of market functioning that does not expect a secure long-term market equilibrium that will *necessarily* lead to the best collective utility, but finds it necessary to consider a mid-term economic development perspective that has as its reference the observable effects of competition on a local scale. From this point of view, it is unacceptable that the long-term expected local benefits from global competition are achieved with the rapid destruction of the local economy (business failures and high unemployment) and local communities (youth emigration). It seems more realistic to argue instead that the economic and social benefits of market competition can be achieved by progressively strengthening the competitiveness of local companies without blocking external competition or the market selection of companies.

Economic theory prescribes total mobility of goods, capital and labour as the best long-term guarantee of an efficient market, but the economic dynamics of economically marginal and weak regions make options with limited spatial and temporal validity more appropriate. Sardinia's peripheral geographical location, its inadequate infrastructure and the limited social and economic resources available for its development, means the region occupies a marginal position compared to the economically strong and competitive areas within the European market. Sardinian companies are considerably less competitive than their more structured, external counterparts, and historically their economic system is fragile and vulnerable to external competition. The Sardex experience suggests that there may be effective, alternative instruments for local development, that do not increase external competitive pressure on Sardinian companies, but nonetheless manage to make the local economic system more competitive as well as avoiding economic closures.

This approach to competition regulation requires an understanding of how markets function when competition, cooperation and value attribution are equally important operating elements in the market being considered (Beckert 2009). The Sardex experience demonstrates that, for small businesses in weak economies, the ability to cooperate can be fundamental in enabling them to compete with large, better-organised companies. Faced with resource asymmetry for market competition between large trans-national companies and small enterprises in depressed areas, instruments for re-equilibrating the attribution of market value (see Sub-sect. 4.3.2 *Desires*) can be useful in the short-term for encouraging fairer competition, without penalising local businesses and workers, and allowing companies to become more competitive instead of rapidly disappearing.

If modern abstract money, described by Simmel and commodified by the theoretical monetarist approach, is associated with the functioning of abstract markets that are indifferent to the short-term economic and social effects of competition, then the conceptualisation of the Sardex project's community money has to be associated with a market in which trust and cooperation are as necessary to its functioning as competition. If community money in the form of mutual credit is to exist and function, it requires a regulatory form that creates high levels of interpersonal trust among network members and a spirit of solidarity at least towards the network group (see Sub-sect. 4.1.3 *Reciprocity*). Community money does not foster weak social ties like modern money does, but rather it promotes strong social ties and a strong attachment to the local dimension.[19] Sardex currency is thus associated with a community-oriented model of social action that is

[19]The strong social bonds associated with this form of money are not always desirable in all historical and geographical contexts. For example in the presence of social trends tending towards identitarianism, community money might reinforce normatively undesirable trends.

neither atomistic nor utilitarian—in this model individual and collective utility are linked together (see Sect. 4.3 *Solidarity*).

The Sardex experience has clearly demonstrated how, and the extent to which, the form and functioning of money have the capacity to change society. A theory of money that regarded money as an instrument for cooperation, instead of competition, could support institutional change and a change in social interactions that would enable political goals such as wealth redistribution and social justice to be pursued instead of only individual enrichment.

5.4 Further Research

A comparison of the functioning of the Sardex currency with the effects produced by similar local currencies in other regions with different cultural and economic backgrounds (e.g., with Liberex and Venetex (Italy), Bristol prospect (UK), Sonnantes (France)) would make it possible to definitively exclude exogenous cultural influences in the social mechanisms described and to verify the possible influence of contextual factors that may guide their functioning as well. The observation of a growth similar to that of the Sardex project, in regions with a less pronounced identitarian tradition than in Sardinia, could further confirm the thesis that the social mechanisms described are not particularly influenced by the cultural context. As Sardex-type currencies expand into different regions it is possible that a significant role emerges for institutional actors in promoting the use of their complementary currency project, something which so far has not happened in Sardinia.

There is currently no historical research available to help explain how the forerunners of Sardex, in particular Wörgl and Wir, functioned. These two cases are emblematic for the history of complementary currencies and for the importance of their economic effects. An archival search on the Wörgl case and historical research and contemporary analysis for the Wir case could be useful for hypothesising further possible social effects for the development of CCs similar to Sardex. Sardex operations have many elements in common with the functioning of Islamic finance which is now widespread in Western countries. Given the long history of Islamic finance, a comparative study of the principles and operations of Islamic finance and Sardex could provide useful information for the development of complementary currencies.

The research undertaken made it possible to describe the social functioning of the Sardex currency and to gather evidence on how positive economic results can be the effect of specific sets of social mechanisms that do not coincide with the traditional utilitarian interpretation of economic activity. The Sardex experience demonstrates how a currency can have characteristics and social effects that are very different from those of the ordinary money of the modern state, and also very different from microcredit and ethical finance because Sardex also acts on the demand side. These findings suggest the need for dedicating more theoretical and empirical attention to understanding the social effects of money and the specific mechanisms through which it operates. From the point of view of economic policies, the Sardex experience should be followed with interest for its anti-cyclical effects on the economic recession, and for the local development it stimulates in economically depressed areas. The distinction between providing support for local development and adopting protectionist policies is sometimes a subtle line of demarcation that does not allow easy generalisations. In general terms, it seems possible to support a substitute effect between protectionism and innovation for local economic systems, even if the real economic and social effects of unconventional policies such as in the Sardex experience are difficult to classify into ordinary categories of economic policies. The orientation that one draws from this research is however that of empirically observing with a fine-grained view the performative effects of the theoretical principles on which economic policies are based.

Finally, the Sardex experience could be considered as a laboratory for experimenting with more complex forms of money functioning than current monetary policies take into consideration. The potential for Sardex-type currencies to function as a mediator of social bonds could be used for unconventional monetary policies whose objective would be to foster cooperation among companies to facilitate innovation, or to regulate access to collective goods or to deploy monetary policy to further social justice.

References

Alchian, A. A., & Demsetz, H. (1972). Production, information costs, and economic organization. *The American Economic Review, 62*(5), 777–795.

Aspers, P. (2007). Theory, reality, and performativity in markets. *American Journal of Economics and Sociology, 66*(2), 379–398.

Atkinson, A. B., & Stiglitz, J. E. (1969). A new view of technological change. *The Economic Journal, 79*(315), 573–578.

Barney, J. B., & Ouchi, W. G. (1986). *Organizational economics*. San Francisco-London: Jossey-Bass Publishers.

Barrell, R., & Davis, E. P. (2008). The evolution of the financial crisis of 2007–8. *National Institute Economic Review, 206*(1), 5–14.

Barro, R. J., & Lee, J. W. (2005). IMF programs: Who is chosen and what are the effects? *Journal of Monetary Economics, 52*(7), 1245–1269.

Becattini, G. (1989). Riflessioni sul distretto industriale marshalliano come concetto socio-economico. *Stato e Mercato, 25*(1), 111–128.

Becattini, G. (2004). *Industrial districts: a new approach to industrial change*. Cheltenham: Edward Elgar Publishing.

Beckert, J. (2009). The social order of markets. *Theory and Society, 38*(3), 245–269.

Beckert, J. (2016). *Imagined futures*. Cambridge, MA: Harvard University Press.

Blanchard, O. J. (2008). Neoclassical synthesis. In S. Durlauf & L. Blume (Eds.), *The new Palgrave dictionary of economics* (2nd ed.). London: Palgrave Macmillan.

Block, F. (2001). Introduction. In K. Polanyi (Eds.), *The great transformation: The political and economic origins of our time*. Boston, MA: Beacon press. (First Publication 1944).

Bottazzi, G. (1999). *Eppur si muove. Saggio sulle peculiarità del processo di modernizzazione in Sardegna*. Cagliari: CUEC.

Braun, B. (2015). Governing the future: The European central bank's expectation management during the great moderation. *Economy and Society, 44*(3), 367–391.

Braun, B. (2016a). From performativity to political economy: Index investing, ETFs and asset manager capitalism. *New Political Economy, 21*(3), 257–273.

Braun, B. (2016b). Speaking to the people? Money, trust, and central bank legitimacy in the age of quantitative easing. *Review of International Political Economy, 23*(6), 1064–1092.

Çalışkan, K., & Callon, M. (2009). Economization, part 1: shifting attention from the economy towards processes of economization. *Economy and Society, 38*(3), 369–398.

Callon, M. (Ed.). (1998). *The laws of the market*. Oxford: Blackwell Publishers.

Callon, M., Millo, Y., & Muniesa, F. (Eds.). (2007). *Market devices*. Oxford: Blackwell.

Cheah, E. T., & Fry, J. (2015). Speculative bubbles in Bitcoin markets? An empirical investigation into the fundamental value of Bitcoin. *Economics Letters, 130,* 32–36.

Cho, D., & Rhee, C. (2014). Effects of quantitative easing on Asia: Capital flows and financial markets. *The Singapore Economic Review, 59*(03), 1450018.

Crouch, C., Le Galès, P., Trigilia, C., & Voelzkow, H. (2004). *Changing governance of local economies: Responses of European local production systems*. Oxford: Oxford University Press.

Crotty, J. (2009). Structural causes of the global financial crisis: A critical assessment of the 'new financial architecture'. *Cambridge Journal of Economics, 33*(4), 563–580.

Dei Ottati, G. (1995). *Tra mercato e comunità: Aspetti concettuali e ricerche empiriche sul distretto industriale*. Milano: FrancoAngeli.

Dore, R. (1983). Goodwill and the spirit of market capitalism. *The British Journal of Sociology, 34*(4), 459–482.

Eggertsson, G., Ferrero, A., & Raffo, A. (2014). Can structural reforms help Europe? *Journal of Monetary Economics, 61,* 2–22.

Epstein, G. A. (Ed.). (2005). *Financialization and the world economy*. Cheltenham: Edward Elgar Publishing.

Eser, F., & Schwaab, B. (2016). Evaluating the impact of unconventional monetary policy measures: Empirical evidence from the ECB′ s securities markets programme. *Journal of Financial Economics, 119*(1), 147–167.

Faini, R., De Melo, J., Senhadji, A., & Stanton, J. (2015). Growth-oriented adjustment programs: A statistical analysis. *Developing Countries In The World Economy, 42*(8), 125.

Fratzscher, M., Duca, M. L., & Straub, R. (2016). ECB unconventional monetary policy: Market impact and international spillovers. *IMF Economic Review, 64*(1), 36–74.

Guseva, A., & Rona-Tas, A. (2014). *Plastic money: Constructing markets for credit cards in eight postcommunist countries*. Stanford, MA: Stanford University Press.

Hall, P. A. (1993). Policy paradigms, social learning, and the state: The case of economic policymaking in Britain. *Comparative Politics, 25,* 275–296.

Hawkins, G. (2012). The performativity of food packaging: Market devices, waste crisis and recycling. *The Sociological Review, 60*(2_suppl), 66–83.

Ingham, G. (2004). *The nature of money*. Cambridge: Polity.

Kapetanios, G., Mumtaz, H., Stevens, I., & Theodoridis, K. (2012). Assessing the economy-wide effects of quantitative easing. *The Economic Journal, 122*(564), 316–347.

Keynes, J. M. (2007). *The general theory of employment, interest and money*. London: Palgrave Macmillan. (First Publication 1936).

MacKenzie, D. (2004). The big, bad wolf and the rational market: Portfolio insurance, the 1987 crash and the performativity of economics. *Economy and Society, 33*(3), 303–334.

MacKenzie, D. (2008). *An engine, not a camera: How financial models shape markets*. Cambridge, MA: Mit Press.

MacKenzie, D., & Millo, Y. (2003). Constructing a market, performing theory: The historical sociology of a financial derivatives exchange. *American Journal of Sociology, 109*(1), 107–145.

MacKenzie, D., Muniesa, F., & Siu, L. (2007). *Do economist make markets? on the performativity of economics*. Princeton, NJ: Princeton University Press.

Moe, T. M. (1984). The new economics of organization. *American Journal of Political Science, 28*(4), 739–777.

Muniesa, F. (2014). *The provoked economy: Economic reality and the performative turn*. London: Routledge.

Ouchi, W. G. (1980). Markets, bureaucracies, and clans. *Administrative Science Quarterly, 25*, 129–141.

Palley, T. I. (2013). Financialization: What it is and why it matters. In T. I. Financialization (Ed.), *Palley* (pp. 17–40). London: Palgrave Macmillan.

Pinna, L. (1971). *La famiglia esclusiva. Parentela e clientelismo in Sardegna*. Bari: Laterza.

Ramella, F., & Trigilia, C. (2010). Strong and weak ties in the social construction of inventions. *Stato e Mercato, 30*(1), 77–112.

Rappaport, S. (1996). Abstraction and unrealistic assumptions in economics. *Journal of Economic Methodology, 3*(2), 215–236.

Reinhart, C. M., & Rogoff, K. S. (2009). *This time is different: Eight centuries of financial folly*. Princeton, NJ: Princeton University Press.

Ricucci, R., & Moiso, J. (2017). *La banca e il minareto. Mondo islamico e finanza etica*. Bologna: Centro Editoriale Dehoniane.

Sartori, L., & Dini, P. (2016). From complementary currency to institution: A micro-macro study of the Sardex mutual credit system. *Stato e Mercato, 36*(2), 273–304.

Scott, A. J. (1998). From silicon valley to hollywood: Growth and development of the multimedia industry in california. In H. J. Braczyk, P. N. Cooke, & M. Heidenreich (Eds.), *Regional innovation systems* (pp. 136–162). London: UCL Press.

Simmel, G. (1990). *The philosophy of money*. London: Routledge. [First Publication 1907].

Soskice, D. (1993). *Product market and innovation strategies of companies and their implications for enterprise tenure: A comparative institutional approach to some cross-country differences*. Berlin: Wissenschaftszentrum.

Streeck, W. (2014). *Buying time: The delayed crisis of democratic capitalism*. London: Verso Books.

Streeck, W. (2015). Why the euro divides Europe. *New Left Review, 95*, 5–26.

Stubbs, T., & Kentikelenis, A. (2018). Targeted social safeguards in the age of universal social protection: The IMF and health systems of low-income countries. *Critical Public Health, 28*(2), 132–139.

Tabellini, G. (2010). Culture and institutions: Economic development in the regions of Europe. *Journal of the European Economic Association, 8*(4), 677–716.

Trigilia, C. (1986). Small-firm development and political subcultures in Italy. *European Sociological Review, 2*(3), 161–175.

Trigilia, C. (1989). Economia dei costi di transazione e sociologia: Cooperazione o conflitto? *Stato e Mercato, 25*, 129–158.

Trigilia, C. (2001). Social capital and local development. *European Journal of Social Theory, 4*(4), 427–442.

Trigilia, C., & Burroni, L. (2009). Italy: Rise, decline and restructuring of a regionalized capitalism. *Economy and Society, 38*(4), 630–653.

Valiante, D. (2017). The 'Visible Hand' of the ECB's first quantitative easing. *International Economics and Economic Policy, 14*(4), 601–624.

Veltmeyer, H., Petras, J., & Vieux, S. (1997). *Neoliberalism and class conflict in Latin America: A comparative perspective on the political economy of structural adjustment.* New York, NY: St. Martin's Press.

Vines, D., & Wills, S. (2018). The rebuilding macroeconomic theory project: An analytical assessment. *Oxford Review of Economic Policy, 34*(1–2), 1–42.

Williamson, O. (1975). *Markets and hierarchies.* New York, NY: Free Press.

Zelizer, V. (1995). *The social meaning of money: Pin money, paychecks, poor relief and other currencies.* New York, NY: Basic Books.

Zelizer, V. (2010). *Economic lives: How culture shapes the economy.* Princeton, NJ: Princeton University Press.

Appendix: Sampling and Methodologies

The collaboration developed with the Sardex broker team was fundamental for organising interviews with Sardex members. The broker team has access to the updated list of members, as well as to all the company data collected daily by the advisors and the broker team, such as geographic location, company size, business sector, when the company was founded and its owner. This data made it possible to construct a purposive sample in which the different characteristics of the member companies were included, although their representativeness was not statistically weighted due to the small size of the sample (37 interviews).

The sample was constructed by differentiating according to the geographical location of the enterprise (Cagliari and metropolitan area versus small rural centres); company size as measured by the number of employees (very few of the companies chosen had a large number of employees, in line with the type of members and with companies operating in Sardinia); age of the company (recently started companies, companies with more than 5 years of activity and those with over 20 years of activity); activity sector (the sectors considered were those most prevalent in Sardinia: construction, catering, industrial production, business services, trade, personal services, tourism); length of time in Sardex (less than three years, over three years) (Table A.1).

After a first list of members was agreed upon with the Sardex Ltd broker team, the remaining members were then obtained from a snowball selection compiled using the direct knowledge and contacts of members who had been interviewed. In fact, after the interview ended, the majority of respondents were satisfied that they had been able to express their opinion on Sardex and they were willing to provide contact details of other members or friends who would agree to be interviewed. Contacts with members increased over the period in which the interviews were conducted. The entrepreneur sample, therefore, was based partially on stratified purposive sampling, supplemented by snowball and convenience sampling.

G. Bazzani, *When Money Changes Society,* Wirtschaft + Gesellschaft,
https://doi.org/10.1007/978-3-658-28533-3

Table A.1 List of members interviewed (the location is not reported to maintain anonymity) (source: own presentation)

N°	ACTIVITY SECTOR	NUMBER OF EMPLOYEES	YEAR BUSINESS WAS FOUNDED	YEAR OF JOINING SARDEX
1	Restaurant	19	1988	2013
2	Restaurant	20	2006	2011
3	Pharmacy	9	1912	2014
4	Carpenter	0	2006	2015
5	Hotelier	3	1985	2014
6	Clothing	2	1988	2014
7	Jeweller	1	1948	2015
8	Jeweller	1	1948	2015
9	Tourist agency	1	2002	2010
10	Perfumery	3	1987	2015
11	Hotelier	7	2009	2015
12	Catering	4	2014	2017
13	Production Merchandising	20	1994	2013
14	Clothing trade, catering, buliding construction	64	1994	2014
15	Optical retail trade	3	1913	2013
16	Catering	8	1981	2014
17	Agriculture	30	1981	2010
18	Hairdresser	1	1990	2013
19	Bookshop	3	1929	2013
20	Catering, building construction	11	1970	2010
21	Dentist	3	2004	2014
22	Food shop	7	1997	2015
23	Paper production	2	1976	2015
24	Industrial laundry	250	1967	2010
25	Plant engineering	8	1991	2010
26	Furniture shop	5	1946	2013
27	Optical retail trade	0	2011	2011

(continued)

Table A.1 (continued)

N°	ACTIVITY SECTOR	NUMBER OF EMPLOYEES	YEAR BUSINESS WAS FOUNDED	YEAR OF JOINING SARDEX
28	Catering	7	2015	2015
29	Clothing trade	0	1996	2014
30	Business services	0	2015	2012
31	Packaging production	21	1976	2014
32	Supermarket	9	1952	2016
33	Catering	10	2011	2014
34	Business consultant	12	1996	2013
35	Clothing trade	7	1926	2015
36	Restaurant	6	2000	2015
37	Typography	49	1981	2012

Prior to the interviews members were contacted by telephone to arrange an interview time. Almost all contacts agreed to be interviewed. Temporary absence of an entrepreneur, or difficulty in establishing a mutually convenient time for their interview, meant a few interviews were not conducted after this first contact. The answers to the interview request were all positive, with interesting notes and emphases.

Some entrepreneurs underlined the fact that although they were very busy, and although they normally declined interview proposals, they would agree to do the interview "*for Sardex*", or, "*I'll do it because I owe it to them [Sardex]*". This attachment and sense of recognition towards Sardex reemerged again during the interviews, where it was often associated with the experiences of firms that had been able to make significant investments and put into place expansion programmes thanks to credit provided by Sardex (see Sub-section 4.1.3). The trust that Sardex gave to these companies did not depend on guarantees backed by the company's movable or immovable assets, and this has generated a strong attachment to Sardex in the owners of these companies who are strongly motivated to support the Sardex project, independently, as in the case of the interview, of any direct advantage for them or their companies.

Most of the information and data collected were inserted into a numerical matrix with 151 variables, while the more qualitative part of the interviews carried out was transcribed and coded. It proved necessary to analyse the qualitative part of the interviews because much of the information regarding motivations, use and other, more general, considerations on Sardex provided by the entrepreneurs could not be contained in the standardised answers provided without losing much of their heuristic value. The interviews were then coded using N-vivo software (Table A.2).

Table A.2 Coding of the interviews with Sardex members (source: own presentation)

SCOPE	NODE
Reasons for joining Sardex	• Economic crisis • Curiosity • Insufficient liquidity • Find more clients • Values • Other
Reasons for using Sardex	
How to use Sardex	• % compensation in € • Search for suppliers • Investing in the business • Immediate payments • Preference for Sardex versus € • Promoting your company • Personal expenses • Employees' salaries
Psychological effects of Sardex	
Economic effects of Sardex	• Clients • Revenue • Suppliers • Investments • Credit • Liquidity • Sardex brings € • Euro • Money comes in • Spending more • Personal expenses • Local development
Social effects of Sardex	• Charity and promoting the region • Ethical code of behaviour • Becoming promoters • Customer loyalty • Trust • Mentality • Relations with clients and friends • Family • Values
Broker service	• Evaluations • Buying • Selling

(continued)

Table A.2 (continued)

SCOPE	NODE
Sanctions and selection in the network	• Reputation on Facebook • Reputation acquired through word of mouth and signalling by Sardex Ltd • Control and exclusion in Sardex • Entry selection
Banks	• Sardex-banks relationship • General considerations
Considerations	• Critical issues ○ Inter-network ○ Different prices ○ Other • Preference for Sardex • Political and economic project ○ Economic crisis ○ Money and work ○ General function of Sardex ○ Business and debts ○ Political economy ○ Political and economic project • Sardex Ltd and its behaviour • Suggestions
Other	

Printed in the USA
CPSIA information can be obtained
at www.ICGtesting.com
LVHW080724161023
761181LV00006B/568

9 783658 285326